The Irish Constitutional Revolution
of the Sixteenth Century

Dom Mhuinntir

The Irish Constitutional Revolution of the Sixteenth Century

BRENDAN BRADSHAW

*Lecturer in History, Queens' and
Girton Colleges, Cambridge*

CAMBRIDGE UNIVERSITY PRESS

CAMBRIDGE

LONDON · NEW YORK · MELBOURNE

Published by the Syndics of the Cambridge University Press
The Pitt Building, Trumpington Street, Cambridge CB2 1 RP
Bentley House, 200 Euston Road, London NW1 2DB
32 East 57th Street, New York, NY 10022, USA
296 Beaconsfield Parade, Middle Park, Melbourne 3206, Australia

First published 1979

Printed in Great Britain at the
University Press, Cambridge

Library of Congress Cataloguing in Publication Data
Bradshaw, Brendan.
The Irish constitutional revolution of the sixteenth century.
Bibliography: p.
Includes index.
1. Ireland – Politics and government – 16th century.
2. Ireland – Constitutional history. I. Title.
DA935.B68   320.9'415'05   78–58785

ISBN 0 521 22206 0

Contents

Do bhíodar caoin sibhíalta tréitheach,
Ba mhaith a ndlithe, a gcreideamh is a mbéasa,
Gach duine d'umhlaigh, do bhí a chuid féin leis,
Do bhíodar ceannsa mar cheann cléire,
Do shíolraigh a bhfuil trí na chéile,
Do bhí an Gael Gallda 's an Gall Gaelach.

Seán Ó Conaill, *Tuireamh na hÉireann*, c. 1640

Preface

Sixty-six years ago now, Philip Wilson, in his book *The beginnings of modern Ireland*, focused attention on the 1530s and the two succeeding decades as the period of crucial significance in early modern Irish history. This study originated in a hunch that Wilson was right in his conclusion but that his unionist sympathies had led his argument astray, and that the theme was worth reworking. It was worth reworking, I felt, not for the satisfaction of revising Wilson – that was entirely incidental – but in order to attempt afresh what he had attempted and what no one had attempted since, to my knowledge. That was to provide a conceptual framework for the discussion of the political and constitutional history of early modern Ireland. I was and remain convinced that such a framework must exist before the themes with which political historians have come to occupy themselves recently – the social and economic dynamics of political history, and the like – may usefully be taken up in the context of early modern Ireland. If, therefore, this study is old-fashioned in its preoccupations and in its methodology, those who are kind enough to give it a second glance may find that it is not, for all that, irrelevant.

It is usual in the preface to a work of this kind to discuss in a general way the sources on which it is based. So let me be general. The list of sources set out in the Bibliography contains little with which any serious scholar of sixteenth-century Ireland will not be familiar. It would serve small purpose to work through the list here. However, a word about the literary material in the Irish language may be in order. I have relied on published works, most of them in print for some time. I mention them only because it may be proper to draw attention to an element of novelty about the way I have handled them as historical sources and about the conclusions I have drawn from them. Their interest for me was not the hard historical facts which could be prised from them but the way in which they reflected a political ethos, and the way in which, by comparative analysis, they could be used to chart changing political mentalities. In theory I am alive to the limitations and the pitfalls attaching to the use of literary material for such purposes. Others will, no doubt, judge how I coped in practice. In any case the exercise was immense fun, and has formed in me the conviction that late medieval and early modern literature in the Irish language is too happy a hunting ground to be left as the exclusive preserve of philologists and grammarians.

The pleasurable task remains of acknowledging the chief debts incurred in the writing of the book. It began as a Ph.D. dissertation at Cambridge, supervised by Professor G. R. Elton. What the book owes to his intellectual inspiration, wise counsel and warm encouragement could not be told without lapsing into an eulogy which I am sure he would feel the better thanked for being spared. The eulogy, therefore, may be taken as read, except to say that had it been delivered it should have concluded, according to the custom of Irish praise-poetry, with a paean to Sheila, his wife.

I want to put on record also my gratitude to Steven Ellis of University College, Galway, who read the original version of the work with a lynx's eye for errors of detail and who helped to broaden my knowledge of the late medieval background; to Ciarán Brady of Carysfort College of Education, Dublin, whose delicately but persistently expressed misgivings about fundamental aspects of my thesis helped enormously in clarifying my thought; to Dr Katharine Simms, who was characteristically patient and generous in placing her expertise as a Celtic scholar at my disposal; to Professor David Quinn and Professor John Bossy, who examined the dissertation and offered helpful advice, not all of which, I acknowledge with regret, was accepted at the time in the spirit in which it was offered; to Dr Nicholas Canny of University College, Galway, for cordial interest at all times. My special thanks are due to the Master and Fellows of St John's College, Cambridge. By offering me the benefits of fellowship in their society without any of the major attendant duties, they made the research project possible. At the stage of publication I had the good fortune to have my typescript seen through the press by an old friend, Mr Eric Van Tassel, and by a new one, Mrs Elizabeth Wetton.

The book is dedicated to 'my folks', the nearest approximation in modern English usage to the Irish term used. The dedication embraces a numerous, ramified and far-flung tribe. But I had especially in mind my mother and my father (*requiescat in pace*). These gave me as a child a sense of the vital continuity between past and present which not all the tedium of school and under-graduate education managed to destroy. I also wonder if they did not contribute something more specific to this book. For from their example I learned that fundamentally different political attitudes, as passionately adhered to as among the Irish they can be, do not preclude the possibility of people living together not merely in mutual toleration but even in love.

Queens' College,   Brendan Bradshaw, s.m.
Cambridge
July 1978

Abbreviations

Add. MSS	Additional Manuscripts (British Library)
A.F.M.	O'Donovan (ed.), *Annals of the Four Masters*★
B.L.	*British Library*
Cal. Car. MSS	*Calendar of Carew Manuscripts*★
Cal. Orm. Deeds	Curtis (ed.), *Calendar of Ormond deeds*★
D.N.B.	*Dictionary of National Biography*
E.H.R.	*English Historical Review*
Fiants, Henry VIII	*Calendar of fiants (Ireland)*★
I.E.R.	*Irish Ecclesiastical Record*
I.H.S.	*Irish Historical Studies*
J.E.H.	*Journal of Ecclesiastical History*
Jour.R.S.A.I.	*Journal of the Royal Society of Antiquaries of Ireland*
L.P.	*Calendar of letters and papers, foreign and domestic, Henry VIII*★
Loch Cé	Hennessy (ed.), *Annals of Loch Cé*★
P.R.O.	Public Record Office, London
T.R.H.S.	*Transactions of the Royal Historical Society*
S.P.	*Public Record Office, State Papers (MSS)*★
S.P. Henry VIII	*State Papers of Henry VIII, i–iii*★
T.C.D.	Trinity College, Dublin

★ For details, see the Bibliography, pp. 289 ff.

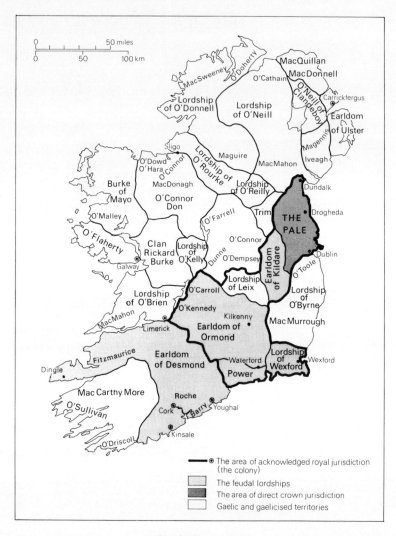

Ireland about 1530

Source: Margaret MacCurtain, *Tudor and Stuart Ireland*, Gill History of Ireland, ed. Lydon and MacCurtain (Dublin: Gill and Macmillan Limited, 1972)

PART I

'A discourse of the cause of the evil state of
Ireland and of the remedies thereof'

I

The medieval legacy

Historiography has highlighted Ireland's sixteenth-century rebellions and ignored its revolution. The transformation of the island's political personality in the course of the middle Tudor period must be the least remarked-upon change in its whole history. Yet it might be claimed to be the most remarkable. It provided Ireland with its first sovereign constitution, gave it for the first time an ideology of nationalism, and proposed a practical political objective which has inspired and eluded a host of political movements ever since: the unification of the island's pluralistic community into a coherent political entity.

The reason for the neglect lies partly in another remarkable feature of the revolution itself, the circumstances of its accomplishment. It was engineered by Anglo-Irish politicians, in collaboration with an English head of government in Ireland, and by constitutional means, in particular by parliamentary statute. Neither the agents nor the means were looked upon with favour by Ireland's latter-day revolutionaries, nor by those who fashioned Irish history in their image, while the more objective school of Irish historiography became settled in the assumption that the Anglo-Irish and their parliament were forces of reaction rather than of revolution in the sixteenth century. It remains to persuade them to the contrary.

Late medieval crown policy in Ireland

The perspective from which the middle Tudor period in Ireland is usually examined tends to obscure its unique significance. The point of reference is established further on, in Elizabethan conquest and colonisation. The middle period is treated as a dark and tangled undergrowth in which the historian gropes for strands of continuity with later developments. The uniqueness of the period itself remains unnoticed. That uniqueness emerges only when the point of reference is situated further back, in the period of the medieval Lordship which it definitely terminated. This study begins, therefore, with an attempt to situate the developments which are its main concern in the context of the medieval background from which they emerged. What follows is not a potted history of the medieval Irish Lordship. The perspective used keeps in view the phase which superseded it. Our special interest is in the origins of those problems of government which caused so much political agitation in the course of the sixteenth century, and of those attitudes which gave rise to the sixteenth-century movement for political reform.

Our starting point must be the strategy for the government of its Irish Lordship devised by the English crown in the course of the second half of the fourteenth century. That strategy produced a body of legislation and certain jurisdictional processes which provided the constitutional framework within which political reformers began their search for a solution to the Irish problem in the sixteenth century. Of central importance here are the celebrated statutes passed by an Irish parliament at Kilkenny in 1366.[1]

The purpose of the statutes of Kilkenny has been the subject of long and agitated controversy. Before launching into those troubled waters one relevant point can be made which is beyond dispute. That is that the statutes represent a body of reform legislation. They strove to eliminate abuses over the whole range of government in the Lordship. A legal historian pointed out in a recent study that sixteen out of the thirty-four acts dealt with problems of government common both to England and Ireland,

---

[1] The significance of the occasion of the Kilkenny enactments has recently been questioned on the grounds that the legislation added little that was new to statutes enacted at various times since the beginning of the century. Our concern here is not with the significance of the event, but with the policy that lay behind the legislation. However, it should be added that despite the legislation's lack of novelty the Kilkenny parliament cannot be deprived of a special significance. It was among the final acts of Edward III's son Lionel, duke of Clarence, preparatory to his departure after five years in charge of the government of the colony. The statutes must be seen, therefore, as reflecting his experience of those five years, and as an attempt to consolidate the arrangements for the government of the Lordship in the light of his imminent departure. This immediate context has a bearing on the long-term significance of the statutes. James Lydon, *Ireland in the later middle ages* (Dublin 1973), pp. 88–97.

the rights of the church, administrative corruption, problems of criminal and civil law, and of social organisation.[2] Many of these simply took over or adapted English legislation, a fact which emphasises that the statutes of Kilkenny were conceived first of all in the context of a comprehensive policy of government reform in the colony.

However, our main interest is in the remaining eighteen enactments which dealt with peculiarly Irish problems, specifically the relationship between the crown, the Lordship, and the Gaelic community. It may be accepted that the legislation here did not mark a new departure in crown policy but rather 'codified the most important parts of existing legislation'.[3] The question is, what was the effect of this code of legislation, and what was the policy behind it?

The interpretation of one of the most influential historians of medieval Ireland, Edmund Curtis, provides the context in which the modern debate on these issues has taken place. Curtis's thesis has three aspects. In his view the strategic consideration behind the formulation of the statutes was a decision by the Anglo-Norman colonists 'to cut their losses', to call off the conquest of Ireland as a whole and to concentrate instead on consolidating the colony within the area already gained. Secondly, he held, they express the colonists' conception of the political community they were attempting to establish, a conception moulded by deep colonial prejudices. Hence, the Kilkenny statutes moulded a political community in which legislation was concerned with the Englishry alone, in which the Gaelic Irish had no status in law, and in which Gaelic culture and customs were proscribed. The final aspect of Curtis's thesis concerns the constitutional implications of the statutes for the two historic communities of the island. Their effect, he suggests, was to provide a system of legal segregation between a privileged colonial community and a Gaelic community which was so far discriminated against as to be placed entirely outside the law, a system which later writers, under the influence of Curtis, have not hesitated to describe as apartheid.[4]

Subsequent research has substantially modified the last two

[2] G. J. Hand, 'The forgotten statutes of Kilkenny', *Irish Jurist*, n.s., i (1966), pp. 299–312.
[3] Lydon, cit., p. 95.
[4] E. Curtis, *A history of medieval Ireland* (London 1938), pp. 231–6. Idem, *A history of Ireland* (rev. edn., London 1950) pp. 113–17.

aspects of Curtis's interpretation, those concerning the motives which inspired the clauses about race and culture and the effect of the legislation as a whole on the Gaelic community. Recent writers, among them Curtis's distinguished successor in the chair of medieval history at Trinity College, Dublin, have emphasised the function of the statutes of Kilkenny as a mechanism of government control rather than as an instrument of aggressive colonial prejudice. They were designed partly to meet a situation in which the pressure of an expanding Gaelic community was threatening to undermine the cultural and political identity of a shrinking colonial community, and partly to secure stability in the political relationships between the two. The effect of the statutes was neither to sever the connection between the two communities nor to outlaw the Gaelic one. A study of the manner in which the sanctions on social intercourse worked in practice shows that they constituted a system of control, not a flat prohibition. In fact, formal processes existed to legalise intermarriage on an individual basis, and to grant full political status to members of the Gaelic community by means of patents of denization. Similarly the provisions concerning political relationships between the two communities did not amount to a 'declaration of war' as Curtis maintained. They were designed to curb arbitrary and unauthorised action from the side of the colonial community – by high-spirited border lords, for instance – and with that object in view, to place the domain of political interaction between the two communities under the control of law and of crown government. Finally, in juridical matters, the effect of the legislation was not to outlaw the Gaelic community. Close scrutiny of the operation of the law within the colony shows that the Gaelic Irish both enjoyed protection and had means available to them to institute proceedings in the crown courts.[5] In this view the conception of the colony expressed in the statutes was not one of withdrawal into hostile isolation, but one of practical accommodation to a situation of coexistence. More recently still, a third distinguished Trinity medievalist has challenged the remaining aspect of Curtis's thesis, the strategic consideration lying behind the statutes. He rejects the view that they mark the abandonment of the long

---

[5] A. J. Otway-Ruthven, *A history of medieval Ireland* (London 1968), pp. 291–4. G. J. Hand, 'The status of the native Irish in the Lordship of Ireland, 1272–1331', *Irish Jurist*, n.s., i (1966), pp. 93–115.

struggle to reduce the whole island to subjection. He argues that 'it was not in the nature of a king such as Edward III to abandon any part of his patrimony', and he points out that 'both he and Richard II spent large sums of money trying to extend the area in which royal writs were effective'.[6]

In the light of these criticisms, particularly the last one, it must be accepted that Curtis failed to establish the significance of the statutes of Kilkenny for the crown's policy towards the late medieval Lordship. The trouble is that his critics made little attempt to replace Curtis's general interpretative scheme which their criticism cumulatively undermined. That is a task which must now be undertaken, since the import of political and constitutional developments in the sixteenth century cannot be grasped unless their precise relationship to the situation in the late medieval Lordship is grasped.

The fundamental weakness of Curtis's interpretative scheme, to which all the criticisms in their various ways draw attention, is its failure to distinguish between the problems of the colonial community and the problems of the crown in Ireland. It is a truism of colonial administration that the home government will tend to differ from the colonial community in its perception of the problems and priorities of government. The late medieval Lordship of Ireland was no exception. Whereas self-interest narrowed the horizons of the colonists to the area of the substantive colony crown government set the problem of the colony in the context of the Lordship as a whole. Even if the colonists were prepared to have done for good and all with the Lordship outside their own area, the king was not. It is relevant to note, therefore, that the statutes of Kilkenny, and the injunctions that foreshadowed them, promulgated at a Great Council in 1351, were both the products of high-powered expeditions from England, which attempted to grapple with the reformation of the colonial area as an aspect of the larger problem of the government of the Lordship as a whole.[7]

Consideration of the special problem posed by the Lordship reveals the function that the statutes of Kilkenny were designed to fulfil. The peculiar problem of governing the medieval Lordship

---

[6] Lydon, *Ireland in the later middle ages*, pp. 94–7. Idem, *The Lordship of Ireland in the middle ages* (Dublin 1972), pp. 220–2.

[7] Above, p. 4, note 1.

was created by the circumstance that a substantial part of it was in the control of Gaelic or Gaelicised Anglo-Norman lords who held their local lordships without a grant of tenure from the crown, and in many cases in defiance of a royal title conferred under feudal law. So long as the crown was incapable of expropriating these, or alternatively of devising a formula for granting them tenure on mutually acceptable terms, the government could not exercise sovereign jurisdiction in their territories.

The statutes of Kilkenny mark an important stage in the development of a system of government designed to cope with this situation. Their special significance in this regard was their exclusive nature. They were framed in such a way as to apply specifically to those 'living amongst the Englishry' because only in the area of the Englishry, the area held under feudal tenure, did the full constitutional relationship of king and subject exist. Only in that area, therefore, did the law provide an effective tool of government, because only there was the crown's claim to sovereign jurisdiction accepted, and only there could the machinery for administering the law operate.[8]

The emergence of this expedient has to be viewed in conjunction with another device of government also developed in the course of the fourteenth century. This addressed itself to the problem of governing the Lordship outside the colonial area. To apply the ordinary processes of government, parliament, statute, the administrative and judicial machinery, to the government of the Irishry, the community which did not possess the status of subjects, was not only politically unrealistic but constitutionally inappropriate. However, it was found possible to make arrangements through which government of the disobedient community might be exercised in a limited way, by means of *ad hoc* agreements with individual local lords, based on the external jurisdictional relationship of protection entered into between an inferior and a superior ruler. Thus in the course of the fourteenth century the government adopted the policy of extracting, wherever possible, formal indentures of submission from local lords in the area of the

---

[8] This was pointed out as long ago as the early seventeenth century in a highly perceptive analysis of the constitution of the medieval Irish Lordship: Sir John Davies, *The discovery of the true causes why Ireland was never entirely subdued* (London 1612), pp. 119–24. I am grateful to Mr Hans Pawlisch of the Institute of Historical Research, London, for reminding me of the relevance of the work of Davies to my own.

disobedient Irishry, as it was called. The indentures provided for a simple act of fealty to the king as overlord, an undertaking to abide by the king's peace, and (if practicable) an agreement to render some modest form of tribute, usually by way of military service. They did not impinge on the lord's internal sovereignty. Reciprocally, the act of submission committed the crown to an obligation of protection towards the signatory. Gradually the policy emerged of establishing by this means a legal framework for the conduct of affairs between crown government and the local non-feudal lordships throughout the island. The arrangement was intended to stabilise relationships between the king, the colony and the 'disobedient' community, complementing the provisions within the loyal area under the statutes of Kilkenny. In this context the undertaking of the lord 'to be on the king's peace' was especially important. Through this he not only guaranteed his own peaceful disposition towards the crown and the colony, but – adapting a feature of the Gaelic Brehon Law and, indeed, of legal systems elsewhere – the lord accepted a corporate responsibility for the behaviour of his followers also. At the same time the indentures were intended to provide the basis on which crown government might aspire to exercise a measure of jurisdiction throughout the island, and in particular to fulfil a peace-keeping role.[9]

Thus the statutes of Kilkenny and the device of submission by indenture combined to provide a legal framework within which the Lordship might be governed on the basis of a system of dual government. The special feature of the system to be noted here is that it in no way altered the ambiguity of the existing constitutional situation. The statutes of Kilkenny did not place the inhabitants of the non-feudal lordships beyond the law. They simply acknowledged the fact that they were beyond it. On the other hand, the indentures entered into with the local lords did not concede the validity of their titles. They were purely *ad hoc* agreements, designed to provide a working relationship irrespective of the conflict over tenure. A special characteristic of the system as a whole, therefore, was its provisional and expediential quality. It provided an arrangement for the government of the

[9] On the adoption of this strategy by Richard II and later monarchs, see Lydon, *Ireland in the later middle ages*, pp. 114–24, 133–4. Robin Frame, 'English officials and Irish chiefs in the fourteenth century', *E.H.R.*, xc (1975), pp. 748–77, especially pp. 759–61.

Lordship in a situation of unresolved conflict, while leaving open to the crown the option of embarking upon a final solution at some future date.

One must, therefore, endorse the criticism of Curtis's view of the statutes of Kilkenny as marking the crown's decision to 'call off the conquest'. However, that is not the end of the matter. As a historian recently observed about another aspect of the Curtis thesis, 'his fault was perhaps more in the terms he used than in the substance'.[10] When one comes to consider what fundamentally the statutes of Kilkenny signify regarding the crown's attitude towards the Irish Lordship, one is driven to the conclusion that Curtis was, after all, right to associate the statutes with the termination of the phase of Anglo-Norman conquest. However, the policy of the crown was more subtle than Curtis suggests. It was rather a question of a shift in emphasis than of a dramatic change in policy. The appearance in the first half of the fourteenth century of the kind of exclusive legislation eventually codified in the statutes of Kilkenny indicates that the main emphasis of crown policy in Ireland had come to centre on consolidating the colony within the area under Anglo-Norman control, and with securing political stability in the Lordship generally. As a corollary, more grandiose notions of conquest and colonisation receded into the background, though they did not entirely disappear from view.

All of this is quite clear from the course of Anglo-Irish relations in the late middle ages. It is true that occasional expeditions from England revived an expansionist policy. However, the strategy informing all of these, with one notable exception, was that of securing the borders of the colonial area. They were set, therefore, in the context of a policy of colonial consolidation rather than of conquest. The exception was Richard II's first spectacular expeditions in 1394–5. But that monarch, having perceived at first hand the enormity of the task, quickly opted for a settlement on the lines indicated above.[11]

Thus Curtis's thesis about the significance of the statutes in the history of the Anglo-Norman conquest, if more carefully formulated, is seen to have substantial validity. What of his thesis

---

[10] F. X. Martin, 'The coming of parliament' in B. Farrell (ed.), *The Irish parliamentary tradition* (Dublin 1973), p. 42.

[11] Lydon, *Ireland in the later middle ages*, pp. 109–20. Idem, *The Lordship of Ireland*, pp. 231–40.

concerning their juridical and constitutional implications? As we saw, he was certainly wrong in maintaining that they encompassed the 'outlawry of the Irish race'. The reason for the exclusive nature of the legislation – framed so as to apply to the colonial community alone – was not to place the Gaelic community outside the law but to leave them beyond it. It did not, therefore, create a constitutional distinction but rather took account of political reality. The purpose here was to promote political stability between the two communities, not to exacerbate tension between them. Similarly, the legislation which Curtis viewed as an attempt to segregate the two communities was in reality intended to control intercourse between them.

Despite all of this, however, Curtis was substantially correct in maintaining that the statutes were conducive to political instability and to the alienation of the Irishry. That is not so much because of the provisions of the statutes themselves as because of the dual system of government of which they were an instrument. As such they served to formalise and emphasise the differences between the two communities. Furthermore, the dual system was in an important respect self-defeating as a formula for peace and stability. It shelved the conquest policy without abrogating it, thus aiming to contain the problem rather than to resolve it, to alleviate the symptoms while preserving the cause.

It is true therefore, as Curtis maintained, that the formula devised for the administration of the Irish lordship in the mid fourteenth century served in important respects to exacerbate the problem. At the same time it must be said that Curtis misconceived the source of the tension, and it is crucial to a study of sixteenth-century political reform to appreciate the nature of his misunderstanding. In a nutshell the conflict was not racial or cultural in origin but concerned validity of tenure. Curtis emphasised the legal and social disabilities arising from the failure to accord those of Gaelic ethnic origin full status under the law. However, as we have seen, means were developed for overcoming such difficulties with relative ease. From the mid fourteenth century onwards there is no evidence of resentment over the issue of personal status under the law.[12] Henceforth, the crucial constitutional problem was not the personal status of the Gaelic before the law, but the status of

[12] G. J. Hand, 'The status of the native Irish in the lordship of Ireland, 1272–1331', p. 115.

the non-feudal lordships. The criterion established by the crown for legal title was inheritance under feudal law. It is true that all the Gaelic lordships were thus excluded: even where twelfth-century submissions could have been cited as a basis for feudal title, tenure was invalidated because the Gaelic system of succession did not accord with the feudal principle of primogeniture. However, the crown's criterion also invalidated all those Anglo-Irish lordships which were not held by feudal tenure, either because such title was lost through non-observance of primogeniture or because the lordship was established as an unauthorised settlement by Anglo-Norman interlopers.[13]

The formal indentures with the local lords entered into by the crown from the fourteenth century onwards did nothing to resolve this problem. They were purely *ad hoc* arrangements and implied no recognition on the part of the crown of the legality of the lord's status or his title. Thus the policy of coexistence was designed of its very essence to maintain the constitutional estrangement between the crown and some of the most powerful political elements in the island at the same time as it was designed, as we have seen, to keep open the crown's option on a policy of conquest. Though dim, the spectre of a revival of a policy of conquest and expropriation prevented the development of an atmosphere of political security and kept resentment smouldering throughout the later middle ages.

The fifteenth century saw one important modification of the fourteenth-century strategy for the government of the Lordship. That was the establishment of a Pale within the colonial area. Precisely the same strategic thinking lay behind this development as produced the policy of colonial consolidation earlier. It was a further expedient to enable the crown to conduct government on the realistic basis of its modest actual capabilities without prejudice to ultimate ambitions.

In the course of the fifteenth century the central administration gradually abandoned the attempt to exercise active and regular jurisdiction over the whole area of the 'Englishry', the area to

---

[13] D. B. Quinn, 'Anglo–Irish local government, 1485–1534', *I.H.S.*, i (1938), pp. 354–81. Professor Quinn traces a very tenuous link between the Gaelicised Anglo–Irish lordships in Connacht and Ulster and crown government. These were the petrified residue of the former feudal lordships. In the late medieval period neither area was feudal in its government or was linked with the crown in the same way as the subsisting earldoms of Kildare, Ormond and Desmond.

which it had confined its direct jurisdiction under the system of dual government. As crown government in England became less interested in Irish affairs, and less willing to subsidise its counterpart in Dublin, the latter became less and less capable of involving itself in the administration of the outlying feudal lordships and their adjacent shires. The defence and government of these areas was perforce left to the feudal magnates while crown government confined the area of its own regular administration to the four shires in the hinterland of Dublin where the administration was centred. This Pale now became the focus of the crown's policy of consolidation. Defence works were undertaken to ring it round, as at Calais, with a system of dykes and castles. The policy of securing indentures of submission from the non-feudal lords came to be concerned less with the concept of a national network, and to concentrate instead on the lordships on the borders of the Pale.[14]

Thus the Pale, where alone crown government was regularly and directly operative, came to dominate crown policy. This did not imply the abandonment of the concept of the colony as the area of the crown's direct jurisdiction. Legislation continued to be framed on the basis of its applicability to the area of the Englishry as a whole, and crown government continued to aspire to exercise some measure of direct jurisdiction throughout the whole area.[15] Neither did the concept of the Lordship fade from view completely. Submissions continued to be sought from the non-feudal lords. When Henry VII ascended the throne and turned his attention to reform in Ireland, he thought in terms of the Lordship as a whole, though eventually he settled for something more modest.[16] Thus the crown's strategy of government in Ireland at the beginning of the sixteenth century was conducted on the basis of a threefold distinction between the Pale, the colony, and the Lordship. Meanwhile Irish politics, as distinct from Irish policy, were conducted on quite a different basis.

[14] Lydon, *Ireland in the later middle ages*, pp. 130–3.
[15] Quinn, 'Anglo–Irish local government, 1485–1534', pp. 354–81. Idem, 'The Irish parliamentary subsidy in the fifteenth and sixteenth centuries', *Proceedings of the Royal Irish Academy*, xlii, sect. C (1935), pp. 215–46.
[16] Lydon, *Ireland in the later middle ages*, pp. 171–5.

The anatomy of Irish politics in the late medieval period

In the late medieval period, as in modern times, the most obvious characteristic of Ireland's political anatomy was its partitioned structure. On one side of the divide was the land of the Englishry, to use the collective noun that occurs in contemporary documents. In constitutional terms the Englishry comprised 'the king's faithful subjects', to use another contemporary appellation. This description signified not so much an attitude of docile service as, on the one hand, the community's acceptance of the sovereign claims of the crown and, on the other hand, the crown's acceptance of the rights of the community as subjects. It indicated also, as a corollary, adherence to a particular form of political organisation within the community, one that corresponded to the English system in all essentials. The legal and historic basis of all of this was, of course, the feudal ties established between the English crown and the Anglo-Norman adventurers in Ireland in the course of the late twelfth century.

On the other side of the divide was the land of the Irishry, otherwise referred to as 'the king's Irish enemies' or 'the king's Irish rebels'. Much ink has been spilt in the attempt to define the gradations of meaning between the latter two terms, but they were usually interchangeable in sixteenth-century documents. The description signified not so much a state of open war with the king as one of radical estrangement based on incompatible constitutional claims. Among the Irishry the twelfth-century conquest and feudal law were not accepted as the criteria by which political status and tenure of property were established. Such titles were validated instead in accordance with criteria provided by Gaelic law and custom. As a corollary, the area was organised politically according to the Gaelic system, not in accordance with the English feudal system. Necessarily, the sovereign jurisdiction of the crown was inoperative throughout the area, but individual territorial lords might establish a tenuous relationship of fealty and protection with the king by means of the kind of legal indenture mentioned earlier.

It should, perhaps, be emphasised that the basis for the medieval partition of Ireland was not a racial conflict but a constitutional one, involving issues of political status and property tenure. As already noted, the area of the 'disobedient Irishry' comprised not only the territories of the Gaelic septs but also those territories occupied by so-called degenerate English, the descendants of Anglo-Norman colonists who had established local dynasties without a valid title in feudal law and in defiance of the claims of the crown to be the sole dispenser of political title and land tenure. However, it should also be emphasised that the pursuit of politics on the basis of this national division was secondary, indeed incidental, to political activity at the local level. One reason for this was the increasing ineffectualness of crown government in Ireland in the late medieval period, to which attention has been drawn already. Another was the peculiar characteristics of the political systems that existed on each side of the constitutional divide.[17]

Turning first to the Gaelic system which dictated the form of political organisation that prevailed among the Irishry, the point of greatest significance is the absence of any centralised institutions of government to give the community as a whole coherence as an organised political entity – though a common heritage of culture and social institutions provided a strong sense of collective identity. There existed the concept of a high-kingship; but the twelfth-century Anglo-Norman invasion arrested the development of that institution at the point of transition from a device of particularist dynastic supremacy into a genuine national monarchy. In any case it ceased to have political reality after the disastrous experiment of conferring it upon the brother of the Scottish king, Edward Bruce, in 1314–17.[18] Subsequently it was preserved as a nostalgic memory in the encomiastic political verse of classical Irish. But its common currency in that medium serves only to emphasise its political debasement. It was employed merely as a poetic conceit, resonant with flattering historical associations. The bard flattered the subject of his ode by urging his claims to the

[17] Despite differences of emphasis and of conceptual framework the following analysis seems to find general corroboration in the more specialised – and more expert – studies of Robin Frame: 'English officials and Irish chiefs in the fourteenth century', cited above (note 9), and 'Power and society in the Lordship of Ireland, 1272–1377', *Past and Present*, no. 76 (1977), pp. 3–33.

[18] The Gaelic political system in the late medieval period is brilliantly analysed in Dr Katharine Simms's unpublished Ph.D. dissertation 'Gaelic Ulster in the late middle ages', Trinity College, Dublin, 1976. Cf. Donncha Ó Corráin, *Ireland before the Normans* (Dublin 1972), pp. 168–73. Michael Dolley, *Anglo-Norman Ireland* (Dublin 1972), pp. 178–89. Lydon, *Ireland in the later middle ages*, pp. i–111. D. A. Binchy, 'Secular institutions' in Myles Dillon '(ed.), *Early Irish society* (Cork 1954), pp. 54–5.

high-kingship, but the exhortation to realise those claims was neither intended nor taken seriously.[19]

In consequence the Gaelic political system remained locally orientated, centred on the local dynasty. Its organisation was more tribal than territorial in character. The political unit, the lordship, was constituted by 'a complex of rights, tributes and authority' which bound lord and individual landholder to each other, rather than by 'a closed and defined territory'.[20] The same system of clientship and vassalage was used to bind lesser lords to a more powerful ruler of an adjacent lordship as their overlord. The format of the Gaelic political structure, therefore, was in strong contrast to the feudal pyramid, constructed on the basis of territorial units, and cemented by right of tenure from the king. The Gaelic system produced an erratic pattern of personal political relationships, forming loosely bound clusters of lordships in which the more powerful dynasties provided the nuclei. It should be added that the pattern was a shifting one since the nature of the relationship of overlord with lesser lords depended largely on their relative military strengths at any given time.[21]

This last remark draws attention to the style of politics which the Gaelic system dictated. Although the claim of subordination of one lord to another was almost invariably asserted in the name of ancient customary right, and in many cases backed up by formal legal agreement, the system lacked the clearcut structure of the feudal hierarchy. Consequently the gradation, and even composition, of the local power structure was always open to question, and dispute was practically interminable in the absence of central institutions of government to arbitrate and impose a settlement. Ultimately the argument that really mattered was power, the capacity of the lord either to exact the dues claimed from inferiors or to repudiate the exactions claimed by others upon him.

Thus the Gaelic system dictated an intensely local style of politics, focused on the issue of dynastic power within the local structure of government. As a system it seems more than a little

---

[19] Brian Ó Cuív, 'Literary creation and the Irish classical tradition', *Proceedings of the British Academy*, xliv (1963), pp. 256–7.

[20] Kenneth Nicholls, *Gaelic and Gaelicised Ireland* (Dublin 1972), pp. 21–5.

[21] Nicholls, cit. G. A. Hayes-McCoy, 'Gaelic society in Ireland in the late sixteenth century', *Historical Studies*, iv (1963), pp. 45–58.

conducive to political anarchy. A reading of the Gaelic annals gives some credence to that impression. However, the resultant social evils can be overdrawn. A number of factors served to compensate in practice for the structural weaknesses of the system. In the first place Irish warfare was, on the whole, fairly innocuous in character. It was the business of an elite, limited in scale and in style of operation, and confined to an open season between late spring and early autumn. It normally caused no great interruption to the lives of the ordinary population, the vast majority of whom were not eligible to be called to the lord's hosting. The evidence suggests, furthermore, that internal security, law and order were generally maintained at an acceptable level. This was for two reasons. One was the power of tradition and convention as a sanction for the legal code, as well as reverential awe for the professional class, the brehons, who applied it. One of the earliest Anglo-Irish treatises of the sixteenth century on the subject of political reformation refers with envy to the situation in the Irishry where 'divers Irishmen doth observe and keep such laws and statutes which they make upon hills in their country, firm and stable, without breaking them for any favour or reward'.[22] The other factor making for internal social order was the influence of the lord himself, who took responsibility for the internal peace and the external security of his lordship. In the late medieval period the more powerful local rulers came to involve themselves increasingly with law-making and law enforcement, and the local magnates began to provide mechanisms of social security and order normally associated with the machinery of centralised government. The arrangement seems to have been effective, to judge by another of the early-sixteenth-century century treatises on the reformation of Ireland. The author considered it necessary to meet the objection that there was no need for a reformation since the great Gaelic magnates such as O'Byrne, the McCarthys and O'Donnell 'keepeth and preserveth...their room and countries in peace, without any hurt of their enemies, so that their lands be tilled and occupied with the plough'. The author met the objection not by rejecting the description of the lordships but by

---

[22] Baron Finglas's 'Breviat of the getting of Ireland, and of the decaie of the same' in W. Harris (ed.), *Hibernica*, i (Dublin 1747), p. 551. Binchy, 'Secular institutions', pp. 62–3.

retorting that the magnates secured such conditions only the better
to despoil the people themselves by exactions and tributes.[23]

The Gaelic political system, therefore, was particularist and
dynastic in structure. The nucleus was the local dynasty. In terms
of internal social stability the system seems to have worked well
enough. However, it lacked the institutions of centralised
government, and consequently the means to control the disorder
and violence which characterised the external political relations of
the lords – though the scale of disruption was limited by the
conventions of Irish warfare.

In the feudal colony a sharply contrasting picture might be
expected. The colony possessed both the concept and the institutions of centralised government, as well as a full constitutional
link with the crown. However, all of this represented more the
potential for the creation of a cohesive polity than the actuality
of one. It may be doubted if the feudal lordships established by
the original Anglo-Norman colonisers ever cohered as a single
political unit under the central government of the crown. By the
end of the thirteenth century, at any rate, the picture is one of
largely autonomous local units fending for themselves, even in
external relations with bordering Gaelic communities, and of a
central government scarcely in touch with them, and having no
option but to accept the situation because of its own weakness.[24]

In the course of the two succeeding centuries the structure of
the two systems, Gaelic and feudal, underwent a parallel development, towards the entrenchment of the power of the great
magnates. Significantly, the feudatories adapted the devices that
emerged within the Gaelic system for buttressing the power of the
great lords. One was the recruitment of retinues of professional
soldiers, which made it possible to relegate the less efficient and
limited general hosting, whether Gaelic or feudal, to a secondary
position in military organisation. The new professionals were partly
companies of freelancing indigenous kerns and partly the famous
galloglasses, originally mercenaries from Scotland. These made
their appearance at the end of the thirteenth century in the Gaelic

[23] *S.P. Henry VIII*, ii, p. 1. *L.P.*, ii(i), no. 1366. Lydon, *Ireland in the later middle ages*,
pp. 143–4. Nicholls, *Gaelic and Gaelicised Ireland*, pp. 44–57.
[24] Lydon, *Ireland in the later middle ages*, pp. 47–50. Idem, *The Lordship of Ireland*, pp.
194–201. See also Frame, 'English officials and Irish chiefs'; idem, 'Power and society'.

areas of the north and west. In the course of the fourteenth century Desmond, Ormond and Kildare, the great Anglo-Irish feudatories, took over the system, and adopted the Gaelic exactions – which came to be known as coyne and livery – by which the military force were maintained.[25] A second feature was the development under the Gaelic system in the late medieval period of a method of clientship which enabled the landholder or petty lord to go over the head of his immediate suzerain and to secure the protection of a more powerful ruler, as an indemnity against the lesser lord's oppression or neglect. Evidence of the widespread use by the great Anglo-Irish feudatories of this device, known as 'buyings' (ceannaíocht), exists from the second half of the fifteenth century, and demonstrates their political prestige not only among the Englishry, but among the Irishry also.[26]

The culmination of these developments may be expressed in the words of a recent study of Ireland in the later middle ages. Summing up the situation in the fifteenth century the author declares that 'a new equilibrium was being achieved which had little to do with the Dublin government. The lords, Gaelic as well as Anglo-Irish, were organising their own communities to be as self-sufficient and autonomous as possible. The rights of the lord in his own territory were being more closely defined...In return, the lord offered protection to his people and their leaders.'[27] With the continued ineffectualness of central government Ireland was well on the way towards fragmenting politically into a number of sovereign dynastic principalities by the accession of Henry VIII.

A further symptom of development in that direction was the diplomatic missions of the magnates furthest from the centre – Desmond, O'Brien, O'Donnell, O'Neill – in search of an alternative overlord. These initiatives, it should be noted, were undertaken on an individual basis, with the Emperor and with the French and Scottish kings. From the point of view of changing political attitudes among the great lords these individual initiatives provide an illuminating contrast to the collective alliance that

---

25 Nicholls, *Gaelic and Gaelicised Ireland*, pp. 87–90. Frame, 'Power and society'. On the adoption of coyne and livery in the earldoms, see the articles of Sir William Darcy (1515), Lambeth, Carew MS 635, pp. 188–9 (*Cal. Car. MSS*, i, no. 2).

26 Nicholls, *Gaelic and Gaelicised Ireland*, pp. 41–3. Cf. Frame, 'English officials and Irish chiefs'; idem, 'Power and society'.

27 Lydon, *Ireland in the later middle ages*, p. 143.

attempted to establish Edward Bruce as high-king at the beginning of the fourteenth century.[28]

In view of all this it may seem perverse to suggest that the problem of government and administration presented to the crown by sixteenth-century Ireland tends to be exaggerated. Of course the problem was serious. However, it was not unique. Considered in terms of the crown's effective jurisdiction Ireland scarcely presented a greater challenge than did England and the principality of Wales at the accession of Henry VII. The developments in Ireland in the late medieval period may be compared to the emergence in England and Wales at the same time of the features associated with bastard feudalism: the enhancement of the power and status of the magnates at the expense of monarch and lesser lords alike, this facilitated by a new system of military organisation which enabled the magnate to base his political power on a standing army rather than on the feudal host.[29] The 'overmighty subject' scarcely constituted a more serious challenge to the restoration of royal authority in Ireland than he did in England at the beginning of the Tudor period.[30] Yet by the time of Henry VIII's death the crown's control of England and Wales was no longer a critical problem, though the work of consolidation was far from complete. The principality had been quietly absorbed into the kingdom, and the crown's jurisdiction was sufficiently reestablished to survive unimpaired the turbulent reigns of Edward VI and Mary. This must serve as a warning against the too ready invocation of 'dynastic independence' as an explanation of the failure to establish the crown's unilateral jurisdiction in Ireland in the Tudor period by the ordinary means of adminis-

---

28 *S.P. Henry VIII*, ii, p. 198n. *L.P.*, iii(ii), nos. 2799, 2937, 3118, iv(ii), nos. 3818, 4878, 4911, 4919, 5002, 5062, iv(iii), nos. 5322–3, 5501, 5620, 5756, 5938. J. O Donovan (ed.), *Annals of the kingdom of Ireland by the Four Masters*, v (2nd edn, Dublin 1856) (hereafter cited as '*A.F.M.*'), pp. 1322–3, 1364–5. The evolution of the Gaelic system in the late medieval period is examined in detail in Simms, 'Gaelic Ulster in the late middle ages'. Dr Simms's treatment, though different in perspective, corroborates the views expressed here.

29 D. M. Loades, *Politics and the nation, 1450–1660* (Brighton 1974), pp. 21–99.

30 Professor Quinn puts the emphasis rather differently when he states that 'feudal honours and liberties had, in the absence of direct and effective royal power, grown in the Anglo–Irish colony to an extent rarely paralleled in England', 'Anglo–Irish local government, 1485–1534', p. 363. Of course, as McFarlane pointed out so trenchantly, the concept of the overmighty subject has validity only when the late medieval nobility are considered from the perspective of constitutional history, K. B. McFarlane, *The nobility of later medieval England* (Oxford 1973), pp. 2–4.

trative reformation and statute. The Tudor conquest and colon-isation has been mistakenly regarded as a dictate of political necessity, following upon the half-failure of the Anglo-Norman invasion, and the fragmentary nature of the Lordship that resulted.

Ideology and politics in late medieval Ireland

If the jurisdictional problem bequeathed to the Tudors from the late middle ages was not substantially dissimilar in Ireland and in England, the constitutional and ideological problems were. The nature of the constitutional problem has already been discussed. The ideological problem remains to be examined in concluding this account of the medieval Irish Lordship's legacy to the sixteenth century.

Here a problem about sources arises. Little in the way of personal correspondence, political tracts or speeches – the kind of source to which the historian might turn for evidence of ideological attitudes – survives from late medieval Ireland. Fortunately, how-ever, a massive body of political literature of a rather different kind is available, though it has been shamefully neglected by historians. This is the *genre* of encomiastic verse of Irish bardic poetry. Analysis of the themes of that literature is essential to an under-standing of the ideological mentality of late medieval Ireland.

Such analysis serves to corroborate in a striking way the exposition earlier provided of the political anatomy of the Lordship. In that exposition the dominant element in the political life of the Lordship, both in the area of the Englishry and of the Irishry, was seen to be the great territorial dynasties. These also provide the focus of bardic encomiastic verse, each encomium being composed in honour of a particular magnate, to whom it is offered in anticipation of reward. Hyperbole is piled upon hyperbole in praise of the subject of the poem and of his lineage. His power is extolled by chronicling his prowess in exacting tribute and gaining booty. The security of his territories and their fertility is cited in praise of his virtuous rule.[31] It should be

---

[31] On the ideology of late medieval Gaelic lords, see Simms, cit. For a discussion of encomiastic verse, see Osborne Bergin, *Irish bardic poetry*, ed. D. Greene and F. Kelly (Dublin 1970), pp. 3–22; E. Knott, *Irish classical poetry* (rev. edn, Dublin 1960); J. Carney, *The Irish bardic poet* (Dublin 1967), passim; D. Greene, 'The professional poets' in B. Ó. Cuív (ed.), *Seven centuries of Irish learning* (Dublin 1971), pp. 38–50; Caerwyn Williams, *The court poet in medieval Ireland* (London 1971), passim.

emphasised that bardic encomiastic verse serves to illustrate the ideological climate not only of the territories of the Irishry but of the colonial area also. Just as the great Anglo-Norman feuda-tories consolidated their power in the late medieval period by adopting the appropriate military and fiscal measures developed in the lordships of the Irishry, so also they took enthusiastically to the cultural counterpart of these, bardic encomiastic verse. Thus they became subjects for odes of praise in precisely the same style as those addressed to Gaelic rulers. Although the historical and political references were deftly reworked to suit the background of the feudatories, the sentiments expressed were the same, emphatically particularist and dynastic. The opening stanza of an ode to the earl of Desmond, written in the middle of the fifteenth century, provides a good example of the tone. 'Of all the invasions of Ireland,' chants the bard, 'that of the Geraldines, the last, was the best'.[32] As in the odes to Gaelic lords the claims of the subject of the encomium to the rule of Ireland are urged as the height of flattery, though in the case of the feudal magnates that glory is seen to reside in the office of king's deputy or justiciar, not in the high-kingship.[33] Clearly the outlook which the bardic poets cultivated was congenial to their Anglo-Irish patrons. How pervasive it became in the territories of the feudal magnates is indicated in a treatise on the reformation of the colonial area dating from the 1520s. Here it was urged that the first task was to change the outlook of 'the king's erroneous subjects which so far be in error of their natural duty of allegiance, not knowing their prince, but rather reputing their governors [i.e. the magnates] as their sovereign than the king'.[34]

Greater attention to the ideological content of Irish bardic poetry might well have saved historians of late medieval and early modern Ireland from one of the most persistent myths regarding the political history of the period. This concerns the nature of the relationship between the two 'nations' or ethnic groups. The presentation of Irish history from the twelfth-century Anglo-Norman invasion to the establishment of the state in 1922 as an epic struggle of resistance against a foreign invader has proved

[32] Quoted in Paul Walsh, Irish men of learning (Dublin 1947), p. 38.
[33] For an example urging the Ormond claim, see L. McKenna (ed.), Aithdioghluim Dána (Dublin 1939), i, no. 36. For similar sponsorship of the Geraldine claim, see Idem, Dioghluim Dána (Dublin 1938), no. 67. Bergin, Irish bardic poetry, no. 17.
[34] B.L., Lansdowne MS 159, fo. 9.

a popular, if unwholesome, brand of nationalist historiography. No doubt it is a tradition from which responsible academic historiography has long since dissociated itself. Nevertheless its influence lingers in a number of too easily accepted hypotheses. One such is the received view of race relations in late medieval Ireland. It seems to be agreed that the war of the Gaeil (Gaelic Irish) against the Gaill (Anglo-Irish) was prolonged throughout the span of some five hundred years, well into the seventeenth century. The Confederation of Kilkenny of the 1640s is taken as the first serious attempt at *rapprochement*, one that was eventually unsuccessful. The view is that racial antagonism between the Gaelic Irish and the Anglo-Irish constituted a major factor in Irish politics until political and religious discrimination drew the two ethnic groups gradually to make common cause in the course of the seventeenth century.[35]

An obvious anomaly in the theory of the struggle of the two nations is the openness of the Anglo-Irish to Gaelic social and cultural influences. The theme of *Hibernicis ipsis hiberniores* – Gaelicisation or Anglo-Irish degeneracy, as it is variously described – need not be laboured here. It need only be said that recent research serves to emphasise the degree of cultural and social intercourse between the two ethnic groups at all levels, and not only in the outlying Anglo-Irish earldoms but also in the towns and in the heartland of the Pale, the bastions of English culture.[36] Resistance to this process can be traced to two elements – both of them minorities. One was the political reformers of the colony who had about the same popular mandate for this aspect of their programme as had, for instance, the American prohibitionists in the 1930s. The other, closely related to the first, was an elitist element in church and state, closely involved in administration, for whom the matter was partly one of political reformation, and partly a kind of social snobbery. None of this provides evidence of a general racial struggle. On the contrary, the treatises of the political reformers testify to the imperviousness of popular attitudes to the legislation which attempted to curb cultural Gaelicisation.

[35] This is the thesis presented in R. D. Edwards, 'Ireland, Elizabeth I and the Counter-Reformation' in S. T. Bindoff et al. (eds.), *Elizabethan government and society* (London 1961), pp. 314ff. Also P. J. Corish, *The origins of Catholic nationalism* (Dublin 1968), passim.
[36] See below, pp. 25–6.

The other aspect of the question that needs to be examined is that of the attitudes expressed through the ideologies of the two ethnic groups. Here historians tend to impose a closed outlook of racial conflict between a Gaelic 'native' ideology and an Anglo-Irish 'colonial' one. The former is supposed to have been characterised by resentment of the invader and an aspiration towards his complete expulsion; the latter by abhorrence of native barbarity, and an aspiration towards complete conquest.

In this connection a study of the encomiastic verse of the period is particularly useful. Until the latter half of the sixteenth century the theme of racial struggle occupies a definitely subordinate and usually incidental place in such compositions. Furthermore, the nonchalant attitude of the bards themselves towards the subject emphasises its lack of political significance. This is reflected in the celebrated remark of Gofraidh Fionn Ó Dálaigh, one of the great masters of the *genre*, to the earl of Desmond in the mid fourteenth century. Apparently the earl was peeved by the tone of Gaelic bravado found in the odes composed by Ó Dálaigh to Gaelic lords. Ó Dálaigh explained the approach of his colleagues and himself: 'In our odes we promise the Gaelic a rule they never attain. You must take no notice of this, it is merely a usage with us.' With disarming frankness he went on to explain how they altered the ingredients of the recipe to suit the taste of their patron. To a Gaelic lord they struck the note of routing the Gaill (the Anglo-Irish) back eastwards over the sea; with the Anglo-Irish lord they cheered for the banishment of the Gaelic lords from Ireland.[37] What Ó Dálaigh indicates is that both prospects were so far removed from fourteenth-century realities that they had become poetic conventions. Their invocation involved a celebration of identity, rather than a call to arms. It is certain that this is the spirit in which such trumpeting was responded to by the lords to whom it was directed. It almost invariably occurs in the process of urging the claims of the patron to supreme political power in the island – which, as already noted, was itself a poetic conceit, intended not as a serious political proposition but to enable the patron to preen himself and his lineage.

One highly influential piece of colonial literature may be cited as evidence of the same attitude. This is the *Expugnatio*, the account

[37] McKenna, *Dioghluim Dána*, no. 67. Cf. Knott, *Irish classical poetry*, pp. 72–3.

of the original Anglo-Norman invasion provided by Giraldus Cambrensis at the end of the twelfth century. It is clear that when he wrote the colonists were already adjusting themselves to the idea of coexistence with the Gaelic inhabitants. The objective of complete conquest was rapidly becoming remote and unreal, but it was retained as a means of enabling the community to inflate its ego by fantasising about its destiny. Giraldus quoted scripture and old Gaelic prophecies in support of the view that the coexistence of the two races in Ireland was the design of divine providence until shortly before doomsday, when victory would be granted to the newcomers.[38] In this as in many other matters the views of Giraldus spoke to the situation of the later Anglo-Irish community and won ready acceptance.[39]

An illuminating example of Anglo-Irish racial attitudes is provided by that earl of Desmond who reproved Gofraidh Fionn Ó Dálaigh for the jingoism of his verse. Earl Gerald was a major figure in Anglo-Irish politics in the early decades of the fourteenth century, as his appointment as head of crown government in Ireland indicates. At the same time he provides a classic instance of *ipsis hibernicis hiberniores*. He was a prolific author of poetry in Irish – Ó Dálaigh, in fact, was his tutor. His dearest friend was the lord of the neighbouring Gaelic sept of the MacCarthys, to whom several of his poems are dedicated. And if he made war on the Gaelic Irish, as he did, a poem of his is extant which apologises to Gaelic friends for this breach of friendship, protesting that these hostile acts were forced upon him by the English king who suspected his Gaelic sympathies. In this light the earl's reproof of Ó Dálaigh appears not as an example of Anglo-Irish petulance but as an example of the way in which such jingoism grated upon those Anglo-Irishmen who had come to cherish the Gaelic heritage as well as their own.[40]

One would not wish to deny that both Gaelic Irish and Anglo-Irish had a highly developed sense of ethnic identity, which

[38] J. F. Dimock (ed.), *Opera omnia Giraldi Cambrensis*, v (London 1867), p. 385.
[39] See Dimock, cit., pp. x, lxxvi–lxxviii, xciii–xcviii; a copy of the Anglo-Irish redaction and translation of the *Expugnatio* is in Lambeth MS 598 (*Cal. Car. MSS*, v, pp. 261–317); the 'Book of Howth', Lambeth MS 623 (*Cal. Car. MSS*, v, pp. 1–260), used this redaction for its account of the Anglo-Norman colonisation. Cf. Whitley Stokes, 'The Irish abridgement of the Expugnatio Hibernica', *E.H.R.*, xx (1905), pp. 77–115.
[40] Thirty of Earl Gerald's poems are published in Gearóid MacNiocaill (ed.), 'Duanaire Ghearóid Iarla', *Studia Hibernica*, iii (1963). The poem of apology is no. 5 of the series.

Ó Dálaigh and his colleagues were expected to flatter. Indeed, this was an element in social turbulence where the two ethnic groups were in close contact. But none of this prejudices our case. A distinction must be made between the deep-rooted cultural and social antagonisms which the theory of racial conflict presupposes and the kind of group *parti pris* which can be socially disruptive without, however, possessing major political significance. The scale on which social and cultural intercourse is known to have taken place at the same time indicates that the evidence of race-consciousness, and of its socially disruptive consequences in later medieval Ireland, must be placed in the latter category. It reflects much the same mentality as, for instance, caused a sporting wrestling competition in 1305 between 'the country men of the barony of Naas and the men of the town of Naas' to degenerate into a violent riot between the townsmen and their country neighbours and, indeed, produced such an aftermath of bitterness that a judicial commission had to be sent to the area in order to restore peace.[41] The juxtaposition of this evidence of social conflict between town and country within the Anglo-Irish community with the evidence of economic cooperation between Anglo-Irish towns and their Gaelic hinterlands provides a useful commentary on the significance of racial tension in the history of late medieval Ireland.[42]

In any case, when the record of actual political activity in the late medieval period is examined it reflects consistently only one ideological influence. That is the particularist and dynastic one. The laconic accounts of the Gaelic chroniclers provide little evidence of a racial struggle at the national level, or indeed of advertence to national issues at all. The record of incessant political struggle which they chronicle, spanning the twelfth to the sixteenth century, is concentrated upon issues of local dynastic hegemony and upon the internal disputes of the septs. A few notable episodes might be cited by way of exception: the initial resistance to the Anglo-Norman colonisers, the episode that culminated in the Bruce bid for the high-kingship at the opening of the fourteenth century, and the movement of opposition to Richard II at the end of that century. That politics in Ireland

---

[41] Lydon, *Ireland in the later middle ages*, p. 22.
[42] Nicholas Canny, *The Elizabethan conquest of Ireland* (Hassocks, Sussex 1976), pp. 7–10.

throughout the later middle ages were preponderantly local in character is demonstrated not only by the paucity of episodes such as these but by the history of the episodes themselves. Although the issues on these occasions were national, the alignment of forces they produced were not. On no occasion was there a clearcut confrontation between the two ethnic groups, and the so-called national movements quickly lost momentum as local politics reasserted priority.

The conclusion from all of this is that one legacy which the late medieval period did *not* bequeath to the sixteenth century was racial tension of major political proportions. There existed no 'native' Gaelic movement of national liberation on the one hand, nor any 'foreign' Anglo-Norman movement of colonial domination on the other; neither was the idological climate dominated by the theme of racial struggle. At the social and cultural levels the evidence is of attitudes of openness and considerable actual intercourse. One important qualification must be added. Both ethnic groups retained a strong sense of their individual cultural identities. Given the appropriate political conditions this could provide the material from which ethnic ideologies of Gaelic nationalism and Anglo-Irish colonialism might emerge – the ideologies which historians have imposed on the two communities in the late medieval period, but which did not then exist.

It remains to point out the manner in which the twelfth-century Anglo-Norman invasion did, in fact, impinge at the ideological and political level in the late medieval Lordship. Here, once more, attention must be drawn to the importance of distinguishing between the colonial community and the English crown. Undoubtedly the distinction was relevant within the community of the Irishry. Gaelic writers differentiated between the colonists (whom they referred to as 'Gaill') and the English ('Saxain') and their king, though the fact escaped translators, and Celtic scholars in general, until very recently. This must be considered significant, since the source of Gaelic contention in the late medieval period was fundamentally a constitutional issue between themselves and the English crown regarding the validity of political and tenurial titles.

As we have seen, relationships between the crown and the non-feudal lordships were radically vitiated because of this conflict. The matter had no practical political importance so long as the crown refrained from exercising its sovereignty in the affected areas. Nevertheless there remained an underlying sense of insecurity which is reflected in the political verse of the bardic poets. In these the 'paper charters' of the English king are vehemently denounced, and the legitimacy of swordland as the principle of tenure is vindicated. An ode to O'Reilly of Cavan towards the middle of the fifteenth century elaborated the argument fully. First the poet attacks the injustice of the English titles, pointing out that they were granted only to the Gaill (the Anglo-Irish) so that it was obvious that under such charters none of the Gaelic would succeed to their ancient patrimonies. Secondly he attacks their legality. The Gaelic Irish first won the land by conquest, and ever since have adhered to the principle of swordland as the basis of title: 'The broad spear in the hand, the weapon from Vulcan's smithy, the sword, this is your charter.'[43] This was not just another poetic conceit, like references to the high-kingship, or the glorification of the race. That the poet here was treating a sensitive political issue is indicated by the way the sentiments of the ode are echoed a century later in quite a different part of the country, and in a real political situation. When Lord James Butler challenged McCarthy Reagh to submit the question of his tenure to the judgement of the Irish council he retorted 'with a proud countenance...that which he hath won with his sword, he will hold it with his sword'.[44] This incident occurred in 1535 in the aftermath of the Kildare rebellion, a time when considerable doubt existed about the government's good faith. A decision by the crown to make an issue of the question of legal title suggests one situation in which a Gaelic 'native' ideology of nationalism would be likely to develop.

The constitutional implications of the link with the crown established in the twelfth century were also a source of tension within the colonial community. The issue was less fundamental but scarcely less explosive. It concerned the question of jurisdiction. It has two aspects. First, relationships between the crown and the feudal magnates, Ireland's 'overmighty subjects', provided a source of tension. In the latter half of the fifteenth century the

---

[43] McKenna, *Aithdioghluim Dána*, i, no. 30. For the elaboration of a similar argument at the same time for the benefit of McWilliam Burke, see Knott, *Irish classical poetry*, p. 71.

[44] *S. P. Henry VIII*, ii, p. 281 (*L.P.*, ix, no. 556).

struggle for control of crown government in Ireland provided a major flash-point.[45] Secondly, the nature of the relationship between the institutions of crown government in England and Ireland provided a general source of resentment in the colony. Without questioning the constitutional position of the crown itself in Irish government the colonists resented the subordination of their institutions of government to English jurisdiction. In the course of the fifteenth century there was a growing tendency towards separation – not from the crown, but from English domination. A statutory declaration of the Irish parliament of 1460 might serve as the movement's manifesto: 'That whereas the land of Ireland is, and at all times has been, corporate of itself by the ancient laws and customs used in the same, freed of the burden of any special law of the realm of England save only such laws as by the lords spiritual and temporal and commons of the said land had been in great council or parliament there held, admitted, accepted, affirmed and proclaimed, according to sundry ancient statutes thereof made'.[46] Since the struggle between king and magnates centred on the question of control of crown government in Ireland, the two issues of magnate power and institutional autonomy tended to merge, though it is clear that a reforming element among Anglo-Irish politicians saw the distinction clearly enough.

The legacy of Henry VII

In establishing the background against which political reform took place in sixteenth-century Ireland, the reign of Henry VII deserves special mention, partly because it highlights the plight of the Lordship as it entered the century that was to witness its total transformation, partly because the king's own crude stop-gap effort at reform introduced a special constitutional complication into the situation.

We shall deal with the latter first. It resulted from the mission to Ireland of Sir Edward Poynings in 1494. In the aftermath of the Irish sojourns of Lambert Simnel and Perkin Warbeck, Poynings'

[45] Lydon, *Ireland in the later middle ages*, pp. 145–54.
[46] On the separatist tradition manifested in the history of parliament in the late medieval period, see F. X. Martin, 'The coming of parliament' in B. Farrell (ed.), *The Irish parliamentary tradition* (Dublin 1973), pp. 37–56. *Statute rolls, Ireland, Henry VI* (Dublin 1910), pp. 646–7.

primary task was to render the Irish Lordship ineffectual as a
springboard for pretenders to the English throne. The task had two
aspects. One was to curb the loyally Yorkist Fitzgeralds. To deal
with this the earl of Kildare was ousted as lord deputy, arrested
and attainted of high treason. The second aspect was to prevent
the exploitation of the institutions of government in Ireland for
subversive purposes. This was done partly by introducing English
personnel into the major administrative posts and partly by means
of parliamentary legislation. An act of parliament stipulated that
all the major government offices could only be held 'at pleasure'
– a measure designed to end Kildare monopoly of office through
life grants. Meanwhile parliament was bullied into enacting a
number of measures which explicitly affirmed the subordination
of crown government in Ireland to its English counterpart. These
included acts ensuring the jurisdiction of the English seals in
Ireland and the famous Poynings' Law which withdrew the power
of initiating legislation from parliament in Ireland to the Irish
council, which in turn was required to obtain formal approval for
its legislative proposals under the English great seal.[47]

It was suggested earlier that although the Gaelic and Anglo-Irish
communities were not in conflict at the beginning of the sixteenth
century it was possible to envisage such a conflict developing,
based on a Gaelic 'native' ideology of liberation on the one hand
and an Anglo-Irish 'colonial' ideology of conquest on the other.
The Poynings episode suggests another possibility for ideologically
based political conflict. The total subjection of colonial government to English control opened up the prospect of a popular
separatist movement developing in the colony, under magnate
leadership which, if pushed to extremes, would be likely to direct
itself not only against English jurisdictional interference, but
against the constitutional link with the English crown. In this way
Gaelic insecurity and Anglo-Irish resentment could make
common cause in a national movement of secession.

The course of future political development in Ireland at the
beginning of the sixteenth century was, therefore, highly prob-
lematic. It held the possibility of a native–colonial conflict or,
alternatively, of a native–colonial combination in a movement of
secession from the English crown. These were possibilities. The

47 Lydon, *Ireland in the later middle ages*, pp. 171–8.

probability was something different: it was that the island would complete the process of fragmentation into dynastic principalities, bringing the course of political development in the late medieval Lordship to its logical culmination. The ineffectualness of Poynings' reforming expedition seemed to escalate this process. The English lord deputy was called home at the end of 1495 and was followed in 1496 by the English troops and administrative personnel who had enabled him to maintain Irish government in tight English control. Bowing to economic considerations Henry VII restored Kildare as lord deputy, and allowed him to regain all his old control over government.[48]

The pattern of development for the next two decades confirmed the trend of the previous two centuries. The earldom of Desmond drifted further from jurisdictional contact with crown government, and, like some of the Gaelic lordships, began the search for a continental overlord as an alternative to the English king. The earldom of Ormond entered on a new phase of consolidation and expansion under the driving force of a junior branch of the family who as resident heirs male claimed the inheritance against the absentee heirs general. The Kildare earldom went from strength to strength. The drive towards magnate autonomy was sharply underlined by the establishment of the Kildare liberty jurisdiction at the turn of the century, on a trumped-up legal claim. At the same time the earl set about using his control of the Dublin government to turn the Pale into a Kildare annex.[49]

That the course of political development in Ireland took none of these directions was partly the result of extraneous influences, the Tudor reformation in church and state and the emergence of a new colonialism in England. However, that Ireland emerged in the early modern period with a new constitutional status, as a sovereign kingdom under the crown, and that a new ideology of nationalism emerged which aspired to unite Gaelic and Anglo-Irish alike in common devotion to the native land – that this was the direction of Ireland's political development was the achievement of local forces. It was the work of a political element in Ireland which has received little attention in this survey so far, the Anglo-Irish of the Pale and of the towns.

[48] Ibid., pp. 179–80.
[49] Quinn, 'Anglo-Irish local government, 1485–1534', pp. 366–81.

2

The Anglo-Irish movement for political reform

The origins of the movement for political reform in Ireland

One purpose of this study is to draw attention to a much-neglected – indeed largely unsuspected – aspect of sixteenth-century Irish political history, its indigenous movement for political reform. That the movement should have escaped the notice of historians is perhaps not surprising. Studies of government and society in Tudor England, despite an increasing concentration on the localities, generally envisage the dynamism for reform as emanating from the centre. The remoter regions – the north, the west, Wales – are depicted as backward and unruly. The achievement of Tudor government was to sow or – to give Edward IV his due – to resow the seeds of reform in this inhospitable soil and to bring them to fruition. Ireland being most remote, it follows that its plight was worst – culturally archaic, intellectually moribund, politically anarchic. One would all the more readily take for granted, therefore, that local stirrings of enthusiasm for political reform were by way of a reaction to stimuli provided by crown government in England.

Whatever may have been the case in the English regions, to make such an assumption about the dynamics of political reform in Ireland would be grossly distorting. As we saw, the reign of Henry VII produced only one excursion into Irish reform on the part of the Crown, one that was generally ineffectual apart from the doubtful achievement of reducing parliament to an instrument for the approval of the annual subsidy. We shall see later that the reign of Henry VIII up to the 1530s follows a similar pattern. Apart from the single, unsuccessful, expedition of Surrey in 1520–1 the crown's involvement in Irish government for the first twenty years or so of the reign suggests an attitude fluctuating between

32

apathy and feeble interest.[1] On the other hand, there is evidence of sustained pressure for reform within Ireland itself from the second decade of the century onwards. It is true that this is the period when Wolsey finally came to dominate English government and that his administration was marked by occasional assaults upon Kildare's regime in Dublin – none of which quite managed to bring the earl to heel. It may very well be, though there is no evidence to show it, that in order to discomfit Kildare the cardinal encouraged the kind of bleak surveys of the state of Ireland that provide the first evidence of local concern for reform. Nevertheless, the picture that the evidence suggests at this period is of an active local lobby attempting to exert pressure on a habitually passive crown administration in England. We shall see that with the advent of Thomas Cromwell the situation changes. Henceforward the London government was to apply itself, more or less consistently, to the task of reform in Ireland. Nevertheless, much of the initiative in the formulation and execution of reform policy continued to come from within the Anglo-Irish reforming milieu. It was not the case, therefore, that the centre of gravity of the movement shifted to crown government in England from the 1530s onwards. Indeed, it is crucial to a proper analysis of the history of political reform in sixteenth-century Ireland to take account of the fact that it came under the influence of two gravitational pulls, one located within government, the other within the Anglo-Irish reforming milieu. This study will attempt to analyse the interaction of these two forces for reform and its consequences for the programme of reform itself, fruitful at first, but less and less so from the mid Tudor period onwards as each side became increasingly committed to incompatible concepts of reform. Ultimately the local movement failed to influence the course of Tudor policy in Ireland. That does not justify its neglect by historians since, as we hope to show, the history of this movement also constitutes the history of the formation of the mainstream Anglo-Irish political tradition in the early modern period.

The immediate task is to account for the appearance in Ireland of a milieu sympathetic to political reform. Such a development

---

[1] D. B. Quinn, 'Henry VIII and Ireland, 1509–34', *I.H.S.*, xii (1961), pp. 318–45. An even more emphatic statement of the crown's lack of interest in Ireland at this stage is S. G. Ellis, 'Tudor policy and the Kildare ascendancy, 1496–1534', *I.H.S.*, xx (1977).

might not seem to be within the bounds of reasonable expectation
in the light of the political anatomy of Ireland earlier provided.
However, one area of the Lordship developed along different lines
– the four fertile shires of Dublin, Kildare, Meath and Louth,
which constituted the hinterland of the seat of crown government
at Dublin. The Pale existed as a socio-economic reality long before
it became a strategic concept in crown policy in the fifteenth
century. For a variety of reasons that reality approximated more
closely to conditions in the south of England than did any other
area of the colony. Its economy was substantially a monetary one,
in contrast to the barter system prevalent elsewhere throughout
the island. Society was organised on an agrarian basis, with market
towns, villages, and solid farmsteads, rather than on the largely
scattered and less stable pastoral system that obtained in the Gaelic
and Gaelicised areas. It was unique also in possessing a substantial
stratum of lesser nobility, landowning gentry and town
merchants.[2]

Political attitudes in the Pale were, in the nature of things,
conditioned by these factors. Its socio-economic organisation was
geared towards stability in contrast to the mobility that characterised the pastoral system. At the same time the social stratum
referred to above showed the commercial enterprise and the
enthusiasm for social and economic advancement characteristic of
their peers in England. These had a vested interest in peace and
political stability. The socio-economic structure of the Pale was
much influenced by the fact that it constituted the hinterland of
Dublin, the seat of crown government. This factor conditioned
the political attitudes of the Pale community in a direct way also.
The four shires constituted the area with which the central
administration had always been most intimately involved, and in
which its machinery of government operated most continuously
and relatively effectively. Thus it was the area most amenable to
the jurisdiction of crown government, and also the area most
immediately responsive to the cult of the sovereign. As a corollary
it was the area least open to control by a feudal magnate, despite

---

[2] D. B. Quinn and K. W. Nicholls, 'Ireland in 1534' in T. W. Moody *et al.* (eds.), *A
New History of Ireland*, iii (Oxford 1976), pp. 4–6. Another recent survey emphasises
the disparity between the Pale and southern England without, however, vitiating the
thesis of a relative correspondence, especially in contrast to the socio-economic
organisation of the Gaelic territories, Canny, *The Elizabethan conquest of Ireland*, pp.
18–20.

the strong influence of the earl of Kildare, whose seat was at Maynooth on its western border.

Amenability to government under the crown, and to its system of centralised administration, was strengthened by a tradition of participation in the operation of government. The Pale gentry provided a pool from which the crown administration in Dublin was staffed. Among the most influential elements of the Pale community was the type of professional gentry who, besides managing substantial landholdings on their own behalf, made a career either in government administration or as lawyers in the crown courts. Since facilities did not exist in Ireland these were forced to go to England for professional training. Their career outlet, the legal profession or government administration, as well as their private landed interests, dictated a stint at the Inns of Court in London, and these, rather than the universities, drew increasing numbers of students from the Pale from the beginning of the sixteenth century. Legal training, exposure to the cultural and intellectual currents of London, and involvement in government all served to emphasise the political attitudes already noted. They were also conducive to a sharpened political perception, and to practical reflection upon the performance of the government machine.

Bearing this background in mind it is not difficult to understand the alarm with which the political leaders of the Pale community contemplated the trend of developments in the opening decades of the sixteenth century. Without immediate action it seemed that the momentum of the historical process would deprive the crown of the last vestige of its Irish Lordship. The steady accumulation of magnate power threatened to subvert the existing form of government organisation from within while simultaneously raising the spectre of extinction under the weight of Gaelic pressure from without. Thus vested interest – the concern of the Pale's social and political establishment about the plight of their own four shires – provided the initial impetus for the movement of political reform in Ireland. It began with their attempts to elicit relief from the guarantor of their freedom and their security, the crown.

With these must be joined one other group: the patrician class of the royal towns, the major ports of Waterford and Cork in the south, Limerick and Galway in the west, and some half dozen other centres, mainly dotted along the coast from Wexford in the

southeast to Kinsale in the southwest. As in the Pale, the political, social and economic environment of the towns moulded an ethos favourable to reform. Their royal charters provided a direct link with the crown, and they looked naturally to royal government to protect their prerogatives against the increasing encroachment of neighbouring magnates. In the nature of the case also the merchants of the towns sought conditions of social and political stability which would be conducive to trade. Finally, close contact with major centres of trade in southern England and the continent, including lengthy sojourns by merchants overseas, provided the kind of broadening experience which members of the Pale community obtained through attendance at the London Inns.[3] This serves to explain the stirrings of enthusiasm for political reformation which can be discerned among the town patricians almost as soon as the movement emerged in the Pale. Nevertheless, it will be seen that the Pale political milieu was from the beginning, and remained, the heart of the movement, the main source of its dynamic energy and of its most creative and original thought.

'Of the cause of the evil state of Ireland and of the remedies thereof'

In Ireland as in England and, indeed, generally throughout western Europe, the movement for political reform generated a considerable body of literature: letters, treatises, projected programmes. Elsewhere this material has attracted considerable scholarly attention,[4] but students of Irish history have shown less patience with it than they might. Admittedly, the combination of verbosity, pedantry and banality that is sometimes encountered – Polonius prattling on through several folios – can be stultifying. Admittedly also, in the case of Ireland, the impact of the whole corpus on the crown's policy bears little relation to its considerable volume. Nevertheless it must be studied. By the reign of Elizabeth a veritable revolution had taken place in the political mentality of the Anglo-Irish community. The course of that revolution can

---

[3] Quinn and Nicholls, 'Ireland in 1534', passim. Canny, *The Elizabethan conquest*, pp. 3–4, 6.

[4] The modern literature on the phenomenon in England is tersely surveyed in G. R. Elton, *Reform and renewal* (Cambridge 1973), pp. 1–8.

be most fully traced by observing the shifts in political philosophy and ideology, the changing perception of the problem of reform, that are reflected in the reform literature. It will also be found that a careful comparative analysis of this literature provides new insight into the general political history of the period, not only illuminating what happened but also drawing attention to what failed to happen, the latter frequently a matter of no less historical significance than the former.

Our present concern is to sift the earliest contributions to the literature in order to elucidate the attitudes and the mood within political circles in the Pale and in the towns on the eve of the great phase of sixteenth-century development.

Underlining what was said earlier about the origins of the reform milieu, among the earliest surviving contributions to the literature are one from Sir William Darcy, for many years the treasurer of the Dublin administration, and another from Sir Patrick Finglas, the chief baron of the exchequer about the same time. These were among the most politically influential of the Pale's professional administrators in the second and third decades of the century. The earliest datable composition devoted to the problem of reform is the set of articles submitted by Darcy to the English council on 24 June 1515. So far as the evidence will allow us to judge, therefore, Sir William Darcy appears as the father of the movement for political reformation in Ireland. He came into government service under the patronage of the earl of Kildare, but he fell from favour when the Great Earl died in 1513 and his heir, Garret Óg, took over the office of lord deputy virtually as part of his patrimony.[5] Though Darcy managed to retain office, relations between himself and the eighth earl were always uneasy. Perusal of Darcy's set of articles on the 'decay of Ireland' suggests why.[6]

Darcy's articles are briefer than the treatises that came later. They differ also in confining themselves to an analysis of the root causes of the problem, leaving the remedies to be inferred. Nevertheless they are worthy of study since they provide an analysis of the Irish political situation which may be regarded as the most prevalent one within the Pale political circle at this time. They indicate, therefore, the outlook which lay at the source of

[5] 'The book of Howth' in *Cal. Car. MSS*, v, pp. 192–3.
[6] Lambeth, MS 635, pp. 188–9 (*Cal. Car. MSS*, i, no. 2).

the movement for political reform in Ireland. On this last point it will be well, before discussing the details, to note the general approach.

Not untypically for a highly placed government administrator with a legal background, Darcy's articles display a rather narrow conservative outlook. His limited vision is indicated by the scope of the articles. They are confined to the area of the traditional colony, the area to which crown government had limited its direct jurisdiction under the fourteenth-century arrangement. Ignoring conditions in the rest of the island, Darcy surveys the situation in the Pale, the three earldoms, Kildare, Ormond and Desmond, and the virtually defunct earldom of Ulster. His conservatism is indicated by the historically bound nature of the analysis. He portrayed the existing situation in terms of a deterioration from a previous perfect state. The underlying assumption – of highly dubious validity, as we noted earlier – was that the colony had once constituted a viable political unit under the jurisdiction of crown government.

The premise was shaky, but it enabled Darcy to construct a persuasive thesis about the existing situation. In the first place it highlighted the humiliating plight of crown government in existing circumstances, and implied that political reform was urgently needed to restore the colony to its historic dimensions. Secondly, it enabled him to focus attention on the two features of the present situation which, as it seemed to the Pale reformers, were the root causes of all the trouble. These were the phenomenon described by historians as bastard feudalism, and the irresponsible attitude in England towards the Irish Lordship. He proceeded to demonstrate how these two factors undermined the fourteenth-century experiment in government described in the opening chapter. With telling effect he was able to show their pernicious consequences in the contraction of the crown's jurisdiction. In the course of the fifteenth century the three existing earldoms had been transformed into self-contained lordships, autonomously organised for military, tax and judicial purposes. They had absorbed the adjoining shires in the process. Thus central government was extruded. At the same time English negligence accounted for the withdrawal from the fourth earldom, Ulster, with its adjoining shires. When the inheritance passed to English absentees, and eventually to the crown, they were so preoccupied with English affairs that they allowed their Irish inheritance to be overrun by Gaelic and illegitimate Anglo-Irish encroachers who did not acknowledge the sovereign jurisdiction of the crown. Against this historical background Darcy could highlight the present predicament of the Pale. The last bastion of the crown's sovereignty was undergoing the same process as had already taken place in the three earldoms. The magnates who had been allowed to act as lord deputies for the crown were exploiting their authority to introduce the same organisation of government in the Pale as already existed in their own earldoms. The consequence must eventually be the annexation of the four shires in the same way as the outlying shires had earlier been annexed into the adjoining earldoms. The attack here, of course, was directed particularly against the earl of Kildare, who enjoyed practically a monopoly of the office of lord deputy. However, there was also an underlying reproach, more explicit in later treatises, against royal irresponsibility, since the four shires of the Pale had always been governed under direct crown control.

That Darcy's articles reflect a characteristic attitude within the Pale reforming circle in the opening decades of the sixteenth century is indicated by subsequent treatises from the same milieu. In general they approach political reformation from the same standpoint, displaying interest only in the situation of the substantive colony, and follow Darcy's historical method of analysis. Like him also they focus attention on bastard feudalism and the irresponsibility of England as the root causes of the colony's decline. However, where Darcy described the decline simply in terms of the contraction of crown government, later treatises drew attention to two other aspects which obviously bulked large in the preoccupations of the Pale group generally. These may be illustrated by reference to a treatise composed by Sir Patrick Finglas, a contemporary and colleague of Darcy, promoted chief baron of the Irish exchequer in 1520.[7]

One additional aspect of the problem was the defence of the Pale borders. Finglas introduced this to the discussion by taking the story of the colony back from the fourteenth century, which Darcy had used as his historical backdrop, to the twelfth, showing

---

[7] Finglas's 'Breviate' in Harris (ed.), *Hibernica*. Another version is in Lambeth, MS 600, p. 204, MS 621, p. 92 (*Cal. Car. MSS*, i, no. 1). A manuscript copy of the *Hibernica* version is in T.C.D., MS 842, fos. 25–36.

how Leinster, the first Gaelic kingdom to be gained by the Anglo-Norman colonists, was also the first to be lost. Like Ulster, it collapsed through the neglect of English absentees. The result was that the four shires of the Pale were now surrounded by Gaelic septs who preyed upon the loyal community and extorted blackrent (protection money) from them. The other problem was internal political disruption, which Finglas ascribed to bastard feudalism. According to him the colony began to disintegrate from within when the magnates took over control of the defence and military organisation of their areas. In pursuit of greater personal military power they joined Gaelic alliances, disregarding their common loyalty to the colony, and wrecking any possibility of a common policy supervised from the centre.

To complete the picture of the way in which the problems of the colony were envisaged initially by Anglo-Irish political reformers, attention must be drawn to one other feature of their analysis. This was the evil of Gaelicisation, the spread of Gaelic culture (using the word in the wide sense) within the colony. Darcy had highlighted this evil, and it is clear that his attitude was typical because he is almost invariably echoed in this respect in subsequent treatises. Since hostility to Gaelicisation was such a prominent feature of the attitude of Anglo-Irish reformers at this stage it would be well to devote some time to an attempt to understand their attitude, especially since it easily lends itself to misunderstanding.

One of the accepted truisms of sixteenth-century Irish historiography concerns the attitude of the Anglo-Irish of the Pale and of the towns towards the Gaelic Irish. Historians have felt able to pronounce upon this in the most general and unequivocal terms. These represented the colonial hard core of the Anglo-Irish community. Therefore, in contrast to the softening of the Anglo-Irish of the outlying earldoms to Gaelic cultural influences, the Anglo-Irish of the Pale and of the towns retained their cultural purity and their prejudices. Their attitude to the Gaelic was set in a mould of colonial contempt and hostility.[8] In this respect, as in regard to the supposed racial struggle discussed earlier, the

---

[8] E.g., D. B. Quinn (ed.), 'Edward Walshe's "Conjectures concerning the state of Ireland"', *I.H.S.*, v (1947), pp. 303–4, 311. Idem, 'Ireland and sixteenth century European expansion', *Historical Studies*, i (1958), p. 22. Edwards, 'Ireland, Elizabeth I and the Counter-Reformation', pp. 319–21, 323–4, 329–30.

psychological block seems to exist in the mind of the modern historian rather than in the contemporary Anglo-Irish community. The evidence overwhelmingly shows a high degree of social, cultural, and economic intercourse in the Pale as elsewhere during the sixteenth century. Darcy himself testified that 'all the king's subjects of the said four shires be near-hand Irish and wear their habits and use their tongue'.[9] He was not here referring to cultural mongrelisation in the lower social stratum as a result of the migration of Gaelic labourers. A treatise composed in the 1520s makes it clear that the process was general. It declares that 'except in Dublin, Drogheda, and a very few lords' houses in the English Pale all the English Pale of late time be transposed from English to Irish'.[10]

The evidence – and it can be multiplied – of widespread predilection for the Irish language and Gaelic cultural forms at all levels of society in the Pale flatly contradicts the conventional picture of hostility and contempt. The attitude of the reforming elite is another matter, of course. It is largely through their expressions of hostility that we know of the predilections of the majority. Nevertheless, it must be asked if their hostility was as absolute and as sweeping as at first sight appears. Darcy's own behaviour, for instance, does not suggest social or cultural intolerance. Like the vast majority of the Pale nobility and gentry he was bilingual and regularly acted as interpreter for the earl of Surrey in the course of his expedition to Ireland in 1520–2. More revealingly, he married off one of his daughters to a Gaelic magnate, O'Donnell.[11] Finglas shows a similar open-mindedness. He did not regard the Gaelic Irish as primitive savages, as the Elizabethan colonisers did. He praised the industry of their 'poor commons' and the respect for law which Gaelic society exhibited, contrasting them favourably in this respect with the community of the colony.[12]

This shows the invective of the reform treatises against Gaelicisation in rather a different light. It has been supposed that these attacks were culturally and socially grounded, that the denunciation of Gaelicisation as a political evil sprang from

[9] Lambeth, MS 635, pp. 188–9 (*Cal. Car. MSS*, i, no. 2).

[10] B. L., Lansdowne MS 159, fo. 8v.

[11] *S. P. Henry VIII*, ii, pp. 35, 42. *L.P.*, iii(ii), app. no. 15.

[12] 'Breviate' in Harris (ed.), *Hibernica*, p. 51 (*Cal. Car. MSS*, i, no. 1).

cultural and social prejudices. In fact the converse was the case. The criticism of Gaelic culture and society was politically motivated. Furthermore, what was under attack was not the Gaelic community as a rival political community, but Gaelic dynasticism as a rival political system. At this point it is necessary to refer again to Darcy's account of the disintegration of the colony. As already indicated, one of the two fundamental causes ascribed to the process in his description was the appearance of bastard feudalism. However, he described that development in terms of the adaptation by the feudal magnates of those features of the Gaelic political system which particularly suited the consolidation and extension of their own power, principally by the introduction of the Gaelic exactions known as coyne and livery which enabled the magnate to maintain a standing army. He further implied that Gaelicisation at the social and cultural level buttressed dynasticism at the political level by fostering a mystique of the local dynasty, rather than of the crown, and by conditioning the community to accept those features of the Gaelic socio-political structure on which the power of the dynastic lordship was based. This charge was made explicit in a treatise of the 1520s which declared, 'This vulgar Irish tongue induceth the habit, the habit induceth the conditions and inordinate laws, and so tongue, habit, laws and conditions maketh mere Irish.'[13] The object of the attack here was not Gaelic culture or society, but Gaelic dynasticism, a political system that was incompatible with the form of centralised government to which the Pale reformers were totally committed. In coming to grips with the problem of reform in practice, as we shall see, the priorities of the reformers reveal comparative indifference to the purely cultural forms of Gaelicisation. They addressed themselves to those features of the Gaelic socio-political system, such as buyings, coyne and livery, and the galloglass, which were directly inimical to the stable and centrally governed community they were striving to achieve. The reform of matters of language, dress and similar social customs was put on the long finger. The attitude of these practical politicians towards Gaelic culture was tolerant – indeed, one suspects, in many cases sympathetic. The same attitude was characteristic of the reform movement at all stages.

Having discussed the problem of the Irish Lordship as it was

---

[13] B. L., Lansdowne MS 159, fo. 8r (*L.P.*, iv(ii), no. 2405).

initially conceived by Anglo-Irish reformers we must turn to the programme of reform which they advocated to remedy the situation. Examined from this point of view Sir William Darcy's brief disquisition is more reminiscent of the 'complaint' typical of late medieval political literature than of the *genre* of reform literature which developed in the early modern period and which owed much to humanist influences. He draws attention to evils in the body politic without presuming to advise about appropriate remedies. Few of his fellow advocates of reform displayed such reticence. Despite the risk of tediousness, their proposals must be considered in some detail if we are to be able to trace through its various stages the transformation in mentality and in the practical approach to reform that occurred over the succeeding half century. What follows is an attempt to summarise the lines along which reform was approached at this time, rather than to describe any particular programme.[14]

With regard to the mentality they reflect, two characteristics stand out, already evident in the analysis of the problem: these are a narrow range of interest and a conservative disposition. Discussion of the first feature provides an opportunity to draw attention to a distinction made by writers at this time which remained as a basic concept in reformation thought and which figured prominently in reform vocabulary – the distinction was between a general reformation and a particular one. By a general reformation was meant the reform of the Lordship as a whole, while the term 'particular reform' referred to a project of limited scope. Though the meaning of the latter term altered to take account of a new situation in mid century, for most of the period it imported the reform of the traditional colony, the political entity constituted by 'the king's faithful subjects', as distinct from that other component of the Lordship, 'the disobedient Irishry'. The limited political horizon of the early Anglo-Irish reformers is reflected in the fact that they used this distinction to focus attention narrowly on the colony, to the almost total neglect of the larger

---

14 The discussion here is based mainly on two lengthy treatises. One is Sir Patrick Finglas's 'Breviate', which can be taken as representative of the Pale milieu. It is clear from the relatively large number of surviving copies (see note 7 above), and from references to it later in the century, that it enjoyed a wide circulation. The second treatise is anonymous, but internal evidence indicates a town rather than a Pale provenance, B. L., Lansdowne MS 159, fos. 9 ff. (*L.P.* iv(ii), no. 2405). Significantly, the two differ substantially in points of detail while closely corresponding in general line of approach.

problem of the Lordship. The usual approach was to acknowledge that a thorough reform must extend to the whole island, but it was argued that the reform of the colony ('particular reform') took precedence both as a priority for government policy and as a necessary preliminary before general reform could be undertaken. In practice the programmes advanced were preoccupied with reviving the colony as a viable political entity and made no suggestions for a programme of general reform aimed at reviving the Lordship as a whole.

The preoccupation of these early reform programmes with the restoration of the traditional colony indicates not only the limited range of their authors' interests but also their conservatism. Their political thinking was bound by a conceptual framework dating from the fourteenth century, described in the opening chapter. This is emphasised by the lines along which the strategy of reform was conceived. Once more the authors thought within the fourteenth-century framework. And they did so with full awareness. Sir Patrick Finglas's treatise explains how, in the days of Edward III, Lionel, duke of Clarence, made certain statutes at a parliament at Kilkenny 'for the common wealth, for the preservation of English order...[which] if they had been kept, this land had been obedient to the king's laws hitherto'.[15] This extolling of the statutes of Kilkenny as a panacea was typical of reform thought at the early stages.

The specific proposals fell into four main categories. One category concerned the curtailment of magnate power, most especially the exploitation of the office of lord deputy. Another related to the revival of the traditional system of defence. The main defensive burden was to be assumed once more by the landholders of the locality rather than by the great lord of the region. Thus, the massive retinues maintained by the lord deputy and the magnates on the plea of defensive needs could be eliminated, as well as the burden of 'Gaelic exactions' imposed to sustain them. Thirdly, there were prescriptions of a social character for the maintenance of law and order, for the control of relationships with the Gaelic borderers, and for the revival of agriculture, trade and market towns. Last but not least, there was a series of proposals aimed at revitalising the machinery of crown government, both at the centre and in the localities.

[15] The 'Breviate' in Harris (ed.), *Hibernica*, p. 41.

Two matters subsumed under these categories call for special comment. One concerned the preservation of the office of lord deputy from exploitation by the magnates. Opinion within Anglo-Irish reforming circles quickly settled against the practice of appointing a local magnate to head government in Ireland.[16] It is important for an understanding of the intrigues within the Irish executive in the reign of Henry VIII to appreciate that not only English-born administrators but Anglo-Irish reformers strongly favoured an English head of government. This view gradually changed in the mid Tudor period, partly as a result of the very success of the movement itself. Less powerful magnates, and an executive more capable of asserting itself, afforded a better prospect of keeping under control a lord deputy appointed from among the Anglo-Irish magnates. The change of view was partly also as a result of a changing political atmosphere in which Anglo-Irish reformers found their own great nobility better attuned to their line of thought than English lord deputies of the colonial type.

A second aspect of the programmes which calls for special comment is related to the defensive strategy. Here some expansion of the colony beyond its present limits was envisaged, and the ominous theme of colonisation, dormant throughout the late medieval period, was revived. It is important to distinguish such proposals, made in the context of a 'particular' reformation, from calls for a thorough-going conquest as a strategy of general reformation. What was involved here was a plan to extend the colonial area to its strategic borders. The recovery of the mountainous region of south Leinster from the Kavanaghs, the O'Byrnes and the O'Tooles was frequently urged, in view of its strategic location between the Pale and Ormond. There was also a more ambitious proposal to extend the western border of the Pale to the natural boundary of the Shannon. But even this proposal was formulated within the framework of the late medieval strategy of government. The plan was to expand 'that narrow English Pale to make a large English forest'.[17] The notion was retained of two substantive, coexisting communities, a

[16] For a full expression of the reformers' case on this point see *S. P. Henry VIII*, ii, p. 169 (*L.P.*, vi, no. 1587). See also B.L., Lansdowne MS 159, fos. 9v, 13v, 17v (*L.P.*, iv (ii), no. 2405).

[17] B.L., Lansdowne MS 159, fo. 9. Richard II had attempted a similar scheme in south Leinster but it got nowhere, Lydon, *The Lordship of Ireland*, pp. 234–6.

community of subjects under the sovereign jurisdiction of the crown and a community beyond the law.

The process by which it was proposed to assimilate these areas to the existing colony deserves special attention, because throughout the sixteenth century it was to remain representative of the approach of an influential group of Anglo-Irish reformers to the mechanics of colonisation. Once more the influence of historical precedent is evident. Obviously the administrative and legislative devices of the fourteenth-century reform programme would not serve as a model in this instance, since they were concerned only with the government of the existing colony. However, an historical model was available from two centuries earlier. This was provided in the description by Giraldus Cambrensis of the scheme of the Anglo-Norman Hugh De Lacy for the settlement of Leinster and Meath. The plan was in three parts: a land settlement in which the rights of Anglo-Norman and Gaelic holders alike were protected against illegal privateers; the establishment of a network of castles and walled towns to underpin the land settlement; and, flowing from these, the transformation of the area into a land of peace, in which the inhabitants turned from warfare to agriculture.[18] The special feature of De Lacey's scheme was its moderate attitude towards the Gaelic Irish, demonstrated by his willingness to extend his protection to their possessions against opportunistic Anglo-Norman land-grabbers – and even if Giraldus himself was not explicit on this point, the Anglo-Irish redaction of the *Expugnatio* was.[19] The scheme of the sixteenth-century reformers was designed according to the same basic conception.[20] They envisaged a moderate land settlement through which Gaelic landholders, secure in their possessions, would live side by side with new colonists – the latter acting as a leaven within the community as a whole. There was to be a minimum of disruption to the existing population. Those lower down the social scale were to suffer no disturbance, 'for there be no better labourers than the poor commons of Ireland, nor sooner will be brought to good frame, if they be kept under a law'.[21]

[18] Dimock (ed.), *Opera omnia Giraldi Cambrensis*, v, p. 352. As mentioned earlier, the *Expugnatio* was widely known in the Pale in the later middle ages.

[19] *Cal. Car. MSS*, v, p. 308.

[20] B.L., Lansdowne MS 159, fos. 12–13 (*L.P.*, iv(ii), no. 2405). 'Breviate' in Harris (ed.), *Hibernica*, pp. 44–5. *Cal. Car. MSS*, i, no. 1.

[21] *Cal. Car. MSS*, i, no. 1.

The ruling dynastic septs themselves would be treated in accordance with the principle of legality of title. They would be required to yield wherever their claims conflicted with authentic feudal titles and to hand over their castles to the crown; but beyond that they would not be dispossessed. The properties thus recovered by the crown – augmented, Patrick Finglas suggested, by the confiscation of derelict monastic properties – would provide a land pool through which new settlers could be infiltrated into the area. These were to be English and of gentle class, but younger sons and such like whose lack of possessions in England would provide an incentive to establish a family tree in Ireland. Complementarily the ruling septs were to be transformed from a warrior oligarchy into civilian landowners. Their lands would be permanently divided into individual freeholds under English tenure, instead of the Gaelic system of corporate ownership, with individual use on the basis of a life interest only, and consequent redivision of holdings at death. They would be required to relinquish the right to levy exactions from their tenants for the maintenance of military retinues, and to disperse their bands of galloglasses and kerns, 'putting them to husbandry and other labour'.[22] Thus a reformed Gaelic landowning class would live side by side with a new English gentry class, the latter providing a strong influence in favour of loyalty, order, and agricultural enterprise as the aspirations appropriate to a ruling elite rather than military prowess.

The arrangements proposed for the government of the new areas followed the Anglo-Norman model also. A constabulary system was to be established. The network of walled towns and castles first built by the Anglo-Norman settlers were to be reconstructed. The castles would be placed in charge of constables upon whom the government of the area would primarily devolve. At the same time both castles and towns would provide a refuge for the peaceful inhabitants of the area in time of attack.

The uniqueness of this approach to colonisation stands out in contrast to what was proposed as an alternative, should the inhabitants show themselves impervious to reformation. This was the expulsion of the dynastic septs and the settlement of a completely new set of loyal landowners on their traditional

---

[22] B.L., Lansdowne MS 159, fo. 15v.

territories. A second, even more radical, alternative was mooted but was dismissed as impracticable: the root-and-branch expulsion of the entire Gaelic population, and the planting of a new community.[23]

This completes the analysis of the kind of reform thinking that was typical in Anglo-Irish circles in the early part of the sixteenth century. A narrowness of concern and a strongly traditionalist cast of mind was displayed both in the formulation of the problem and in the approach to a solution. Nevertheless, it would be a mistake to deprive these schemes of all novelty. No doubt in previous generations the elite elements in the Pale and in the towns grumbled about their plight and, perhaps, even attempted to secure succour from the crown, though the tale cannot now be told for lack of evidence. Yet the proclivity which these grumblers of the early sixteenth century displayed for systematic analysis of the problem in writing, and for the formulation of extensive proposals for a solution, seems to suggest a new influence. It is hardly a coincidence that these first stirrings of the agitation for reform within the Anglo-Irish community follow close upon the outpouring of reform literature that marked the growth of humanism in England in the opening decades of the sixteenth century. It is hardly a coincidence either that many of the hallmarks of humanistic reform – concern for the state of the Church, the commonwealth, education – are to be found in these writings, though the imprint is not as strong as in a typical humanist literature. Earlier it was argued that it would be wrong to regard the reform ethos as an element essentially extraneous to the Anglo-Irish community, artificially engendered by crown government in England for its own ends. In assessing the external forces at play in generating the movement, humanist influences imbided by students of the law in London – contemporaries of Thomas More – seem more significant than the desultory attention of crown government. Be that as it may, the fact is incontrovertible, as we shall now see, that it was the influence of humanism that enabled reform thought in Ireland to break out of the traditional mould and to achieve a radically new formulation.

23 B.L., Lansdowne MS 159, fo. 9.

Humanism and reform: the commonwealth

To turn from the tracts analysed in the previous section to the anonymous treatise which opens the first volume of Irish material in the published state papers of the reign of Henry VIII is to find oneself in a strangely different environment.[24] The subject matter is the same – reform in the Irish Lordship – and so, more or less, is the material: the crown's political system was disintegrating, and the causes as well as the symptoms were plain enough. The chronological period is the same also, corresponding roughly to the administration of Cardinal Wolsey. Yet the way the discussion proceeds in the state papers' treatise is strikingly different and so are the conclusions. What makes the difference is a new concept, and this, in a word, is the commonwealth.

True, that term crops up in the other writings. But here it is used with a difference. An analogy with contemporaneous reform literature in England may serve to illustrate. It is the same difference that can be observed between the concept as employed in Edmund Dudley's *Tree of commonwealth* and in the *Utopia* of More or Thomas Starkey's *Dialogue between Pole and Lupset*.[25] No doubt in Dudley's book the term has become something other than the cart-horse of common fifteenth-century speech. It has been groomed for special service as part of the vocabulary of political discussion. Yet, despite its prominence in the title of the work, the concept makes little impression on the discussion itself, which amounts to a conventional moral exhortation in the medieval tradition. For More and for Starkey, on the other hand, the term is literally a cardinal philosophical concept, a hinge on which a whole political disquisition pivots. So is it also for our latest contributor to Anglo-Irish reform literature.

His work must be examined in some detail since it stands at the source of the Anglo-Irish commonwealth tradition. But before

---

[24] *S.P. Henry VIII*, ii, pp. 1–31 (*L.P.*, ii(1), no. 1366). The original survives in two slightly different versions; S.P. 60/1, no. 9; B.L., Add. MS 4792, fos. 96ff.

[25] Edmund Dudley, *The tree of commonwealth*, ed. D. M. Brodie (Cambridge 1948). Thomas More, *Utopia*. Thomas Starkey, *A dialogue between Cardinal Pole and Thomas Lupset* (London 1878).

    Utopia was written originally in Latin, but for More, as for sixteenth-century political commentators generally, the Latin *res publica* and the English 'commonwealth' or 'common weal' were equivalent terms. This is exemplified in the translation of *Utopia* itself made by Ralph Robinson in 1551.

doing so, a brief diversion is called for in order to explore the
concept that the term 'commonwealth' expressed in the literature
of political reform that burgeoned in western Europe in the first
half of the sixteenth century.[26] It should be noted that our concern
is with the sixteenth-century concept. The term itself has been
made to serve for a variety of political concepts since then which
have little more in common with each other, and with the original
sixteenth-century concept, than their name. A way into the
discussion is to make a comparison between the present usage and
the sixteenth-century one. In the sixteenth century the term had
no connotation that would associate it with an international
federation of states such as the phrase 'British Commonwealth'
conjures up today. At the same time it is instructive to note the
tenuous link between the modern and the sixteenth-century
notions. Both embody the idea of group solidarity, of a commitment to the promotion of the *common* wealth or weal, i.e. of the
welfare of the community as a whole. To divide the composite
noun into its component elements in this way – the form in which
it was usually written in the sixteenth century – is to recover its
roots in ordinary speech and to take the first step towards
elucidating the meaning it bore for sixteenth-century political
reformers. A second step is to distinguish the constitutional entity
to which the first element in the component made reference. This
was not a community of *peoples* (nations), as the modern usage
envisages, but a community of persons, the individual political
community or body politic, to use the contemporary term. Thus,
the sixteenth-century concept referred to the welfare of the
community that constituted the state. Thirdly, the rich philosophical tradition to which the term made reference must be borne
in mind. The *bonum commune* – which the term 'commonwealth'
readily translated into sixteenth-century English – was a basic
criterion of social and political morality both for the authors of
classical antiquity and for the medieval scholastics. Set against this
background, a very visible one in the sixteenth century, the term

26 Professor Elton discusses this subject with customary incisiveness in *Reform and renewal*,
    pp. 1–8. For earlier discussions from varying perspectives, see W. K. Hancock, 'A veray
    and true comynwele' in *Politics in Pitcairn* (London 1947), pp. 94–109. W. Southgate,
    Erasmus: Christian humanism and political theory, pp. 249–52. A. B. Ferguson, *The
    articulate citizen and the English renaissance* (Durham, N.C. 1965). J. K. McConica,
    English humanists and Reformation politics (Oxford 1965), pp. 29–31. W. R. D. Jones, *The
    Tudor commonwealth 1529–59* (London 1970), pp. 1, 6, 13.

assumed a deep moral resonance which had to do with the notion of a justly ordered and justly governed society. Lastly, the particular ethos within which the term was developed as a political concept in the sixteenth century must be taken into account. This was the ethos of Christian humanism, which was characterised by enthusiasm for social, political and religious renewal. In the light of what has been said already it is easy to see how the humanists could exploit the concept of the commonwealth as the pivot of their programmes of reform. They made the term encapsulate an ideology – one less concerned with politics than with society, less concerned with forms of government than with its social function; an ideology which proposed public service as the motive and social welfare as the object of political involvement, and which, above all, was committed to achieving a true commonwealth by means of social, political and ecclesiastical reform.

The impact of this full-blown humanist concept on the discussion of reform in Ireland becomes evident in the treatise which is the subject of this section. In the first place it altered the perspective, adding a philosophical and social dimension to a problem which had been considered hitherto in narrowly political and historical terms. Thus, where other writers made their case for reform by providing a history of the decline of crown government in the Lordship, this author did so by examining the existing political organisation of the Lordship, assessing it in the light of the requirements of the commonwealth. The result was to present the root problems of magnate power and the ineffectualness of crown government in a new context.

Stress was laid on the impossibility of providing good government in the territorial lordships because of the inherent inadequacies of the systems of political organisation through which they were administered, whether bastard feudalism or the Gaelic system. Both methods of political organisation were designed, the treatise argued, to advance the private good of the lord, not the common good of the community. Even where the lord pursued the common good, as in the defence of the territory, it entailed placing an inordinate burden on one section of the community, the commons, the non-gentle classes. For the system depended heavily on the maintenance of a large private army by the lord, and the burden of maintaining it fell on the commons, so that there was 'no common folk in all this world so little set by, so greatly despised, so feeble, so poor, and so greatly trod under foot.'[27] Turning to the central administration itself, the problem was set once more in the context of the commonwealth. The author lost little time in recounting the historical circumstances in which crown government had declined, indicating that he regarded that exercise as speculative and largely irrelevant. What mattered was the quality of the crown's present performance in government and this was clearly unacceptable. The nobility were allowed to pursue their private advantage to the detriment of the public good and the oppression of the common people. Ultimate responsibility for reforming this situation rested with the king. He had a strong moral obligation to act; the alternative was to relinquish his claim to the Lordship. 'It were more honour and worship to surrender his claim thereto...than to suffer his poor subjects always to be so oppressed, and all the noble folk of the land to be at war within themselves...the lord must render account of his folk, and the king for his.'[28] Similarly the lord deputy stood in 'perdition of his soul' for exploiting his office for the augmentation of his personal wealth and power.[29]

Thus by assessing the manner in which the Lordship was governed by the complementary criteria of the commonwealth – public service and the welfare of the community – the author was able to highlight its major defects: the irresponsibility of the crown and magnate domination, both at the centre and in the localities. It may be questioned whether in doing so he advanced the cause of political reform to any substantial degree. The problems besetting government in Ireland were obvious enough, and their root causes well enough perceived. The application of the criterion of the commonwealth simply provided a further motive for attending to them. And it might well be doubted if morality, based on the principle of the commonwealth, provided a more persuasive argument for the king and his council than expediency, based on the lessons of history. The real significance of the introduction of the concept of the commonwealth lay not in its greater persua-

---

[27] *S.P. Henry VIII*, ii, pp. 17–18. Emphasising the humanist provenance of this treatise, its author, echoing Plato's simile of the shepherd who fattens his flock to devour them, describes the ruler who protects his subjects from external dangers while exploiting them himself. Plato, *The Republic*, I (3).

[28] Cit., p. 14.

[29] Cit., p. 15.

siveness, or in its power as an analytical tool, but in facilitating a radical alteration in the manner in which reformers themselves viewed the problem. This needs further comment.

One of the things that make the treatise under discussion so evidently different from those discussed hitherto is the shift of the temporal focus from the past to the present and the future. The emphasis is on the needs of the present community, and on plans for future improvement. Thus, the historical excursus with which the other treatises were largely taken up was here replaced with a detailed examination of existing structures of government, drawing attention to their inadequacies, especially the reliance of the great lords upon might as a sanction rather than law, and the consequences of this in the disproportionate burden of military taxation, and in public disorder. This shift had obvious advantages. Little time was lost in lament or recrimination over past mistakes. Attention was concentrated on the existing deficiencies and their remedy, rather than on the historic development of the problem.

Along with the shift in the temporal perspective went a revolutionary change in local perspective. The problem was now set in a nation-wide context rather than in the limited context of the colony. The nature of the author's concerns was incompatible with the traditional exclusivism. The solidarity of the commons as a class transcended the political frontiers. The spectacle of their plight in both areas of the Lordship prompted the author to indiscriminate criticism of the self-interest of their rulers, the magnates, whether Gaelic or Anglo-Irish. Similarly, as he saw it, the political disorder resulting from the incessant power struggles of the lords was equally inimical to the commonwealth whether the disorder emanated from the Irishry or from the Englishry. Furthermore, the king bore charge for the land as a whole, not for the colonial community; the commonwealth which he was responsible for advancing was that of the Lordship, not the colony. Indeed, the author announced this, and established the context in which his discussion was to take place, in the first paragraph of the treatise. It opens with a declaration of intent to 'make surmise to the king for the reformation of his land of Ireland'. It then proceeds to a systematic account of the political geography of the island, beginning with the area governed under the Gaelic system, progressing to the area of the feudal magnates, and lastly to the state of the Pale.

The primary significance of the introduction of the common-wealth concept, therefore, was that it enabled a new conception of the problem of reform to develop within Anglo-Irish reforming circles. When the full implications of the commonwealth were accepted, the goal of reform could no longer be set merely at the restoration of the colony. In the contemporary terminology, the particular reformation could no longer be given precedence over the general one. Reform must be concerned with providing good government, prosperity and peace for the community of the island as a whole. Furthermore, an obvious tension existed between the constitutional formula under which the Lordship had been partitioned since the fourteenth century into two distinct political entities and the conception of a single social entity, to which the commonwealth was conducive.

In strategic conception it was equally revolutionary. It did not envisage the completion of the twelfth-century conquest by extending the pattern of the existing colony, with great colonial lords, and layers of colonial settlers pushing out the indigenous inhabitants, over the island as a whole. Rather, the Gaelic and Gaelicised area was to be assimilated to the colonial one, more or less intact – constitutionally and jurisdictionally at first, and gradually culturally also. The 'Irish great landlords' were to receive noble status and a title of inheritance in their possessions under royal patent, and to 'enjoy all the prerogatives of the king's parliament, as other lords doth'. Lesser lords would receive a patent and knighthood, thus assimilating them to the colonial gentry class. All of this would be accompanied by assimilation within the crown's jurisdictional system also. They would attend parliament in virtue of their status, and participate in the admi-nistration of the crown's judicial machinery as justices of the peace in their localities.

The attending support programme is noteworthy for the way it is influenced by humanistic notions about political reformation through social engineering, another novelty of this treatise. Characteristically, in this sphere there was a strong emphasis on education. All the assimilated lords were to send their heirs to school to one of the Anglo-Irish towns to be taught to read, write, and speak English, and 'to learn also the draught and manners of English men'. The emphasis on vocational occupations was also typical. The lord's second son was to be put to learn 'some clergy, or some craft, whereby they may live honestly without vices'. A general programme of vocational training of the same kind was to be implemented among the common people 'so that no man be found without some craft, or without a master'. One other measure of the social programme may be mentioned as an example of the affinity with English humanist proposals for social legislation. It was a proposed injunction that '[no] idle man, stranger ne vagabond be found in any place through all the land, Irish or English, upon pain of his life'.[30] Apart from this programme of social reformation the strong influence of humanism upon the author is revealed in his concern for reformation of the clergy. He categorises the abuses of the Irish clergy in typical humanistic fashion: a lack of pastoral concern among both higher and lower clergy; inattention to preaching and teaching; over-attention to the more profitable business of canon law; and the engagement of local pastors in mundane pursuits to the neglect of the cure of souls – 'they cowde more by the plough rustical, than by lucre of the plough celestial'.[31]

Despite the revolutionary conception of the programme in its objective and in its strategy, it is important to note that in certain fundamental respects the attitude of the author remained conventional. These related to the sphere of tactics, the means by which the programme was to be implemented. Most fundamental of all, he was convinced that 'if the king were as wise as Solomon the sage, he shall never subdue the wild Irish to his obeisance, without dread of the sword'. He dismissed the possibility of conciliation as impracticable. The only realistic basis on which to secure the general subjugation of the island was by conquest. As already noted, this was not a revival of the twelfth-century formula. The general conquest was not to be followed by a general scheme of colonisation: instead, it was to be followed by a programme of reformation, designed to secure the assimilation of the indigenous community. Here also, however, it is necessary to add a qualification. Although the author's strategic formula was conquest and reformation rather than conquest and colonisation, he provided for fairly extensive colonisation of the tactical kind proposed in the schemes for the expansion of the colony discussed earlier. This was to take place along the borders of the Anglo-Irish

---

[30] *S.P. Henry VIII*, ii, pp. 28–31.
[31] Cit., pp. 15–16.

area. Finally, the author retained the traditional tactical approach in maintaining the necessity for a particular reformation, for the restoration of a strong and united colonial community, as a necessary preliminary to the general one. The difference was that he envisaged the latter not as the optional extra of the traditional treatises, but as the necessary sequel, following immediately and automatically. Thus, on the one hand, the author clearly perceived the nub of the Irish problem, and the only feasible basis on which it could be resolved, namely, by offering the non-feudal lords status and title within the constitution. On the other hand, he found it impossible to break with convention in devising the tactics to give effect to his revolutionary strategy.

In the perspective of hindsight we can see that the least important aspect of the treatise was its immediate impact on the development of crown policy. The possibility of a policy of assimilation was mooted by the king himself in 1520–1, but with a tactical approach substantially different from that suggested here. In any event that proposal never got beyond the discussion stage. Such a policy was not taken up until the 1540s, and then it differed both from the scheme proposed here and from the king's own proposal of 1520–1. The treatise has greater significance as a contribution to the literature of the movement for political reformation in Ireland. It marks the beginnings of a radical shift in perspective within that movement. The objective and the strategy of the programme here proposed were set in a national context, rather than in the traditional colonial one. It was pervaded by a sense of moral purpose. The motivation for reform was provided by an appeal to altruistic ideals and moral sanctions concerned with social welfare and development, rather than by the considerations of expediency and the interests of the crown, emphasised in the treatises discussed earlier. All of this was made possible by the introduction of a new political concept into the discussion, that of the commonwealth. On the basis of that concept a new political ideology was being moulded within the Anglo-Irish reform movement. It goes without saying that not all who used the jargon subscribed to the ideological outlook it implied. Nevertheless the increased currency of the word undoubtedly contributed to bringing a particular attitude and set of values to the forefront of political consciousness. A remark in a letter from Norfolk to Wolsey, in 1528, may serve to illustrate the attitude that lay behind its invocation, at least in some cases. It concerns a member of the Bathe family, Thomas, who called on the duke on his way back from a pilgrimage to Walsingham. His purpose was to discuss the Irish political situation. Norfolk referred him to Wolsey, commending him as a man who 'doth more love the wealth of that land, than any of the parties of the Garentines, or Butlers, and hath done more to cause O'Neill contain from war, than any man of that land, to his great charges'.[32] Norfolk knew Bathe from of old, for he had used him in making contact with the Gaelic in 1520–1.[33] The picture reflected in this incident, therefore, is likely to be true: a man sincerely devoted to the public service, critical of the exploitation of public office by the great feudal magnates, solidly working for political stability based on conciliation with the Gaelic Irish. From this milieu was to emerge the Anglo-Irish nationalist ideology of the 1550s. Meanwhile, its growing presence must never be forgotten when examining the interplay of political forces in Ireland.

[32] *S.P. Henry VIII*, ii, pp. 135–6 (*L.P.*, iv(ii), no. 4459).
[33] S.P. 60/1, no. 60 (*L.P.*, iv, no. 4302).

3

Henry VIII's Irish policy:
Surrey's Irish expedition, 1520–2

Against the background outlined in the last chapter, of the ineffectualness of early Tudor government in Ireland, of the continuing consolidation of magnate power, and – in reaction to this situation, and under the influence of humanism – of a developing movement for reform, Henry VIII's first serious attempt to attend to the problems of his Irish Lordship must be considered. It originated in 1518–20, a period marked by a new though transitory zest on Henry's part for the role of active ruler. It was a period of grandiose schemes in external affairs, most of which came to nothing, the period of his candidature for the imperial crown and of Wolsey's for the papal tiara, the period of the plan for a crusade against the Turk, and of his first projection of a theological polemic. Side by side with these pretentious designs went an uncharacteristic interest in the practice of government. The king had lengthy memoranda prepared for the consideration of his council, outlining schemes for the reform of government, and envisaging a more active function for himself in the routine of administration. One of the few resulting projects to reach finalisation was the expedition of the earl of Surrey to Ireland in 1520.[1]

Among the memoranda drawn up in 1519 was one setting the king and his council 'to devise how Ireland may be reduced and restored to good order and obedience'.[2] The decision was to send a military and administrative expedition, on the same lines as that sent by Henry VII in 1494–6 under Sir Edward Poynings. The earlier expedition had been largely ineffectual, but this one was

---

[1] Quinn, 'Henry VIII and Ireland, 1509–34', pp. 318–24. J. J. Scarisbrick, *Henry VIII* (Harmondsworth 1971), pp. 135–67. G. R. Elton, *The Tudor revolution in government* (Cambridge 1953), pp. 36–40.

[2] *L.P.*, iii, no. 576.

to be more high-powered. It would be led by a great nobleman, not a mere administrator, and he would take the title of lord lieutenant of Ireland, not the more usual one of lord deputy. The man in question was Thomas Howard, earl of Surrey, later to become duke of Norfolk, a central figure in English politics, indeed the most powerful challenger of Cardinal Wolsey's dominant position in government. That he was later to be instrumental in bringing down Henry's two great ministers, Wolsey and Cromwell, and in securing the marriage of two of his nieces to the king, while surviving the disgrace of both, suggests a formidable personality and a more than usually shrewd political intelligence.

Despite these auspicious augures Surrey got no further in solving the Irish problem than his less distinguished predecessor in 1494–6. He slunk home sick and sorry in the spring of 1522, after a two-year stint which cost the crown some £18,000, without making any substantial impact on the Lordship, politically, militarily, economically or administratively.[3] To that extent Surrey's expedition, like Poynings', takes its place as an historical episode with the series of ineffectual intrusions by English government into the affairs of the Irish Lordship which punctuated the later middle ages.

Nevertheless, in an important sense it also heralds the dawn of early modern Irish history, the period of uninterrupted English involvement which began in the 1530s, and the phase of conquest and colonisation, the context in which the modern history of Ireland is set. This is not because of the significance of the episode in itself. Its importance lies in extraneous factors. First, it gave rise to a prolonged correspondence between the king and his lord lieutenant on the subject of Irish policy, in the course of which all the main paths open to the crown were surveyed. Thus the episode illuminates the attitudes of two of those who were to be major figures in the formulation of Irish policy in the crucial decades of the 1530s and the 1540s. Secondly, the episode brings into sharp relief the nature of Irish politics and of local political attitudes on the eve of the Tudor conquest, the most momentous event to occur in Ireland between the Anglo-Norman invasion of

---

[3] For a detailed examination of the administrative and economic aspects of Surrey's expedition, see D. B. Quinn, 'Tudor rule in Ireland, 1485–1547', London Ph.D. thesis, 1933.

the twelfth century and the creation of the free state in the twentieth.

The Henrician 'new departure' – 'policy' and sovereignty

Like every major expedition from England since that of Richard II in 1395, the strategy of Surrey's campaign was directed towards constructing a legal framework for the conduct of crown government on the dual basis already outlined. He arrived late in May 1520 and spent the following four months in military and diplomatic activity, reconciling the feudal magnates to the crown and to each other, and extracting submissions from the non-feudal lords.[4] By the end of August he was able to report to Wolsey that peace, however fragile, was restored, and he turned his attention to the other aspect of the strategy, the consolidation of government in the obedient territories, the area of the crown's internal jurisdiction. It was proposed to place the whole organisation of civil government under review, judicial, administrative, and financial, paying special attention to the possibility of increasing the revenue. The objective was the same as in the fourteenth century, to establish the area occupied by the crown's subjects as a cohesive and viable political entity, with the resources to maintain and defend itself, and to provide revenue for the crown.[5]

Surrey's letter to Wolsey late in August had been preceded by a number of earlier dispatches to the king. He was still without reply when he wrote to Wolsey and was clearly anxious for comment. When it came it was disconcerting. The brunt of the king's dispatch was to propose a radical departure from the policy on which Surrey was engaged. He noted the lord lieutenant's efforts to reconcile the disaffected earl of Desmond, but the king stressed that no distinction was to be made in the nature of the submissions to be extracted whether from feudal or non-feudal lords. All captains of the Irishry, as of the Englishry, were to 'come in . . . as our obedient subjects'. In this way Henry VIII envisaged reducing all the land to 'civility and due obedience'.[6] As well as proposing a new goal the king proposed a new strategy, the famous policy of 'politic practices'. Surrey was to soften up the opposition initially by diplomacy, winning some over by generous

---

[4] S.P. Henry VIII, ii, pp. 31, 35.   [5] S.P. Henry VIII, ii, pp. 38, 41.
[6] S.P. Henry VIII, ii, p. 31.

offers, bringing others to terms by force, and neutralising the danger of combined opposition by keeping the lords at odds with one another. When they had been sufficiently addled by these means the king would send further reinforcements to enable the lord lieutenant to scoop the lot into his net.

The two elements of Henry VIII's new departure, the jurisdictional end and the strategic means, need to be underlined. The concept of the coexistence of the obedient and disobedient communities under the crown's overlordship, and the dual system of government based upon it, as well as the legal framework which supported it – all of these were to be dropped. In place of this the king proposed a new model according to which the inhabitants of the island would form a single community of obedient subjects, and the government of the island would be conducted under the unilateral jurisdiction of the crown. Thus the total subjugation of the island was restored as the *immediate* objective of crown policy. But the king did not simply restore the objective of the twelfth-century English monarchs who claimed an overlordship in Ireland. With Henry VII a new emphasis had come to be laid on the dignity and power of kingship in England. As will become plainer in examining the subsequent correspondence, it was this concept which his son read into his title of lord of Ireland. He replaced the medieval notion of lordship with the concept of kingly sovereignty just as that concept was in the process of development towards a new and more modern formulation.[7] Furthermore he proposed a different strategy than the medieval one for the attainment of his object. 'Policy' was to replace straightforward conquest. It must be said that this was not the approach of enlightened statesmanship for which a succession of commentators since the nineteenth century – particularly English ones – have showered bouquets on Henry VIII. As outlined by the king himself the main features of politic ways were bribery, trouble-making and bullying, a good example, as Eoin MacNeill pointed out, of renaissance statecraft. Nevertheless there was also a modicum of shrewd good will. In any case, however motivated, and however modified, it was a strategy based on diplomacy and conciliation rather than on a war of conquest and colonisation.

The feasibility of the end and the practicality of the means

---

[7] G. R. Elton, *England under the Tudors* (London 1974 edn), pp. 42–6, 160–2.

proposed by the king were to form the major theme of the correspondence between himself and Surrey for most of the latter's stay in Ireland. The indications are that the lord lieutenant was already aware of the direction in which the king's mind was moving before he set out for Ireland. In a letter written in July, before he received his first communication from Henry, he seems to be anticipating the king's proposal. He indicates his intention of assembling the Irish council to consider 'what ways were best to be taken to bring the Irishmen to some good order', and he declares that from preliminary discussion of the matter he and others of the council were of the opinion that 'the said Irishmen will not be brought to no good order, unless it be by compulsion, which will not be done without a great puissaunce of men, and great cost of money, and long continuance of time'.[8]

In order to understand the ensuing correspondence it is necessry to distinguish the matters that were in debate between the king and his lord lieutenant. Surrey did not ostensibly reject the objective of the king's policy, nationwide recognition of the crown's sovereignty and government based on the unilateral jurisdiction of the crown throughout the island. What he questioned was the proposed strategy. To Henry's 'policy' Surrey opposed 'conquest'. Already in July he made his position clear: 'whensoever it shall please your highness to be content to put to your royal power, no doubt but your grace shall, at length, obtain the conquest of this land'.[9] However, the course of the correspondence was to make clear that behind the argument about means there lay hidden an argument about ends. Here we see used for the first time a favourite ploy of those who were opposed to the objective of complete subjugation as unrealistic. To avoid the appearance of lacking enthusiasm for the king's rights they questioned the means rather than the end. The tactic was to persuade the king that the only way of securing his claim was by conquest, confident that he would baulk at the cost.

Henry VIII was not easily put off. He followed up the letter in August with another dispatch in October in which he outlined his views more fully and with greater insistence. Surrey was told frankly that the kind of pacification policy he had set about would not justify the expense of his expedition. There were certain

<hr />

[8] *S.P. Henry VIII*, ii, p. 35.   [9] Cit.

essential conditions without which the submissions obtained from local lords were the 'appearance only of obeisance . . . a thing of little policy, less advantage, and least effect'.[10] The reality of obedience centred on the recognition by the lord of the rights of the crown within his territories in two respects. One was the jurisdiction of crown government in the judicial sphere, its laws, and the courts through which they were implemented. The other was the ownership of land. In singling out the issues of internal jurisdiction and land title, the king confirmed his intention of coming to grips with the root conflict between the crown and the lords of the Irishry.

At the same time he developed his ideas on the strategy of the new departure. 'Policy' was here summed up in the much-quoted phrase 'sober waies, politique driftes, and amiable persuasions founded in lawe and reason'.[11] What this meant in terms of diplomacy has already been pointed out. Here Henry VIII devoted more attention to its conciliary aspect, the 'amiable persuasions, founded in law and reason'. Recognition of the crown's right in the spheres of judicial jurisdiction and land title were to be the essential conditions of the form of submission. However, the precise terms of the settlement were subject to negotiation, and the king put forward a basis for compromise on each issue. So far as the judicial system was concerned he showed commendable flexibility. He envisaged a special legal code for the newly reconciled territories, a code worked out in consultation with the local leaders and adapted from both Gaelic and English practice. But the basis for conciliation proposed by the king on the crucial question of land title fell far short of realistic compromise. The criterion he proposed was legality of title: 'though of our absolute power we be above the laws, yet we will in no wise take any thing from them, that righteously appertaineth to them'.[12] The king's conciliatory gesture here was to provide an assurance that the conquest was at an end. Thus local lords would no longer live under the threat of indiscriminate expropriation. But the king's gush of magnanimity begged a crucial question, that of ancient titles. Much of the area staked out for themselves by the first Anglo-Norman feudatories had since become part of the patrimony of the crown by feudal inheritance. But the same circum-

---

[10] *S.P. Henry VIII*, ii, p. 51.
[11] Cit.   [12] Cit.

stance which gave title to the crown – the failure of the male line of the feudatory – gave actual possession to expanding Gaelic septs, or to upstart Anglo-Irish families. Henry VIII made it clear that he intended to hold out for the rights of the crown. Thus his formula would have entailed the surrender in whole or in large part of the territories of the O'Neills, the O'Donnells and the Maguires in Ulster, the Burkes in Connacht, the McMurroughs in Leinster, and the McCarthys in Munster, to name only some of the most powerful families affected.

At the same time it is necessary to underline the contrast between the king's approach and that of Surrey to the general subjugation of the island. Just as for the phase of initial subjugation the lord lieutenant opposed conquest to the king's conciliation, so for the ensuing phase of consolidation he opposed colonisation to Henry VIII's scheme of assimilation. Here he did not have in mind the kind of limited, tactical colonisation put forward in the Anglo-Irish treatises discussed earlier. What he envisaged was the introduction of a whole new community of loyal subjects throughout the Gaelic areas. He supported his proposition with two arguments. First the Gaelic Irish were irreformable. Their areas could be made 'obedient' – that is, subject to the ordinary jurisdiction of crown government – only by populating them with already obedient subjects. Secondly, the density of the population of the areas was far too low, only a third of what would be required to create an agrarian type of socio-economic structure on the English model, in place of the Gaelic pastoral one.[13]

The particular interest of Surrey's proposals is that already at this stage they outline the strategy of the classical colonial policy developed under the Elizabethan *conquistadores*. However, Surrey's personal commitment to it may be questioned. It would be difficult to reconcile such an uncompromising approach to Irish politics with the reputation he gained, according to a number of contemporary sources, for fair and courteous treatment, as well of the Gaelic as of the Anglo-Irish.[14] Very likely he believed that the scheme he outlined was the only way to achieve the general

---

[13] *S.P. Henry VIII*, ii, p. 72.
[14] On Surrey's reputation see, for instance, (i) the contemporary chronicler Walter Hussy, *Cal. Car. MSS* (Book of Howth), v, pp. 190–2, (ii) an anonymous reformation treatise of 1533, *S.P. Henry VIII*, ii, p. 169 (*L.P.*, vi, no. 1587), (iii) the commendation of the Irish council in 1521, *S.P. Henry VIII*, ii, p. 91 (*L.P.*, iii(ii), no. 1888).

subjugation of the island. But it seems clear that his purpose in outlining the scheme was to put Henry VIII off such a venture. He was at pains to emphasise its daunting nature in case the king might find the prospect attractive. He stressed the difficulty of financing, feeding and equipping the army of 6,000 that would be required, and then the problem of finding new settlers. The latter, he insisted, would have to be recruited from among the king's own subjects, for in the uncertain state of Ireland the introduction of colonisers from Germany, Holland or some other continental country could not be risked. Finally he was not prepared to estimate how long the initial military operation would have to be sustained, but he mentioned ten years as a minimum.[15] Simply by the way he presented the facts, Surrey makes clear his lack of enthusiasm for conquest and colonisation.

Sometime in the first half of December Surrey composed a detailed reply to the king. Unfortunately it does not survive, but its message was summed up in an ensuing letter to Wolsey on 16 December. It was that 'this land will never be brought to due obeisance, but only with compulsion and conquest'.[16] The lord lieutenant was sick − the 'disease of the country' − and tired of the Irish venture, and he pressed Wolsey to obtain licence for him to call it off, unless the king proposed to embark on a conquest. At the same time he sent over Sir Patrick Finglas, the newly appointed baron of the exchequer, urging Wolsey to consider what he had to say about the nature of the land and the disposition of its inhabitants.[17]

The effect of all of this was seen in a secret dispatch brought by Sir John Peache early in the spring of 1521.[18] It indicated a dramatic shift in the king's position, both as to the end and the means of crown policy. The subjugation of the whole island was not abandoned as an ultimate goal, but it was put once more on the long finger, where it had dangled since the days of Edward III. On the question of the appropriate strategy for the achievement of that end the change of mind was more radical. The letter tacitly indicated that Henry VIII had come to accept Surrey's viewpoint. The strategy of 'policy', diplomacy and conciliation, which figures so prominently in previous letters, now disappeared from

---

[15] *S.P. Henry VIII*, ii, p. 72.   [16] *S.P. Henry VIII*, ii, p. 61.

[17] *S.P. Henry VIII*, ii, p. 63. *L.P.*, iii(i), nos. 1099, 1180.

[18] *S.P. Henry VIII*, ii, p. 65.

view. Instead the king contemplated at some future data sending 'thither a great army for the total and final subduing of that land'. The army never came, of course, and it maybe doubted whether the king had any real intention of sending one. Meanwhile his scheme for a new departure in Anglo-Irish politics was abandoned before it got off the drawing-board.

The Henrician alternative

The curing of Henry VIII's naive optimism about the prospects of securing a general reformation in Ireland by means of a policy of conciliation is one fact of significance for the future that emerges from a study of the Surrey episode. Another, which emerges as a natural sequel to the first, is his view of the policy to be adopted towards Ireland in the absence of a programme of general reformation. Peache's dispatch which conveyed the decision to abandon the king's new departure also provided a fresh policy brief for the lord lieutenant. From this it was clear that the abandonment of the proposed general reformation was not to result in the adoption of the formula which Surrey had endeavoured to implement. Instead the king favoured an alternative approach to government within the late medieval framework, in which the crown assumed a more restricted role.

The brief outlined in Peache's dispatch followed logically from the attitude to the Irish Lordship revealed in earlier dispatches by the king. As we have seen, he dismissed the kind of external jurisdiction over the Irishry which Surrey endeavoured to achieve as the 'appearance only of obeisance...a thing of little policy, less advantage, and least effect'.[19] This was a half-loaf for which he had no appetite. So long as the goal was not full sovereignty, then the object of crown policy must be to retain the necessary minimum control at the least possible cost. Surrey's request for reinforcements to bring his task-force up to strength was flatly turned down on the grounds that the cost would 'much diminish and decay the king's treasure, and serve for none other purpose, but only to defend the Englishry'. The focus of the lord lieutenant's strategy was to be the Pale not the colony. He was 'to keep himself in the limits of defence for the tuition and safeguard of the four

---

[19]   *S.P. Henry VIII*, ii, p. 51.

shires'.[20] The dispatch of further troops was not envisaged until the king was in a position to send 'a great army, for the total and final subduing of that land'.[21] In the meanwhile government was to be conducted there with absolute parsimony. Though the king had come to accept the impracticality of 'policy' as a strategy for subjugating the island as a whole, he refused to adopt any other means of preserving the crown's minimal hold. Accordingly the lord lieutenant was 'by all politic ways, drifts and means to him possible to provide that his grace be not put to further charges'.[22]

Thus in the spring of 1521 the lord lieutenant found himself hamstrung. In any case, he had long ago lost heart for the Irish adventure, and he feared the effect that a prolonged stay would have on his political fortunes in England. In fact he had initiated moves to secure his recall as early as the autumn of 1520. But then England's embroilment with Scotland complicated the situation. There was rumour of a Scottish invading force, and of an alliance of Irish dissidents.[23] Accordingly he was forced to soldier on through the summer of 1521, doing what he could to secure the defences of the Pale. There was a hosting to curb the obstreperousness of the bordering lords, O'Connor, O'Carroll and O'More.[24] Further beyond, the policy was one of soft diplomacy. Surrey described what this involved in explaining his handling of O'Donnell. The lord of Tirconnell did not keep trust, for he allied with the government's enemies and made war on its friends. Nevertheless Surrey proposed to 'handle him with fair words, for though he do little good it is good to keep him from doing hurt'.[25] By October he had made peace with the border chiefs also on whatever terms he could get, having to be content with an oath as bond, where hostages were not forthcoming.[26]

As the campaigning season drew to a close in September he renewed his suit for recall and the king responded favourably. That was entirely consistent with the progression of his thoughts on Irish policy. Once he became convinced that the only way to secure the subjugation of the island was by conquest, Surrey's presence with his retinue there became an unnecessary extravagance in his eyes, temporarily justified over the summer by the

[20] *S.P. Henry VIII*, ii, p. 65. [21] *S.P. Henry VIII*, ii, p. 51.
[22] Cit. [23] *S.P. Henry VIII*, ii, pp. 65, 70.
[24] *S.P. Henry VIII*, ii, p. 75, 77. [25] *S.P. Henry VIII*, ii, p. 82.
[26] *S.P. Henry VIII*, ii, pp. 84, 85.

political crisis. However, it took almost another six months to decide on an alternative form of government and to arrange for the transfer. Henry VIII toyed briefly with the idea of appointing an Englishman as lord deputy, on a more modest basis than the existing arrangement. The idea was to avoid placing Irish government once more in the hands of an Anglo-Irish magnate. However, Wolsey persuaded him to opt for the most economical course. Reluctant to restore Kildare, who had been displaced by Surrey's appointment, the king turned to the Butlers of Ormond.[27] Meanwhile Surrey slipped out of Ireland unobtrusively at the end of December. He returned only fleetingly in March to take his army home.[28] On this mute note ended the enterprise which had been launched with such a fanfare.

The experiment of substituting Ormond for Kildare was soon in difficulty. Ormond was at a disadvantage because of the distance between his earldom and the Pale; both needed his personal presence. Besides, the Fitzgeralds did not want the arrangement to work, and did everything possible to thwart it. By 1523 Henry VIII and Wolsey had begun to reconcile themselves to the inevitable. The earl of Kildare was allowed to return to Ireland from London, where he had been detained throughout Surrey's administration. In 1524 he was reappointed lord deputy.[29]

The new arrangement was not quite a repetition of the pre-Surrey situation. An attempt was made to prevent Kildare from assuming absolute control of the Dublin administration by the association of Ormond with him as treasurer. The 1520s were marked by closer supervision from England, and punctuated by revisions of the arrangement. At the end of 1526 Kildare was summoned to England once more. In 1527 the Butlers gained fleeting control of the Irish executive only to be displaced in favour of a new experiment, the appointment of Henry VIII's illegitimate son, Richmond, as lord lieutenant in absentia, and the delegation of his authority to a bureaucratic 'secret council' of three. Wolsey's fall from power and the restoration of Norfolk's influence resulted in the termination of this experiment also, in favour of the suggestion mooted by the king himself in 1522 – the appointment of a non-noble English lord deputy with a modest

[27] L.P., iii(ii), nos. 1630, 1646, 1675, 1709, 1719, 1774, 2086.
[28] S.P. Henry VIII, ii, pp. 91, 92, 95.
[29] Cal. Car. MSS, i, no. 27. L.P., iii(ii), nos. 2197, 2693, 3048.

retinue of 200 to support him. However, that scheme too proved unworkable. The lord deputy, Skeffington, became too closely identified with the Butlers and lost the confidence of the Dublin executive, in addition to that of the Fitzgeralds which, of course, he never had. By 1532 Norfolk himself was convinced that the experiment would not work, and there was a return to the 1524 arrangement. Kildare was restored as lord deputy with Lord James Butler as treasurer.[30] But Nemesis was already at the door – in fact in the council chamber itself – in the person of Thomas Cromwell, rapidly rising to a prominence less spectacular but more efficient than Wolsey's. Under Cromwell the first sustained attempt to reform Irish government began. A new phase in the history of political reformation in Ireland opened with the breaking of the hold of the Anglo-Irish magnates over the Dublin executive and, as an incidental consequence, the total collapse of Geraldine power.

None of the experiments just outlined indicate that Henry VIII had second thoughts about Ireland after he expressed favour towards Surrey's request to be recalled and offered a final rueful reflection on that episode: 'We and our council, taking regard as well to the marvellous great charges that we yearly sustain, by entertainment of you, our Lieutenant, with the retinue under you there, as also the little effect that succeedeth thereof. . . have clearly perceived. . . that to employ such sums of money yearly upon any other English Lieutenant, with like retinue as ye have now, should be frustratory and consumption of treasure in vain; which being by politic provision reserved and saved, might stand in good stead for the advancement of other higher enterprises that may percase be set forward in few years hereafter.'[31] The king's attitude in the 1530s and the 1540s will show that the effect of the Surrey episode upon him was not to whet his appetite for 'higher enterprises' in Ireland at a later date, but to relegate the Irish question from the sphere of immediate to eventual attention, and to determine him to involve himself there as little as possible unless he could see his way to launch a conquest. So far as it depended on the will of the king, a substantial change in the government of the Lordship was as unlikely after 1522 as it had been at any stage since 1366.

---

[30] On all of this see Quinn, 'Henry VIII and Ireland, 1509–34', pp. 330–40.
[31] *S.P. Henry VIII*, ii, p. 88.

Consideration of the king's Irish policy in one other respect serves to underline his attitude.

From the point of view of the student of Henry VIII's Irish policy – whatever the view of contemporaries – the development of a major imbroglio involving England on the continent and in Scotland, in the course of Surrey's Irish expedition, was a singularly fortunate occurrence. The correspondence between the king and the lord lieutenant preserves an illuminating record of Ireland's place in English foreign policy in the scheme of Henry VIII.

In December 1520 Surrey was endeavouring to push the king into agreeing to his recall by presenting this course as the logical alternative to sending an army of conquest. Then news reached Surrey of a Scottish army of invasion under the earl of Argyle, to join an alliance of dissident Irish lords against the forces of the crown. The genuineness of his concern is evident from his change of attitude. His appeal to return home was suspended, and he sent Sir John Wallop hotfoot after his previous messenger with news of this threatening development and with an urgent request for reinforcements.[32] The background to these events was the breakdown of the arrangements engineered by Wolsey in 1518 to stabilise European diplomacy. France and the Empire were moving rapidly towards open war. Under the treaty of London of 1518 England was committed to joining in an alliance against whichever of the two should be the aggressor.[33] At the same time the Anglo-Scottish treaty was due for renewal, and relations between the two countries were nervous. This was the situation when Surrey's news of the alliance against the crown in Ireland, and his appeal for reinforcements, reached court. The king's response is instructive. He refused to be ruffled by the prospect of an invasion of the loyal territories in Ireland; he hinted that Surrey was over-reacting. He promised to investigate the rumours of a Scottish invading force, but he considered them improbable. In any case the supply of 800 troops as requested was out of the question – though in response to yet another appeal by Wallop he sent some munitions, and 1,000 marks as a reserve for emergencies.[34] The arguments by which Henry VIII justified his

---

[32] *S.P. Henry VIII*, ii, pp. 65, 70,
[33] Scarisbrick, *Henry VIII*, pp. 116–17.
[34] *S.P. Henry VIII*, ii, p. 70. *L.P.*, iii(ii), p. 1544.

parsimony to Surrey indicate the general context within which Irish policy was formulated, and its place in the king's thoughts on foreign policy. In the spring of 1521 he could foresee three possibilities for military involvement in the course of the year: participation in a continental power struggle; a war of defence against the Scots on the northern borders; military action in Ireland to safeguard the crown's interests there. His first concern was to play a major role on the European stage. Peache was instructed to explain to Surrey that on the king's ability to make an impact as a major European potentate 'greatly dependeth his honour and estimation, and consequently the surety of this his land'. Second in priority he felt obliged 'to defend this his realm [England] against the temerity of the Scots'. Lastly, Surrey was assured, the king would 'not...omit to do as much as may lie in the possible power of his grace, to succour his lieutenant there [in Ireland]'.[35] As already noted, what lay in the 'possible power' of the king proved to be extremely limited. The order of priority is enlightening. Faced with a probable alliance of dissidents in Ireland, a possible invasion of the north of England by the Scots, and an opportunity to cut a dash in continental politics, Henry VIII showed least concern about the first – and then only in so far as was necessary to ensure his freedom to concern himself with the other two.

It is easy to understand why the Irish Lordship should have been Henry VIII's most neglected inheritance. Its remoteness on the edge of Europe made it more of a curiosity than a prestigious possession and deprived it of value on the open market. Besides, it was largely in the hands of squatters or inattentive tenants. Convinced that neither was amenable to persuasion he formed the resolution of sending in the bailiffs but, immersed in greater affairs, he shrank from the cost and the bother. Meanwhile, since the property yielded no return, he was understandably reluctant to fulfil his own obligations to the tenants who showed fidelity. This left the latter in a peculiarly invidious situation. The king might push his Irish inheritance to the back of his mind as more of a nuisance than an asset; but his faithful subjects in Ireland had to live with its problems.

[35] *S.P. Henry VIII*, ii, p. 65.

Irish policy and Irish politics

Study of the Surrey expedition is instructive not only for what it reveals of the attitudes of the policy-makers but for the way it throws into sharp relief the complex political situation in the Lordship and the implications of the latter for the implementation of reform. It provides a case study of the interaction of policy and politics which may serve to illustrate in a precise and concrete way the rather generalised and theoretical discussion of the previous chapters.

The most obvious feature of the response to Surrey's visit from the rulers of the great lordships was its lack of uniformity. The Gaelic magnates nearest the Pale, most exposed to pressure from the colony, were initially equivocal and ultimately intractable.[36] The two great Ulster lords, whom Surrey had least power to control, vacillated between extremes of heat and cold. At one time they were going over the lord lieutenant's head, vying with one another in personal letters to the king, for the privilege of bringing the adjacent territories to accept the sovereign jurisdiction of the crown. At another time they were menacingly withdrawn. O'Neill was rumoured to be heading a combination of Gaelic dissidents in league with the earl of Argyle. O'Donnell was reported to have brought in massive reinforcements of Scots mercenaries.[37] At the other end of the country, the McCarthys in the southwest, over whom Surrey had not much greater hold, were positively and consistently enthusiastic about becoming full subjects of the crown.[38] Of the three great feudal magnates Kildare had been removed to London to give Surrey a free hand, but there were good grounds for believing that he was directing a rearguard action against the lord lieutenant from there.[39] Desmond showed initial interest in the lord lieutenant's overtures designed to patch up the sixty-year-old quarrel between his family and the crown. Then he fell away.[40] Ormond nicely illustrates the inconsistencies. He was frequently commended by Surrey for his cooperation. He earnestly supported the candidature of

[36] *S.P. Henry VIII*, ii, pp. 31, 35, 75, 85.
[37] *S.P. Henry VIII*, ii, pp. 35, 51, 65, 71, 77, 82.
[38] *S.P. Henry VIII*, ii, pp. 57, 63.
[39] *S.P. Henry VIII*, ii, pp. 31, 42. *L.P.*, iii(i), no. 972.
[40] *S.P. Henry VIII*, ii, pp. 35, 43, 46, 50.

Cormac Óg McCarthy for status under the crown. Yet, at the same time, he did all in his power to sabotage the lord lieutenant's scheme to reconcile Desmond.[41]

These responses defy analysis in terms of racial solidarity or of colonial loyalty to the crown. They make sense only in the context of a system of interacting alliances, formed without reference to ethnic considerations, or of constitutional status. In the south the submissiveness of the Gaelic McCarthys and the unresponsiveness of the Anglo-Irish earl of Desmond had their source in the rivalry between a Butler (Ormond) – McCarthy alliance and a Fitzgerald (Desmond) – O'Brien one.[42] In the midlands the intractability of O'Connor, O'More, and O'Carroll was determined by the nature of their political relationship with the Fitzgerald (Kildare) – O'Neill alliance.[43] In the north two pressures were at work. The Fitzgerald–O'Neill nexus was one. But even more influential was O'Donnell expansionism. It constituted a threat to the O'Neills in Ulster and to the Sligo O'Connors, as well as to the Gaelicised Anglo-Irish Burkes in Connacht. The same expansionist drive reacted also upon the O'Neill feud with their strategically placed offshoot in Clandeboy, east of the Bann. This complex of local political rivalries explains the game of diplomatic checkmate in which O'Neill and O'Donnell engaged during Surrey's visit.[44]

The magnates' response to Surrey's expedition demonstrates once more the dominance in late medieval Irish politics of local and dynastic issues over national and constitutional ones. So far as the prospects of political reformation were concerned it was a situation both daunting and at the same time encouraging. It was daunting because of the centrifugal pressures thus generated which frustrated the attempt to provide the Lordship with political coherence through the centralised jurisdiction of crown government. These pressures, combined with the failure of English financial support, rendered Surrey's expedition politically ineffectual. Nevertheless, the situation was not without advantage on the side of crown government. It was clear that an ideology of Gaelic 'native' nationalism was not operating within the Gaelic

---

[41] *S.P. Henry VIII*, ii, pp. 57, 63, 75.

[42] On this see particularly S.P. 60/1, no. 60 (*L.P.*, iv, no. 4302); *S.P. Henry VIII*, ii, pp. 46, 57, 116, 120.

[43] On this see particularly *S.P. Henry VIII*, ii, pp. 35, 43. W. M. Hennessy (ed.), *Annals of Loch Cé*, ii (London 1871) (hereafter cited as '*Loch Cé*'), p. 242.

[44] *S.P. Henry VIII*, ii, pp. 35, 65, 71, 77, 82. *Loch Cé*, ii, pp. 236–40. *A.F.M.*, p. 1352.

community. The expulsion of the loyal Anglo-Irish community or the repudiation of the crown's overlordship were not the issues which concerned those who dominated Gaelic politics. Attitudes were flexible, and this could be exploited. The lively interest shown by O'Neill, O'Donnell and the McCarthys in the question of constitutional status might be taken as an encouraging sign that a basis existed for the achievement of a lasting settlement.

At the same time the response to Surrey draws attention to undercurrents of tension which we have already noted running through the history of the late medieval Lordship. One was generated by the failure to solve the conflict over tenure. A letter from Henry VIII – unaddressed, but written either to O'Neill or to O'Donnell – highlights the crux. The king acknowledged the addressees's offer to take all the lands he possessed 'with other parcels' by letters patent from the crown, to accept an English title of dignity, and to pay a rent. His reply was diplomatically noncommittal. In fact, settlement on the basis proposed was impossible so long as the king continued to take his stand on ancient title.[45] The other side of the coin can be seen in the manifestations of anti-English sentiment through which opposition to Surrey was expressed. O'Carroll explained his opposition by saying that 'he was so much hurt by Englishmen in times past, that now he saw good season to revenge his hurts'.[46] Later Surrey reported that a confederation of the Gaelic of Leinster had refused to submit to him, declaring that 'they would never fall to peace with Englishmen, till they had utterly destroyed them'.[47] Implicit in this defiance was a gesture of support for the Anglo-Irish earl of Kildare whom Surrey and his English troops had displaced. O'Neill, it seems, made this explicit in his initial reaction to Surrey's arrival. He was reported to have declared that 'he would chase the English aliens home again in the same ship that they came in. And would make the king to send home his cousin the earl of Kildare. . . which being arrived they would betwixt them rule all Ireland.'[48] One other example is worth quoting for the way it rings an important change. It dates from 1528, but the circumstances were rather similar to those of 1520–1. Once more Kildare had been summoned to London; the baron of Delvin was

[45] S.P. Henry VIII, ii, pp. 59, 71, 82.
[46] S.P. Henry VIII, ii, p. 35.   [47] S.P. Henry VIII, ii, p. 75.
[48] B.M., Lansdowne MS 159, fo. 7v (L.P., iv(ii), no. 2405).

deputed to act as lord justice in his place. Kildare's Gaelic allies were restive, and the king sent a personal message of conciliation to O'Connor through Gerald Delahide. According to the report Delahide proffered the king's greetings to O'Connor in delivering the dispatch. O'Connor 'in derision asked him, "what king?" The messenger said, "the king of England", and O'Connor said with pomp, that he trusted, if he might live a year, to see Ireland in that case, that the king should have no jurisdiction or intermeddling therewith, and there should be no more name of the king of England in Ireland, than of the king of Spain.'[49]

These examples are noteworthy for two reasons. First, they show the clear distinction made by the Gaelic Irish between the Anglo-Irish community and the English foreigners (aliens), with whom they associated the king. Precisely the same distinction is found in Gaelic writers, as we have noted. Secondly, they show how the Anglo-Irish separatist tradition and Gaelic resentment and insecurity could coalesce. None of this is sufficient to endow the resistance to Surrey in 1520–2 with a national dimension: as we saw, it was completely dominated by local power politics. Nevertheless, as we have already noted also, it indicated the presence of the elements of an ideology of national resistance, uniting both Anglo-Irish and Gaelic communities. What lacked were the appropriate conditions of stress and insecurity in which the seeds might germinate.

The correlative of the problem of the 'overmighty subject' in the lordships was the 'all but kingship' of the earl of Kildare at the centre of government. The eighth earl gained a virtual monopoly of the office of lord deputy after the mission of Poynings in 1494–6, and his heir, Garret Óg, held it without interruption from the former's death in 1513. This situation was tolerated by the crown because aristocratic delegation provided the cheapest means of maintaining the government of the Lordship, and because the earls of Kildare were the magnates best placed to involve themselves actively in the government and defence of the Pale. However, a heavy price had to be paid in quality of service for the convenience of a cheap caretaker. The central administration became a theatre of war in the prosecution of the Kildare–Butler feud. Desmond having already withdrawn,

---

[49] *S.P. Henry VIII*, ii, pp. 145–7 (*L.P.*, iv(ii), no. 4688).

government was thus deprived of the cooperation of the only other great Anglo-Irish feudatory besides Kildare. In this way the efficiency of the central administration was vitiated by magnate faction, and the problem of extending its jurisdiction beyond the Pale was compounded. The other drawback of the arrangement has already been noted, the opportunity with which it provided Kildare himself to exploit his public office for the augmentation of his hereditary dignity, by transferring the jurisdiction and the functions of the one to the other. The Surrey episode showed the magnitude of the task that faced the crown in attempting to withdraw from the arrangement. In order to ensure a free hand for the lord lieutenant in Ireland, Kildare was summoned to London and placed under a form of arrest, in effect a hostage to the king. There were precedents for this, and the Fitzgeralds had developed a strategy for dealing with it: that was to manipulate their alliances, especially in the area of the Irishy, so as to demonstrate their indispensability in maintaining political equilibrium within the Lordship. This was done to such good effect, as we have seen, that by 1524 Kildare was again in full control of government.

The auspices were undoubtedly unpropitious for reform. Yet the situation had its redeeming feature. Kildare's efforts to entrench himself in the Pale provoked opposition from within the political establishment of the Pale itself, which found expression in that pressure for political reform which we examined in the last chapter. This had two implications for government in Ireland. It provided the English crown with local allies in its efforts to reassert control over the Dublin administration, allies who at this stage showed more zeal than their mentors for the task. Secondly, it added a new dimension to the intrigue and faction surrounding crown government in Ireland, one that historians are prone to ignore. From the second decade of the sixteenth century the struggles for control of the Irish executive are no longer merely a matter of Fitzgerald–Butler rivalry. A third faction exists, committed to neither side, but ready to exploit their rivalry for the sake of advancing the cause of reform.

The Surrey mission itself has to be seen against the background of a joint alliance between the reforming element and the Butler faction though, as mentioned already, the immediate impulse came from the king's passing enthusiasm for the practice of government. In 1515 Sir William Darcy presented his articles, strongly critical of Kildare's administration, to the English council. On that occasion Kildare came through unscathed, and Darcy lost office as vice-treasurer for his trouble. But Robert Cowley, an Ormond client, renewed the attack in 1518–19, and Darcy again lent support. These were the circumstances in which Surrey superseded Kildare in 1520.[50] The course of the expedition also shows plenty of evidence of mutal warmth and cooperation between Surrey and the Pale administrators. Sir William Darcy, Sir Patrick Finglas and Sir Patrick Bermingham, the chief justice of the king's bench, were all closely associated with his administration. In his initial revival of the policy of coexistence, and his firm repudiation of Henry VIII's scheme for a general reformation by conciliation, he accepted their assessment of the situation. Finglas's mission to Wolsey on his behalf, at a crucial stage of the policy discussion with the king, clearly played a major part in the abandonment of the king's proposal.[51]

Where they differed was on the subject of Surrey's departure. Here the lord lieutenant played his hand very close to his chest. But it is clear that the administrators suspected the worst in the winter of 1521. While Surrey was pressing for immediate withdrawal the Pale-dominated council was writing separately to Wolsey assuring him that the country had been brought 'in towardness of reformation', and that Surrey was uniquely placed to capitalise on the advances already made, since experience had taught him 'the ways how the said reformation may ratherest be brought to effect, of any man, that ever came in this land in our time'.[52] Their plea fell on deaf ears, and by February they were writing in barely concealed reproach, contrasting the 'marvellous towardness' to which the land had recently been brought with the jeopardy in which it was placed 'by reason of this sudden departing of the earl of Surrey and the king's army here'.[53] If the will of crown government for reform had faltered, the will of local reformers had not.

[50] *Cal. Car. MSS*, i, no. 126. *Cal. Car. MSS* (Book of Howth), v, pp. 192–3. Quinn, 'Henry VIII and Ireland, 1509–34', p. 324 and n. 21.

[51] *S.P. Henry VIII*, ii, pp. 61, 63.

[52] *S.P. Henry VIII*, ii, p. 91 (*L.P.*, iii, no. 1888).

[53] *S.P. Henry VIII*, ii, p. 93.

The sequel to the Surrey expedition draws attention to one other relevant factor concerning the interplay between internal faction and the reformation of the central administration – sharp divergence between the reformers and the Butler interest. This is illustrated by the reaction of the Pale administrators to the initial arrangement for the conduct of government made on Surrey's departure. It was decided in London to place Ormond in charge as an alternative to the restoration of Kildare. However, so far as the Pale administrators were concerned, the distance of the Butler power base from the Pale deprived Ormond of the only justification which could be offered for a local magnate as head of government, his ability to protect the four shires. Within two months of Ormond's asssumption of office in March 1522 they were already going behind his back, appealing to Norfolk to have Kildare sent home.[54]

So far the Pale community has been considered as a force for reform within the Lordship. The Surrey expedition also draws attention to an important limitation on that commitment and, by the same token, to an area of extreme sensitivity in Anglo-Irish relations that was to constitute a major issue in the history of political reform in Ireland. This was the problem of finance. Surrey was followed to Ireland by Sir John Stile, a treasury expert, whose task was to survey and reform the revenues. His examination showed that Sir William Darcy had exaggerated their potential – understandably, in order to encourage positive intervention from England. It transpired that a subsidy of £10,000 from England was required to maintain government on the scale of Surrey's administration.[55] Thus the problem was posed of where the money was to come from to pay for reformation in Ireland. From the beginning parliament provided a forum for the debate, and in the parliament of 1521 both sides took up the positions which basically they would retain thereafter. The attitude of the king was that Irish reform was to be financed from Irish resources. Accordingly two bills were drafted, designed to increase the crown's Irish revenues. One was to resume certain custom duties currently conceded to the port towns; the other was to give the crown a salt monopoly. The preambles of both justified the

---

54 S.P. 60/1, no. 60 (L.P., iv, no. 4302).
55 S.P. Henry VIII, ii, pp. 77, 85. Quinn, 'Henry VIII and Ireland, 1509–34', p. 329 and note 43.

proposals as a means of enabling the king to proceed to the reformation of the Lordship.[56] The response of the king's obedient subjects in parliament was to reject both measures. This does not mean that they opposed reformation. Though no record of the parliamentary debate remains, the local argument soon became clear in submissions to England on the subject of financing the reformation. The obedient community was neither able nor prepared to bear the financial burden of reforming the rest of the country. That was the responsibility of the crown. The money should therefore come from the king's resources, as an investment which would pay rich dividends in due course when the unreformed areas were brought to peace and prosperity. Much of the interplay between the monarch, the English administration, and the local movement for political reformation, in the course of the century, was concerned with manoeuvring 'the other side' into conceding virtually what was refused explicitly in the matter of financing reform.

Ostensibly the Surrey expedition achieved nothing. Yet time would show that there had been some important if indirect benefits. It had served to alert the English administration to the dangers of the existing situation. Even if there was no mind for dramatic intervention from that quarter, at least there was better oversight than hitherto, and a search for some means of inexpensive improvement. No less important, it brought the Anglo-Irish reforming movement into the corridors of power in England. Those Pale administrators who had been about Surrey in 1520–2 never allowed the contact to lapse. The example has already been cited of Thomas Bathe, on his return from a pilgrimage to Walsingham, calling in on the duke of Norfolk (as Surrey had then become) to discuss Irish political affairs with him. Apart from those already mentioned, continuing contact can be traced between the former lord lieutenant and a number of other figures actively involved in Pale politics – the influential Barnewall family (barons of Trimletiston), the Dublin merchant Thomas Stephens, and Walter Wellesley, the prior of the monastery of Greatconnell in Co. Kildare. No doubt all of these had an eye to personal

---

[56] These proposals originated in a memo prepared for the consideration of the council preparatory to Surrey's departure for Ireland, S.P. 1/30, pp. 89–90. D. B. Quinn (ed.), 'Bills and statutes of the Irish parliaments of Henry VII and Henry VIII', *Analecta Hibernica*, x (1941), pp. 120–1.

advantage in maintaining the link. Yet it is indicative of the wider political implications of the relationship that in practically every case these men are also known to have incurred the disfavour of Kildare, without acquiring any close association with the Butlers.[57] The mentality of these men is, no doubt, reflected in the fatherly advice of a senior member of the Irish judiciary to a younger colleague visiting London on government business in 1536: 'Principally, I need not advise you to attend the common-wealth of this wretched land, but secondly, I advise you, speed something for yourself and your heirs...that you thereby may be had in remembrance, as other judges, having like room, long gone past this life, now are, by their purpose and shift.'[58] That combination of self-interest and concern for the commonwealth lay behind the dogged persistence of Anglo-Irish reformers in the decade following 1523. It led them to play a major part in launching the new reforming initiative of Thomas Cromwell in 1533, and in finally defeating the Kildare supremacy.

A classification of reform policies

Our examination so far has brought to light a variety of approaches to political reform in the Irish Lordship. In fact, surprising though it may seem, the broad framework within which the debate about policy was to proceed throughout the century had now emerged. At this transitional point, before carrying the examination into the phase of the crown's sustained involvement in Irish reform, it may be useful to summarise and classify the main lines of approach.

In doing so, difficulties of terminology present themselves. At an early stage of his administration Thomas Cromwell posed the question, in a terse memo relating to Ireland, 'whether it shall be expedient to begin a conquest or a reformation'.[59] Historians generally follow this usage, and distinguish between reformation policies and conquest policies in discussing proposals for solving the Irish problem. The snag about adopting that terminology is

---

[57] On the friction between the Barnewalls and Kildare at this time, see *Cal. Car. MSS* (Book of Howth), v. p. 191. In 1523 Surrey was instrumental in obtaining the see of Kildare for Wellesley against Kildare's candidate, *S.P. Henry VIII*, ii, p. 98 (*L.P.*, iii(ii), no. 2824).   [58] *S.P. Henry VIII*, iii, p. 19.

[59] S.P. 60/2, pp. 82–3 (*L.P.*, vii, no. 1211).

indicated in a remark made by an author of 'a treatise of Irlande' at the end of the century. He explained that 'The plots for reformation of Ireland are of two kinds. One which undertake to procure it by conquest and by peopling of countries with English inhabitants... Another kind is of those wherein is undertaken to make reformation by public establishment of Justice.'[60] For this author 'reformation' and 'conquest' were not mutually exclusive categories, since the former referred to the ultimate objective of policy and the latter to one of two possible strategies for achieving it. This was the sense in which 'reformation' was most usually used in the earlier as well as the later part of the century. It would be confusing, therefore, to use 'conquest' and 'reformation' as labels by which to classify Irish policies.

Apart from the difficulty about nomenclature there is also the difficulty about the categories themselves. Here Cromwell and the later author seem to agree in distinguishing between two alternatives, a policy designed to subjugate the island by force and one designed to bring it to obedience by effective government. By the time the later author wrote these did indeed represent the possibilities. In Cromwell's time, however, the question about strategies was anteceded by a question about objectives. As we have seen, the most influential element within the Anglo-Irish movement for political reformation in its first phase did not contemplate a general subjugation of the island. They envisaged a solution based on the concept of coexisting communities that emerged in the course of the fourteenth century. This concept continued to receive powerful support – including that of Cromwell himself – down to the end of the Marian period. It must therefore be comprehended in any classification of crown policy.

Accordingly, the first distinction that is to be made in the discussion of policy in this period is between the late medieval bilateral approach to government and a unilateral conception whereby the crown's sovereign jurisdiction would extend throughout the island. Programmes of the first kind can be labelled *conservative*. This is partly because they represent the traditional late medieval policy, and were put forward, as we saw, by reformers who viewed the problem of reformation from a

---

[60] Quoted in Quinn (ed.), 'Edward Walshe's "Conjectures concerning the state of Ireland"', p. 303.

predominantly traditional perspective. It is partly also because they were orientated so strongly towards consolidation and conservation of the colonial area. Within the category of the conservative approach a further distinction must be made. The fourteenth-century concept of a viable colony extending throughout the area of the Englishry was modified in the fifteenth century by the concept of a Pale, confined within the four shires around Dublin. The examination of the Surrey episode revealed the relevance of this distinction. Surrey strove to promote the broader concept under the influence of the Anglo-Irish reformers, whereas Henry VIII opted for the more limited one as the most economical expedient in that vague interim while awaiting an occasion to launch a conquest.[61] It is proposed to refer to the more ambitious policy as *strong conservatism* in contrast to the *politic conservatism* to which the king reverted.

Turning to the solutions which envisaged the establishment of royal sovereignty throughout the island, a distinction has to be made between those which proposed a forceful (conquest) strategy, and those which proposed to achieve their objective simply by promoting just and efficient government. Again the discussion between Surrey and Henry VIII provides the example of these alternatives in the scheme of conquest and colonisation outlined by the lord lieutenant in opposition to the policy of conciliation proposed by the king.[62] However, examination of the Anglo-Irish reformation treatises provided an example of a programme composed of one element of Surrey's programme and one of the king's. This is the commonwealth treatise which insists with Surrey against the king on the need for an initial conquest, but substitutes for Surrey's subsequent programme of colonisation the king's scheme for the assimilation of the existing lordships and reform by means of persuasion. It is proposed to refer to conquest policies generically as *radical*, distinguishing the strategy of conquest and colonisation proposed by Surrey as *extreme radicalism*, and the strategy of conquest followed by assimilation as *moderate radicalism*.[63]

Finally, the policy of conciliation proposed by the king may be classified as 'liberal'.[64] It proposed to proceed at all stages by appealing to the reasonableness of the Irishry and to their

---

[61] Above, pp. 60, 66–71.

[62] Above, pp. 60–6.

[63] Above, pp. 51–6.

[64] Above, pp. 60–6.

amenability to reform. It reflected, therefore, those optimistic assumptions about the inherent goodness of human nature which are characteristic of liberal humanism, though the depth of the king's own convictions on this score may be gauged from Surrey's success in persuading him to the contrary. In any case, as we noted, Henry's conciliatory gesture did not go nearly far enough to be realistic. A more generous conciliatory formula was to emerge within the Anglo-Irish reform movement in the 1530s. These two approaches to a conciliatory policy may be distinguished as *royal liberalism* and *commonwealth liberalism* respectively.

PART II

The reform of the Lordship in the era of Thomas
Cromwell, 1530–40

4

The revival of crown government

The long tradition of Irish historiography which takes the rebellion of the Fitzgeralds of Kildare in 1534 as marking the transition between the medieval and the modern phase of Irish political history is surely correct. The continuous succession of English heads of the Irish executive, broken only by the appointment of Ormond – an exceptional man in execeptional circumstances – in the reigns of Charles I and his son, begins with the ousting of the earl of Kildare from office in the prelude to the rebellion. Similarly, the continued presence of an English army in Ireland dates from the arrival of the force under Lord Deputy Skeffington in the summer of 1534 to deal with the rebellion. Both phenomena, the succession of English heads of the executive and the continued presence of the army, testify to a new involvement on the part of government in England with Irish affairs, an involvement which profoundly influenced the course of Irish history throughout the modern period.

Thus far the traditional historiography will hardly be challenged. What must be discussed are the circumstances which precipitated this new involvement and its precise significance in the context of Tudor policy towards Ireland. According to the tradition, 1534 saw the culmination of a number of related historical developments in the onset of the Tudor conquest. One was the emergence of the renaissance-style Tudor monarchy which sooner or later had to come to grips with the home rule – as Curtis termed it – of the Anglo-Irish and Gaelic magnates. The showdown between Henry VIII and the Fitzgeralds marks the point at which the irresistible force finally launched itself against the immovable object. The timing of the assault was determined by the Reformation in religion. This brought matters to a head for two reasons: first, because of the need to assert the royal ecclesiastical supremacy in the Irish Church; and secondly, because the heightened threat of invasion by the forces of Catholicism made it imperative to secure the back door.[1]

All of this has come under question in recent years as part of the revival in the study of sixteenth-century Ireland. One historian, looking forward from 1534, has argued persuasively against regarding that year as the beginning of the Tudor conquest. The crown did not commit itself to such a policy until the reign of Elizabeth. What happened in 1534 was essentially a holding operation designed to secure the Pale in new circumstances of threat.[2] Two other historians have examined what happened in 1534 against the background of English policy in the years preceding, and have concluded that the crown at this stage was reacting to rather than determining the course of events. In place of the ruthlessly efficient Tudor machine, setting about the destruction of the overmighty Fitzgeralds, we are presented with a new administration, headed by Thomas Cromwell, unfamiliar and out of touch with Irish affairs and too engrossed in the urgent business of the royal supremacy in England to pay much attention to Ireland. Nothing was done until the situation drifted into rebellion and the crown was forced to intervene or forefeit its foothold in Ireland. Thus, the Kildare rebellion was not just a symptom of the arrival of the 'new monarchy' in Ireland, as the traditional historiography would have it, but its cause. The conflagration drew attention to the urgency of the Irish situation and imposed on the crown the necessity to devise some way of coping with it. It took the Irish crisis of 1534 to produce an Irish policy.[3]

In this section, which is concerned with the significance of the 1530s for the course of Irish history, all of these questions will necessarily come under review. What were the circumstances which precipitated the historic intervention in 1534, and what – if not conquest – was the purpose which sustained the momentum after the Kildare rebellion was crushed? What was the role of the

---

[1] For a modern statement of the traditional interpretation see G. A. Hayes-McCoy 'The royal supremacy and ecclesiastical revolution, 1534–47', in Moody *et al.* (eds), *New history of Ireland*, iii, pp. 39–68.

[2] Canny, *The Elizabethan Conquest of Ireland*, pp. 29–65. Cf. Bradshaw, 'The Elizabethans and the Irish', *Studies*, lxv (1977), p. 41.

[3] Quinn, 'Henry VIII and Ireland, 1509–34', pp. 318–44. Ellis, 'Tudor policy and the Kildare ascendancy'; Ellis substantially revises Quinn but not on the point at issue here.

Reformation in religion, and what place did Ireland occupy in English foreign policy as a result of the new threat of a Catholic crusade?

Before commencing that discussion, however, attention should be drawn to a thesis which is argued more by implication than expressly in what follows. It relates to that long-fought and continuing debate in England about the architect of English policy in the 1530s: king or minister?[4] The present study does not address itself directly to that controversy, but it implies that the architect of Irish policy, at any rate, was Thomas Cromwell. The bias of the evidence is overwhelmingly in this direction. The presence of the king in Irish affairs throughout the period is for the most part invisible. It is to Cromwell that the great bulk of correspondence flows and from him that it emanates, unless he wishes to lend some missive the added authority of the royal signature. Furthermore, it will be seen that what the crown attempted to implement in Ireland at this period is of a piece with what was attempted elsewhere throughout the king's dominions under Cromwell's administration. No doubt it could be argued that the unifying intelligence was the king's not Cromwell's. On the other hand, as we shall see, the formula for an Irish solution at this period is substantially at variance with the views expressed by the king himself in 1520–1. Furthermore, once Cromwell departed from the scene in 1540 Irish policy was again conceived on a quite different basis, and it is clear on this occasion that the initiative in the formulation of policy came from the Irish administration and not from the king. It seems reasonable to infer, therefore, that the Irish policy under examination in the 1530s is that of Thomas Cromwell. The king may be regarded as the maker of policy in so far as his support was essential to the implementation of any major programme.

The third partner in the making of policy was the local movement for reform. With regard to the contribution from this source, three points may be made at this stage. In the first place, it would be a mistake to regard local reformers as a tightly knit body on the lines of a modern political party. They represented the vital current of reforming energy within the colony; but they

---

[4] G. R. Elton, 'King or Minister? The man behind the Henrician Reformation' in *History*, xxxix (1954), pp. 216–32. Idem, *England under the Tudors*, pp. 484–5.

were not united by a common programme of reform. Our examination of early reforming treatises showed two substantially diverging lines of approach, and in the 1530s it will be possible to discern a number of reforming lobbies each advocating a programme of reform that differed in fundamental respects from the others. Secondly, it would be a mistake to regard these merely as Cromwellian agents, acting at the behest of their master. Undoubtedly most of them came to be associated more or less closely with the king's chief minister. But those most prominently involved with reform clearly regarded themselves as collaborators rather than as agents, bound to Cromwell by a common concern for reform in Ireland. Indeed, in many cases the objective was to enlist Cromwell as the sponsor of one particular line of approach rather than another. On the other hand it would be a mistake to identify Cromwell with any one of these lobbies. This brings us back to our starting point. Cromwell listened to – indeed, actively canvassed – advice on all sides and, as we shall see, drew heavily upon it. That was the mark of his stature as a politician. For while drawing freely upon the advice of others he retained his independence of judgement and his own unique conception of the master plan.

The inauguration of reform

So far as the historiographical discussion is concerned, the thesis presented here about the circumstances in which the crown's Irish policy was launched in 1534 consists in a reformulation of the traditional interpretation. The Kildare rebellion was a consequence and not a cause of the crown's new involvement with Ireland. However, this new involvement was not simply the expression of the ineluctable drive of Tudor despotism against overmighty subjects. It expressed rather the constructive concern of the crown for the reform of the Irish Lordship. At this point continuity can be reestablished with the closing discussion of the previous chapter. The new involvement of 1534 resulted from the interaction of two reforming impulses, one located within the administration in Ireland and closely associated with the Anglo-Irish reforming milieu, the other located within the English administration and finding its source in Thomas Cromwell.

It is reasonable to surmise that Cromwell was already well

acquainted with the problems of the Irish Lordship when he entered royal service in 1530. He had been in the inner ring of Cardinal Wolsey's personal servants for at least a decade. It is true that his function was to act as a legal and business agent in the cardinal's personal affairs;[5] nevertheless, in view of the capacity for politics and public administration that he later displayed, it is hardly conceivable that he could have spent so long a period in such close contact with the man who was at the hub of government without becoming familiar with the great problems of state including the problem of Ireland. Interestingly, the first evidence of a direct contact with Ireland is associated with this background.

Prominent with Cromwell in Wolsey's household was the ecclesiastic John Alen, for whom the cardinal obtained the archbishopric of Dublin and the office of Irish lord chancellor in 1528. Their work in Wolsey's household had brought the two into close contact, especially when they collaborated on the project of dissolving the rundown monasteries that endowed the cardinal's college at Oxford. This contact was renewed in 1530 when, on Wolsey's fall, Cromwell had just managed to launch himself on a career in the king's service. Alen was implicated in the charge of praemunire levelled against Wolsey, and like the cardinal he turned to the king's new servant in his distress. Although the only letter from Alen to Cromwell dating from that episode is confined to recounting the archbishop's personal plight, the renewal of the contact could not have failed to deepen Cromwell's knowledge of Irish conditions, especially since Alen was now prominently associated with the cause of political reform in Ireland and with opposition to Fitzgerald hegemony in government.[6]

By this means, at any rate, Cromwell was brought into direct contact with the personnel of government in Ireland as soon as he entered the king's service. His contacts became more extended as his political influence grew between 1531 and 1533. Two of his early petitioners are of special interest in this discussion. One was the clerk of the council, also named John Alen, who came to Ireland as the archbishop's secretary, a circumstance which no doubt explains how he was put in touch with Cromwell. To that connection can be attributed Alen's promotion to the office of

---

[5] Elton, *The Tudor revolution in government*, pp. 71–88.
[6] *S.P. Henry VIII*, ii, p. 158 (*L.P.*, v. no. 878). A. Gwynn, *The medieval province of Armagh* (Dundalk 1946), pp. 63–6. On all of this see the note on Alen in the *D.N.B.*

master of the rolls in July 1533, following a visit to court.[7] The other petitioner provides the first evidence linking Cromwell with the Anglo-Irish movement for political reform. He was Thomas Cusack, a landowner and lawyer from Cosingston in Co. Meath. Sometime before the autumn of 1531 Cromwell is found arranging to obtain the royal signature on a bill on Cusack's behalf.[8] Cromwell's early association with Alen and Cusack has a particular significance. Not only were they closely involved in launching his first reform programme, but they proved to be dominant figures in the history of political reform in Ireland through three succeeding decades.

One other contact dating from Cromwell's earliest years as a royal servant calls for comment. This one is usually emphasised to the exclusion of all others and loaded with misleading implications. In a letter to Cromwell at the beginning of January 1532 Piers Butler, earl of Ossory, referred to the friendship newly established between them.[9] The alacrity with which Ossory attached himself to the emerging administrator indicates his need for a friend at court to counterbalance the influential contacts among the court nobility of his rival, the earl of Kildare. The latter had acquired as father-in-law an English nobleman, the Marquis of Dorset. More recently the dispute between the Butlers and the Boleyns over the Ormond inheritance enabled Kildare to win the good will of an even more important person, the earl of Wiltshire, the father of the future queen, and by Wiltshire's good offices to secure the favourable disposition of the duke of Norfolk. Since Wiltshire and Norfolk were Cromwell's competitors for royal influence, Ossory's intention was of course to establish a Butler–Cromwell nexus to counteract the Fitzgerald–Boleyn–Howard one.

The interaction of the factional struggles within the two administrations seriously complicated the preparations for launching the programme of Cromwellian reform and, indeed, contributed something to the situation in which these preparations

---

[7] *L.P.*, vi, nos. 929(26), 1051.
[8] P.R.O., E. 36/139, p. 17. *L.P.*, vii, no. 923(iv). Cromwell's Anglo-Irish contacts at this time included at least two others who were associated with reform, viz. Thomas Luttrell from the Pale, *L.P.*, vi. no. 727, and William Wise of Waterford, *L.P.*, vi, no. 815.
[9] *S.P. Henry VIII*, ii, p. 153 (*L.P.*, v. no. 688).

precipitated a rebellion. At the same time it would be a great mistake to suppose that Cromwell identified himself with the Butler faction and that his intrusions into Irish affairs at this time can be explained on that basis. If his policy had an anti-Kildare bias it was neither inspired by nor directed towards Butler interests. The dominant local influence upon him was not the Butler faction but the local movement for political reform. As we shall see, the objective he pursued was more comprehensive and more constructive than simply the overthrow of the Fitzgeralds.

Meanwhile Ossory's letter of January 1532 has a more immediate interest. It provides an example of the way in which Cromwell's Irish suitors at this early stage provided him with a flow of information on the local situation. If the earl's account was strongly influenced by his prejudices, Cromwell may be credited with the necesssary acumen to extract its useful content. It is clear, in fact, that from the earliest stages Cromwell used his expanding network of Irish contacts to compile a dossier on the Lordship. A catalogue of documents held by him late in 1534 listed among those he had retained from the two-year period beginning at Michaelmas 1531 a set of articles put in by William Fagan, an Anglo-Irish intermediary with O'Neill, documents and reports relating to the short-lived experiment of installing the Englishman Sir William Skeffington as lord deputy in 1531–2, a deposition against Kildare's liberty jurisdiction, two 'books of the description of Ireland' and a 'device' on Irish affairs by John Alen.[10]

Bearing in mind this steady accumulation of information and of personal contacts from 1530 onwards, we take up the crucial question. At what point did Cromwell formulate and begin to implement an Irish policy? Did preoccupation with the ecclesiastical revolution in England push Irish problems beyond the range of his practical concerns until their urgent need for attention was brought home to him by the rebellion in the summer of 1534? Did it take the Irish crisis, therefore, to produce an Irish policy? The thesis argued in the following pages is that Cromwell embarked upon a policy of Irish reform in the summer of 1533 and applied himself to it steadily thereafter, despite the gravity and urgency of other business claiming his attention. Cromwell's Irish policy was launched, therefore, no more than six months after he

---

[10] P.R.O., E. 36/139, pp. 83, 95, 114 (*L.P.*, vii, no. 923, (xix, xxi, xxxi)).

had succeeded in entrenching himself as the king's chief minister and almost a year before the Fitzgeralds went into rebellion.[11]

Characteristically his reform began with the personnel of the Irish administration. The appointment of John Alen as master of the rolls in July 1533 was the first major step towards refurbishing that body.[12] Around the same time Thomas Cusack was promoted to a minor post in the exchequer.[13] Further proof of the direction in which Cromwell was moving – steadily towards reform – was provided after the death of Sir Bartholomew Dillon, the chief justice of the king's bench, late in the summer. Cromwell proposed to utilise the vacancy to effect an administrative reshuffle which would bring in Sir Patrick Finglas, the veteran reformer, as chief justice, and would enable two other Pale reformers, Gerald Aylmer and Thomas Luttrell, to follow Finglas up the ladder.[14]

That the projected reshuffle in the administration did not take place immediately indicates the way in which factional interests were already complicating the situation. Cusack's preferment earlier had caused a storm since Kildare, acting in virtue of his authority as lord deputy, had allocated the same post to one of his own cronies.[15] Inkling of the proposed Finglas promotion roused the earl into mobilising his English alliance. A letter asking Wiltshire for support played on the Butler–Boleyn dispute over the Ormond inheritance, alleging Finglas's attachment to the Butler interest.[16] Very likely, therefore, Cromwell held over the latest spate of promotions in order not to prejudice the outcome of his next move. This was a summons to Kildare to come to court, which was issued early in the autumn of 1533.[17] The enormity of the complication this caused is indicated by the fact that the promotions proposed in the autumn did not take place until the following summer.

It is customarily assumed that Cromwell's only thought at this

---

[11] On Cromwell's rise to power see Elton, *The Tudor revolution in government*, pp. 71–98.

[12] *L.P.*, vi, no. 929(26).

[13] *L.P.*, vi, no. 105(16), 1250.

[14] B.L., Cotton MS Titus B. I. fos. 453–7 (*L.P.* vi, no. 1381).

[15] Kildare's nominee, Richard Delahide, refused to accept Cromwell's authorisation in favour of Cusack unless supported by a royal patent, *L.P.*, vi, nos. 105(16), 841(i), 1250. *Calendar of patent rolls, Ireland, Henry VIII–Elizabeth*, p. 4.

[16] *L.P.*, vi, no. 944.

[17] The date of the summons cannot be established precisely, but Kildare's wife had appeared at court in response to it by 3 October, *L.P.*, vi, no. 1249.

stage was to break the power of the Fitzgeralds. On the contrary, the evidence indicates that Cromwell did not envisage the dire fate that overtook the family until after they went into rebellion. In fact, as we shall see, what the evidence indicates is that at this stage he was preparing the way for launching a full-scale programme of political reform in the Lordship, in which his plan for the Fitzgeralds was reform not destruction. His anxiety to bring Kildare to London before launching the reform programme can be understood. In London the earl could be exposed to persuasion to accept the disagreeable reforms. At the same time, his presence there would minimise his opportunities for making trouble locally at the crucial initial stages of the reform campaign and would provide the government with a hostage, in effect, for the good behaviour of his kinsmen.

In the same way it would be a mistake to interpret the events that occupied the period from the autumn of 1533 to the following spring purely as manoeuvres in a factional struggle. That is what the Fitzgeralds did at the time, to their cost. It is true that the political pressure against the earl mounted throughout the second half of 1533. Robert Cowley pressed the attack on behalf of the Butlers.[18] Skeffington, whose brief experimental period of office had ended with the reinstallation of Kildare in 1532, submitted his own indictment.[19] The political reformers of the Pale were active through Thomas Cusack and Thomas Finglas (the son of the reforming chief baron of the exchequer), who left for court in the late autumn of 1533. However, this activity was not directed narrowly to the destruction of the Geraldines. Certainly, the purpose of the Pale reformers in London was to argue the case for reform. A surviving copy of Patrick Finglas's treatise on political reform, the 'Breviate', written in the hand of his son may well belong to this episode.[20] The attitude within reforming circles at this period is expressed in the most authoritative indictment relating to the episode, that brought across by John Alen. It took the form of a report on the state of the Lordship supported by an impressive array of signatories, eight high-ranking

---

[18] S.P. 60/6, no. 33 (*L.P.*, xiii(i), no. 883). *Cal. Car. MSS.*, i, no. 126.

[19] *S.P. Henry VIII*, ii, p. 181 (*L.P.*, vi, no. 1347).

[20] S.P. 60/2, no. 7. For the copy in the hand of Thomas Finglas see S.P. 60/2, no. 18 (*L.P.*, viii, no. 1081). Cusack's departure for court in the autumn of 1533 is referred to in *L.P.*, vi, no. 1250.

ecclesiastics, two of the Pale nobility, and three of the Pale's administrators. It vented no personal spites and had no axe to grind except political reform. In this case it was critical of Anglo-Irish magnates in general and of Kildare and Ossory in particular, and pleaded for the rescue of government from their control. The message of this report was spelt out in greater detail in two anonymous treatises submitted during the same period.[21] The weight given by Cromwell to these three documents is clear from subsequent events. To a considerable extent his strategy in the ensuing months and the content of his first programme of political reform followed their recommendations.

Despite the scanty documentation Cromwell can be seen, throughout the spring and early summer of 1534, applying himself to three major projects preparatory to launching the general programme. These indicate how comprehensive and well thought out was his design, in contrast to the ill-considered and shifting attempts between 1529 and 1532. One project was, of course, the installation of an English lord deputy. However, there was no naive expectation that a new head of the administration with the assistance of a small military retinue could accomplish all. As we have seen, the executive was to be thoroughly refurbished by the appointment of suitable personnel to outstanding vacancies. The most novel aspect of the preparations was the determined attempt to come to grips with the problem posed for government by the overmighty earls of Kildare and Ossory. The latter as well as the former was brought to court. The aim was twofold: to pacify the feud between the two which had been the cause of so much political instability in the Lordship, and to secure a formal indenture from both binding them to cooperate with the revival of crown government, including its extension into their territories.[22]

The issue, on 8 May, of a patent on behalf of Sir Patrick Finglas for the post of chief justice of the king's bench – the proposal

---

[21] Alen's 'Instructions' claimed the authority of the Irish council, but this can hardly be accepted. The indictment lacked the support not only of the acting lord deputy, Kildare's son, but of the Geraldine chief justice of the common pleas and of the lord of Howth, *S.P. Henry VIII*, ii, p. *162* (*L.P.*, vi, no. 1586). The two anonymous treatises are not dated, but internal evidence places them in the winter of 1533–4 – i.e., both were written while Kildare and Ossory were on their way to court, S.P. 60/2, pp. 4–13, 30–7. *S.P. Henry VIII*, ii, pp. 166, 182 (*L.P.*, vi, no. 1587, vii, no. 264).

[22] On all of this see my 'Cromwellian reform and the origins of the Kildare rebellion, 1553–4', *T.R.H.S.*, 5th ser., xxvii (1977), pp. 83–4.

against which Kildare had protested so vehemently to Wiltshire the previous August – signalised that the process of finalisation had begun. Finglas's appointment was followed by the reshuffle projected the previous autumn. Aylmer got Finglas's old post as chief baron of the exchequer but, deviating from the original plan, Cusack was put in to fill Aylmer's vacancy instead of Thomas Luttrell. It seems that the latter was held in reserve with a view to higher things, for he got the post of chief justice of the common pleas when the Geraldine Richard Delahide was ousted in October. Finally Thomas Finglas was given a start as protonotary of the common bench.[23] Meanwhile the appointment of Skeffington as lord deputy was also put in train, as letters from him to Cromwell on 24 May indicate.[24]

On the last day of May the Butler earl, Ossory, subscribed an indenture by which he bound himself and his heirs to act 'in all and everything as appertaineth to their duties of allegiance of an English subject'.[25] The various clauses which spelt out in detail what this implied will be discussed later. Here it need only be said that Ossory's indenture provided for a particular application of a general programme of reform outlined in a set of *Ordinances for the government of Ireland* which were intended as a blueprint for the new government.[26] Thus final arrangements for launching a full-scale programme of reform were put in train in May 1534. At the same time the process of launching the programme in Ireland was begun. Early in the second half of the month Thomas Cusack and Thomas Finglas were dispatched with instructions from the king which were to be delivered to the Irish council assembled under Silken Thomas, Kildare's son, whom he had deputed to act for him as lord deputy during his absence at court.[27] Then the whole plan went awry: Silken Thomas rejected the

---

23 Cal. pat. rolls Ire., *Henry VIII–Elizabeth*, p. 12. *Fiants, Henry VIII*, p. 36.

24 *S.P. Henry VIII*, ii, p. 193 (*L.P.*, vii, nos. 704–5).

25 *S.P. Henry VIII*, ii, p. 194 (*L.P.*, vii, no. 740).

26 *S. P. Henry VIII*, ii, p. 207. Because the *Ordinances* are not dated, it cannot be said precisely at what date prior to Skeffington's departure for Ireland, at the beginning of August 1534, they were devised and put into print, *L.P.*, vii, no. 105. However, the complementary nature of the indenture concluded with Ossory on 31 May indicates that the two documents were prepared in conjunction. The fact that Skeffington could bring printed copies of the *Ordinances* – an extensive document – to Ireland at the beginning of August also suggests that a manuscript version must have existed some months previously.

27 *S.P.* 60/2, no. 63 (*L.P. Addenda*, i(i), no. 889); *S.P.* 60/2, no. 63 (*L.P.*, ix, no. 514); *L.P.*, vii, no. 736.

king's instructions to assemble in council and went into rebellion.[28]

It is not necessary to discuss here the circumstances which caused Silken Thomas to make this dramatic if ill-advised gesture.[29] Our concern is with its implications for the inauguration of reform in Ireland. The concentration of effort needed to meet the new situation resulted in the postponement of the programme of reform until the spring of 1535. It was then taken up and pursued relentlessly during the remaining five years of Cromwell's administration, as we shall see. However, it should be clear from the foregoing that the work begun in the spring of 1535 was not a response to the Kildare rebellion but the culmination of a project that the rebellion interrupted. The Kildare rebellion did not elicit Cromwellian reform in Ireland: the reform would have come without the rebellion, and it would have come sooner.

Cromwellian reform: the first phase, the revival of government

It is true that the pre-rebellion programme of reform was to undergo further development in the aftermath of the war. The rebellion produced a new set of circumstances and directed attention to aspects of the problem that had earlier received scant consideration. Nevertheless, the original programme has its own special claim to attention. It provided the blueprint according to which one major task of reform in the Lordship was tackled with considerable success. This was the task of revitalising crown government.

What Cromwell and the reform group had worked towards since 1531 crystallised in the policy inaugurated in May 1534 through the reshuffle of the executive and the programme announced in the *Ordinances for Ireland*. The former project can be dealt with briefly. Two more members of the Pale reform milieu were added to the list of promotions in the autumn, when Luttrell's appointment as chief justice of the common pleas came through. These were Sir John Barnewall, lord of Trimletiston, who was promoted lord chancellor – the most exalted post in the

---

[28] S.P. 60/2, no. 63 (*L.P.*, ix, no. 514). Lambeth, Carew MS 602, fo. 139 (*Cal. Car. MSS*, i, no. 84), *S.P. Henry VIII*, ii, p. 197 (*L.P.*, vii, no. 915).

[29] They are discussed in my 'Cromwellian reform and the origins of the Kildare rebellion', pp. 83–4.

executive – and his nephew, Patrick Barnewall, who became serjeant at law.[30] This spate of appointments serves to draw attention to a serious misunderstanding about Cromwell's approach to administrative reform. Of the whole series of appointments made between May and October 1534 in connection with the inauguration of the reform programme, only two broke the monopoly of the Pale group. One was the appointment of an English lord deputy which, as we saw, was completely in line with the thought of Anglo-Irish reformers themselves at this stage. The other was the appointment in October of a personal servant of Cromwell, Sir William Brabazon, to the post of vice-treasurer, the office which oversaw the crucial area of finance. Brabazon's experience as a surveyor and accountant equipped him in a special way for the post.[31] It is clear, therefore, that the systematic discrimination against the Anglo-Irish in government did not begin with Cromwell. His policy was Anglocentric, as we shall see, but not Anglophile. He was ready to sponsor likely men irrespective of nationality. Positive discrimination against the Anglo-Irish in government does not begin until the administration of the earl of Sussex in 1557.

On the other hand, Skeffington's appointment as lord deputy marks a real transition. The appointment of an Englishman to head the executive was not altogether a novelty. Skeffington himself has already served in that capacity briefly in 1531–2; but the experiment collapsed under magnate pressure. On this occasion the arrangement was not allowed to fail. On the contrary, the Fitzgerald opposition broke the dynasty itself. Thus the appointment of Skeffington in 1534 signalises the end of the era of government by Anglo-Irish magnates and the beginning of the era of English heads of government – an era that was to last into modern times.

Before discussing the provisions of the *Ordinances for the government of Ireland*, attention must be drawn to the fact that many of the detailed provisions were a reponse to advice proffered by reformers in Ireland. One document that exercised a considerable

---

[30] *Cal. pat. rolls Ire., Henry VIII*, pp. 12, 13. *L.P.*, vii, nos. 407, 553, 1122(4), app. no. 30.

[31] *Cal. pat. rolls Ire., Henry VIII*, p. 19. Elton, *The Tudor revolution in government*, p. 86. As we saw, the Englishman John Alen had already been promoted master of the rolls in the summer of 1533.

influence on the content of the *Ordinances* was the communication delivered by John Alen in the autumn of 1533 on behalf of an influential group of ecclesiastics and councillors.[32] The argument of that communication was expressed more trenchantly and in greater detail in the two anonymous treatises submitted during the same period.[33] Thomas Cusack and Thomas Finglas were travelling to and fro between London and Dublin at the time also, and this must account for the fact that some of the proposals in Sir Patrick Finglas's *Breviate* appear more or less verbatim in the *Ordinances*.[34] However, the *Ordinances* were ultimately the work of Cromwell. Referring to them in a letter to Cromwell the following year, John Alen spoke of the 'great pains your mastership did take in the devising and debating of them'.[35] To him must go the credit in the first place for designing the first government programme that came to grips with the situation to which Sir William Darcy had drawn attention nineteen years earlier. Thanks to Cromwell the aspiration towards political reformation in Ireland had at last received practical expression in a government programme.

The provisions of the *Ordinances* were directed to both a positive and a negative end.[36] Positively, they were intended to restore crown government throughout the colony; the complementary negative purpose was to abolish the type of political organisation associated with bastard feudalism.

On the negative side the *Ordinances* attacked all those 'abuses', for long lamented in reform treatises, by which the area of the crown's sovereign jurisdiction had been transformed practically into self-contained local political units on the style of Gaelic lordships. There were three principal targets. One was the military system: the large private armies of the lords, and coyne and livery and the other Gaelic exactions that sustained them. A second was the usurpation of the crown's political jurisdiction – and the political cohesiveness of the colony – by the lords' exaction of tributes of protection (biengs) from neighbouring lordships,

---

[32] On Alen's indictment, see above, note 21.
[33] On the date of these two treatises, see above, note 21.
[34] The correspondence is between the *Ordinances* and the *Hibernica* version of the 'Breviate' (see above, p. 39 note 7).
[35] *S.P. Henry VIII*, ii, p. 226.
[36] *S.P. Henry VIII*, ii, p. 207 (*L.P.*, vii, no. 1419).

whether Gaelic or feudal. The third was the usurpation of the crown's function in local government through the replacement of the machinery of the crown by a locally devised system of judicial and fiscal administration, comprised of a mixture of elements of the feudal and Gaelic systems. As an addendum, following the tradition of the reform treatises, the usual proscriptions were included about Gaelicisation in the cultural sphere, language, dress etc.

On the positive side the *Ordinances* proposed to replace this Anglo-Irish brand of bastard feudalism by the crown's own system of political organisation. Thus, in place of the private armies of the great lords, local landowners were to be required to maintain a small retinue, according to their status, for the defence of their estates and tenants, and farmers were to be required to arm themselves for defence. Local government was to be thoroughly restored. The *Ordinances* provided for the appointment of local officers of the crown, justices of the peace, etc. and for the establishment of gaols in every shire. The judges of the central courts were to go on circuit, to hold quarter sessions and to conduct gaol deliveries. A special feature of the revival of local government was the attack on liberty jurisdictions and special semi-autonomous franchises. The recently established liberty of Kildare was abolished. The liberty of Wexford, the patrimony of the absentee earl of Shrewsbury, was to be administered by officers of the crown. Shire administration was to be restored in Carlow and Kilkenny, where it had been dispensed with in favour of the administrations of the earls of Kildare and Ormond. Finally the royal towns, their charters notwithstanding, were to recognise the jurisdiction of the judges of the central court coming on circuit under commissions of oyer and terminer.

The coping stone of the restored structure was, of course, a reformed central administration. An efficient and well-conducted central administration would provide the colony as a whole with political cohesion, and reassert the authority usurped from the crown by the local feudatories. Capitalising on the reform of the personnel of the administration by means of the new appointments, the *Ordinances* provided for a systematic reformation of the working of the system. Starting at the top, safeguards were provided against arbitrary and autocratic government by the lord deputy. His authority was circumscribed by stipulating formal processes of consultation with the council in the conduct of military affairs and with the affected localities concerning such matters as hostings and the billeting of troops. The *Ordinances* also provided for the overhaul of the machinery of the central administration. A greater degree of formality and specialisation of function was to be achieved by insisting on the use – and the uses – of the great seal, the special functions of each department, and the need for the preservation of the records. On the judicial side the role of chancery as a court of equity jurisdiction was normalised – a provision in line with English developments designed to provide greater efficiency in the administration of justice. Thus the central administration, its machinery revived and its personnel reformed, was to act as the driving force in the restoration of the colony.

To complete consideration of the Cromwellian scheme of 1534 one other document must be mentioned. This is the indenture concluded in May 1534 between the King and Piers Butler – who had temporarily exchanged the title of earl of Ormond for that of Ossory in deference to the earldom's heir general, the father of Henry VIII's new queen. The purpose of the indenture was to spell out in the case of this great magnate the implications of the general scheme of reformation set forth in the *Ordinances*.[37] The first clause set the tone. The earl bound himself and his heirs to continue the king's faithful subjects 'as any other of his nobles and peers within his realm of England, in all and everything, as appertaineth to their duties of allegiance of an English subject'. The ensuing clauses acknowledged the earl's status of leadership in his own locality but redefined it in such a way as to eliminate the elements of sovereignty which adhered to it. So far as his internal jurisdiction was concerned he agreed to the revival of shire government in the counties of Kilkenny, Waterford and Tipperary, and to the admission of the judicial and revenue officers of the central administration. In the external sphere he agreed to desist from exercising personal jurisdiction over local Gaelic lordships. Henceforth in relationships with the Gaelic lordships he would act in subordination to the lord deputy, and in the name of the king. However, here also a special function of local leadership was acknowledged in a provision which bound the lord deputy and the council to regard favourably 'such of the Irish or English' as the Butlers brought to 'good conformity'.

---

[37] *S.P. Henry VIII*, ii, p. 194 (*L.P.*, vii, no. 740).

It can be taken as certain that Cromwell envisaged the arrangements for Kildare along the same lines as those for Ormond. There is no indication before the outbreak of the rebellion in June 1534 that he contemplated the complete overthrow of the family. Piers Butler and Kildare were summoned to court in the winter of 1533 in just the same manner. It can be gathered from Cromwell's memos through the winter and the following spring that his plan was to pacify the quarrel between the two and secure their agreement to his reform of government.[38] No doubt he intended Kildare to subscribe to an indenture along the same lines as Ossory's. However, even had the rebellion not taken place, his terms in the case of Kildare would probably have been more rigorous in two respects. The recently established and legally dubious liberty jurisdiction of Kildare would no doubt have gone in any case. Secondly, it had already been decided to detain the earl in England to give Skeffington a freer hand, whereas Ossory was to be allowed to return to assist the lord deputy. Ironically, the vulnerability of the Butlers proved to be their salvation. Since they had neither allies at court – at variance with Norfolk and with the queen's father, Wiltshire – nor a watertight title to the Ormond earldom, the hope of gaining both through Cromwell disposed them to accept the limitations imposed upon them by the May indenture. By contrast, the strength of the Fitzgeralds, based on a secure title, local hegemony, and court alliances emboldened them to stand in the way of Cromwell's policy and allowed them to be crushed in consequence.

Such was Cromwell's initial blueprint for the reform of the Lordship. By and large it was a conventional programme. Considered in the context of the movement for political reform in Ireland it corresponds to the approach which we have classified as 'strong conservatism'. It is concerned with the revival of crown government in the traditional colonial area. It considers the Irishry only in relation to the colony and to the need for stabilising relationships between the two areas. From this point of view it can be said that the abuses proscribed in the *Ordinances* had been attacked by government before, and that the remedies it provided were not new. It maybe that the indenture subscribed by the Butler earl indicates a new approach to the problem of the overmighty subject. Clearly, the intention here was not simply negative, to

---

[38] B.L., Cotton MS Titus B.I., fo. 463. *L.P.*, vi, no. 1056, vii, nos. 50, 420.

humble the great lord. The purpose was rather to redefine the status of the earl in such a way that he retained hegemony in his locality but functioned within the framework of the crown's system of local government rather than as a rival to it. Despite its novelty in the Irish context this formed a basic feature of a strategy designed to reformulate the relationship between the crown and the nobility which had been in operation in England since the reign of the first Tudor.[39]

The real novelty in Cromwell's scheme for the revival of crown government lay in the determination with which it was applied. Never before in the history of English government in Ireland was a programme of reformation implemented with such tenacity of purpose. This was partly because of the enthusiasm of local reformers. Cromwell's contribution was to sustain the necessary support at the highest level of government in England. The combination of local enthusiasm with determination in the English administration ensured that the momentum did not flag throughout the seven years of Cromwell's administration.

In this respect the pattern for the future was set in the aftermath of the Kildare rebellion. The confusion resulting from that event in June 1534 and the diversion of energy to the war effort meant that the reform policy launched in May did not really get off the ground. However, as the forces of the crown took the military initiative in the spring of 1535, Cromwell's new administration swung into the attack also. The first target was the liberty of Kildare. By May Alen, Aylmer and Brabazon were on progress in Co. Kildare prosecuting a commission of oyer and terminer and surveying the crown lands.[40] In the following winter vacation they proceeded to penetrate the breach in Ormond provided by the indenture of the previous year. With the earl and his heir in tow they traversed the Ormond shires, again prosecuting a judicial commission and conducting an inquisition into the crown's rights by way of lands and dues.[41]

The earldom and shires of Ormond illustrate the sustained nature of the assault to which Anglo-Irish magnate autonomy was subjected under Cromwell. The expedition in the Christmas vacation of 1535–6 set the pattern for annual expeditions of crown

[39] Loades, *Politics and the nation*, pp. 117–20.
[40] *S.P. Henry VIII*, ii, pp. 227, 243 (*L.P.*, vii, no. 1419, viii, no. 755).
[41] *S.P. Henry VIII*, ii, pp. 295, 297, 301 (*L.P.*, ix, no. 1051, x, no. 15).

government into the area. A judicial commission was an invariable feature of these. In addition the commissioners gradually wore down Butler resistance to other aspects of the reform programme. A special commission from England in 1537 had the earl proscribe brehon law and Gaelic exactions throughout his liberty jurisdiction, and persuaded him to agree to the levy of crown taxes in the shires.[42] The commissioners in the winter vacation of 1538–9 made good the ground gained by levying the clerical taxes and compounding with the laity for the subsidy.[43] The circumstances of the expedition in the following year, the year of Cromwell's fall, show that it had now become a permanent feature of government. The colony was in political crisis once again as a result of the activities of the Geraldine League. The exigencies of that situation prevented the expedition to Ormond from taking place in the course of the Christmas vacation. But at the first opportunity in March, a commission made the journey from Dublin to hold judicial sessions as usual and, on this occasion, to implement the commission for the dissolution of the monasteries.[44]

It only remains to note that while crown government was being steadily revived in the localities the reform at the centre was also in progress. The bureaucratisation of the treasury – the department mainly responsible for revenue, and for that reason the object of Cromwell's special solicitude – provides another example of the tenacity of the reform effort. Reform began in October 1534 with the appointment of Cromwell's personal assistant, Brabazon, to head the department. Cromwell drafted an accounting procedure for him in 1535, and gave another personal assistant, William Body, the task of auditing his accounts in 1536. The following year he made provision for an annual public audit of the vice-treasurer's accounts, and got the royal commissioners to undertake a general audit for the three years since Brabazon took up office. The process was repeated in 1540, apparently with the intention of making it a triennial affair.[45]

As was to be expected, the way forward was narrow and steep in places. The bill 'for reformation of officers and clerks' was

[42] *S.P. Henry VIII*, ii, pp. 426, 556 (*L.P.*, xiii(i), no. 497). For the separate judicial commission of that year see *L.P.*, xii(ii), no. 1310, 11(2).

[43] *S.P. Henry VIII*, iii, pp. 108, 111 (*L.P.*, xiii(ii), no. 1032, xiv(i), no. 88).

[44] *S.P. Henry VIII*, iii, pp. 195, 197 (*L.P.*, xv, nos. 455, 594),

[45] S.P. 65/1 (*L.P.*, xii(ii), no. 1310). On all this see Quinn, 'Tudor rule in Ireland, 1485–1547'.

blocked by vested interests in parliament, despite its sponsorship by Patrick Barnewall, one of the most influential members of the commons.[46] However, this obstacle could be circumvented by a careful appointments policy such as Cromwell practised, and by periodic reviews such as those conducted by the royal commissions of 1537 and 1540.

The campaign for the total dissolution of the religious orders which took place in Ireland in 1539–40, in the last year of Cromwell's administration, serves as a tribute to his achievement in the revival of crown government. Although the commission was put into effect at the height of a political crisis, and although the commissioners were interrupted by recurring outbreaks of war, they made practically a clean sweep of the religious houses of the colonial area in a period of twelve months.[47] At the end of Cromwell's career, the campaign for the dissolution of the religious orders testifies to substantial progress towards the objective for which Cromwell and the reform group in Ireland had worked unstintingly – the transformation of the Englishry, the area of the king's subjects, into a cohesive political entity, under the effective jurisdiction of the crown.

Conquest or reformation? Policies and lobbies

When Silken Thomas finally surrendered in the early autumn of 1535 Cromwell turned to consider the way forward in Ireland. A comprehensive memorandum was prepared, corrected in his own hand, which itemised many matters calling for attention in the aftermath of rebellion: the administration of the king's lands, the confiscation of the rebels' property, the compensation to be demanded of Kildare's Gaelic allies, the convening of parliament, the examination of the revenues, the reconstruction of defences, and the military mopping-up that was immediately necessary. Our present interest in the memo is that it shows that as part of his general review Cromwell had begun to consider his policy towards the 'disobedient' territories. One of the items corrected

---

[46] Quinn (ed.), 'Bills and statutes of Henry VII and Henry VIII', p. 138. *S.P. Henry VIII*, ii, p. 570 (*L.P.*, xiii(i), no. 684).

[47] See my *The dissolution of the religious orders in Ireland* (Cambridge 1973), pp. 121, 125–30, 137–45.

by himself posed the question 'whether it shall be expedient to begin a conquest or a reformation'.[48] The precise alternatives Cromwell had in mind in the juxtaposition of 'conquest' and 'reformation' is not clear, and the point is not important. What matters is that it indicates that in the autumn of 1535 he had begun to consider seriously the feasibility of extending reform to the Lordship as a whole.

The question was to be pondered by Cromwell for a period of some two years in the course of which time he was inundated with advice from various bodies of opinion in Ireland. The episode is worth considering. It provides the context in which Cromwell's final plan for the Lordship emerged and reveals the considerations that influenced his thought in that respect. Secondly, the alignments in the debate that took place in Ireland enable us to explore attitudes within the movement of political reform in Ireland at an important stage of development.

As early as the spring of 1535 a divergence of opinion had begun to appear in government circles in Dublin regarding the formulation of a post-rebellion policy. One point of view was that 'in the repressing of this outrageous rebellion...such opportunity, means, and ways for conquesting, subduing and reforming of your whole dominion, or any place within the same, be opened unto Your Grace, as the like hath not been seen these hundred years past, and God knoweth whether the like shall ever be seen again in our days without a further great charge'.[49] Since the crown had gained the initiative in the military campaign, and Kildare's Gaelic allies were in disarray, it seemed opportune to turn this force of some 700, sent to put down the rebellion, into the vanguard of an army of conquest. Thomas Agard, a former servant of Cromwell now in the Irish service, expressed the hope that the opportunity would be grasped, in a letter to his old master as early as April 1535.[50] Indicating the tensions within the executive in Dublin, a different programme was proposed a few weeks later in a letter from Skeffington himself to Henry VIII. He assured the king that 'the land is now in like case [as] at the first conquest, being at your grace's pleasure'. Instead of an army of conquest

---

[48] S.P. 60/2, pp. 82–3. The document is misplaced in 1534 in *L.P.*, vii, no. 1211.

[49] *S.P. Henry VIII*, ii, p. 337 (*L.P.*, x , no. 1210).

[50] *S.P. Henry VIII*, ii, p. 243 (*L.P.*, viii, no. 755).

he requested the dispatch of a bureaucratic commission to put government on a proper footing.[51]

The majority view of the Irish council was elaborated very fully in a letter from most of its prominent members to Cromwell in June 1536. An extract will serve to express their position: 'We affirm plainly that it is feasible and possible enough to the king's majesty to conquest this land having people to inhabit after his conquest. And also we think it is more feasible and possible and with less difficulty and charge, if it please his majesty, to make all the inhabitants thereof obedient subjects...And all the policies that...any can use with Irishmen shall neither get profits ne peace but if it be in respect and fear of force.'[52] In this view the crown had the option of one or other form of radical policy. The extreme radical policy of conquest and colonisation was feasible, but the more moderate one of conquest followed by assimilation was preferable.

Examination of submissions by individuals and smaller groups enables us to distinguish the composition of the two lobbies represented by this compromise formula. The larger group, as the formula indicated, came down on the side of moderate radicalism. It was made up mainly of representatives of the Pale administrative class – to whose entrenched position within government, through Cromwell's patronage, the document incidentally draws attention. Of the seven laymen who signed it four were prominent members of the class, now ensconced in key administrative posts. Sir John Barnewall, lord of Trimletiston, was lord chancellor. The redoubtable Sir Patrick Finglas was chief baron of the exchequer. Gerald Aylmer and Thomas Luttrell were chief justices of the king's bench and common pleas respectively. From submissions made by these individually and jointly throughout the period of indecision, their preferences and priorities are made quite clear. Primarily they wanted the assimilation of south Leinster into the area of the crown's sovereign jurisdiction, according to the scheme envisaged for the expansion of the colony, in Anglo-Irish programmes of 'particular' reformation. The traditional formula which, as we saw, derived from Anglo-Norman precedents was proposed to Cromwell in a letter the previous January. It argued

---

[51]   *S.P. Henry VIII*, ii, p. 247 (*L.P.* viii, no. 885). Cromwell's posing of the alternatives of 'conquest' or 'reformation' (above) may have referred to these two possibilities.
[52]   S.P. 60/3, fos. 89–91 (*L.P.*, x, no. 1196).

against a thoroughgoing colonisation of the area and advocated instead a scheme 'to build and reedify some piles and fortresses among them. . .and having part of the lands which they have now in possession given to them and their heirs male and the name of the superiority and captainship renounced. . .no doubt they will be glad to grant the king rent and other impositions, trusting to be in no worse case than other the king's subjects within the county of Dublin'.[53] The debate about Irish policy in the aftermath of the Kildare rebellion shows that a slow change had taken place in their attitude. The trauma of that experience, the fear of reaction from Kildare's Gaelic allies, the ascendancy of the English army sent to put down the revolt, and, no doubt, the growing influence of commonwealth thought all contributed to advancing their view from a solution based on strong conservatism to one of moderate radicalism. However, their main preoccupation remained the reform of south Leinster. As 1536 wore on, and the prospects for launching a general reform began to fade, they concentrated their energies once more on salvaging the project for south Leinster from the scheme for a general conquest.[54]

This attitude was fully shared by a fifth signatory of the letter in August who, indeed, was fast becoming the major protagonist of the policy. He was the Englishman Sir John Alen, whose early career we have noted as a member of the entourage of his namesake the archbishop of Dublin. Alen became a protégé of Cromwell in 1533 so that his career prospered despite the demise of his original patron at the hands of Silken Thomas's henchmen. He was master of the rolls in 1536 and was destined to become lord chancellor on Trimletiston's death in 1538. His prominence in Irish politics lasted into the reign of Elizabeth. It is, therefore, important to know where he stood on the question of Irish policy. Throughout the period he consistently championed the concept of a restored and expanded colony as the primary aim of government policy. To this he added the corollary of a general reformation along moderate radical lines, as a secondary aim, if and when such a project seemed opportune – as it did in the aftermath of the Kildare rebellion.

Another politically significant supporter of this approach may here be mentioned, though he did not sign the letter of June 1536.

[53] *S.P. Henry VIII*, ii, p. 297.   [54] *S.P. Henry VIII*, ii, pp. 337, 380, 391, 408.

He was Lord James Butler, who was to become earl of Ormond in 1539. In one highly important respect his views differed from those of the Pale group. He wanted the reformation of south Leinster left to the Butlers, so that the area could be included in the Ormond sphere of influence.

The inclusion of the extreme radical solution in the compromise formula put forward in the joint dispatch must be attributed to the influence of Sir William Brabazon, the personal servant whom Cromwell appointed as vice-treasurer in 1534. Although he joined forces with a more moderate element on this occasion there had earlier been tension between them and him. Their letter in January, already referred to, was intended to counter a scheme then urged by Brabazon upon Cromwell for the total expulsion of the Gaelic septs of Leinster, followed by colonisation with English settlers. Brabazon's reaction to the waning prospects of a government policy of conquest towards the end of 1536 is also significant. He suggested that he be allowed to try a pilot scheme of colonisation as a private enterprise in Leinster – the first sinister evidence of the presence of colonial privateers whose greed was to wreak so much havoc, socially and politically, in the second half of the century.[55] As with Alen, Brabazon's attitude has a special importance because he retained political prominence to the end of the reign of Mary.

Here attention may be drawn to another contributor to the debate of 1535–6 whose position approximated closely to that of Brabazon. This was Robert Cowley, the pro-Butler solicitor general. He put forward his point of view in a 'little treatise... concerning the readopting of the king's dominion in Ireland', which he presented to Cromwell while at court in the summer of 1536.[56] Two features of his scheme are of interest. First, he attacked the priority given to the 'particular' reformation by the Pale reformers. He argued – sensibly, despite vested Ormond interest – that the reform of the existing political organisation of the colony would substantially reduce the military effectiveness of the Anglo-Irish feudatories, and thereby not only diminish their contribution to a war of conquest but weaken the colony's capacity to resist Gaelic intrusions. Accordingly, since the 'par-

[55] Lambeth, MS 602, p. 87 (*L.P.*, ix, no. 515). S.P. 60/3, no. 94, 60/6, fos. 104–7 (*L.P.*, xii(i), no. 1027).
[56] *S.P. Henry VIII*, ii, p. 323.

ticular' reformation entailed the reduction of the military power of the feudal lords, it should follow rather than precede the general reformation. The second interesting feature of his scheme is that despite the alignment of the Butlers themselves with the moderate radicals, Cowley propounded a policy of extreme radicalism. The details need not detain us, but one notes with dismay the contrast between the bland tone of Cowley's device, and the horror of the tactic he advocated, the systematic devastation of the crops and herds of the Irishry to starve them into surrender and banishment – a tactic later employed with appalling effect. Cowley, therefore, represents the hard-line minority, within the Anglo-Irish community. His attitude differs from the emerging new breed of English colonisers represented by Brabazon only in so far as Cowley made generous provision for the participation of the Anglo-Irish settlers in the ensuing colonisation.

The debate about Irish policy in 1535–6 was conducted from one other standpoint. Lord Deputy Skeffington died in December 1535, but a lobby continued to defend the policy he had advocated in his letter to the king the previous summer. A device written by Skeffington's son-in-law, Anthony Colley, argued against the radical approach and maintained that the policy of conquest was futile. It would prove 'almost impossible to win lands from Irishmen and keep them'. Furthermore, it was unnecessary because 'profits may be gotten here with policy without force'.[57] Colley here reiterated Skeffington's argument that a proper internal reform of government, coupled with the tributes that the lords of the Irishry could be persuaded to pay as part of the traditional indentures of submission, would provide a revenue capable of bearing the cost of governing the lordship and, 'over and above, great revenues to your coffers'.[58]

The debate over policy in 1535–6 provides an interesting comparison with that of 1520–1. So far as attitudes within the local movement of reform are concerned, an influential element had come to adopt a policy of moderate radicalism in the aftermath of the Kildare rebellion. However, a strong conservative bias still remained even among those who now argued a programme of conquest and general reformation. Their major concern was the project for expanding the obedient area to include south Leinster.

---

[57] S.P. 60/3, fos. 89v, 90r (*L.P.*, x, no. 1196).
[58] *S.P. Henry VIII*, ii, p. 247 (*L.P.*, viii, no. 885).

Their primary aim remained the particular reformation and the consolidation of the colony. The comparison also reveals a conspicuous omission from the later debates. The liberal policy suggested by the king in 1520 found no protagonist in 1535–6. In this context, however, the name of one other member of the local reform movement should be mentioned, Thomas Cusack. If Robert Cowley represents one extreme of the spectrum of local opinion on reform policy, Thomas Cusack represents the other. Unlike the more highly placed members of the Pale reform group in 1535–6, he did not come out in favour of moderate radicalism. He was not associated even with the more limited project for the reduction of south Leinster. Instead his name crops up as a close associate of Skeffington, and as an active promoter of Skeffington's attempt to establish a framework of submissions by indenture with the lords of the Irishry.[59] Cusack's association with the Skeffington lobby is of special significance in the light of later developments. It shows that already in 1535–6 he was convinced of the futility of a conquest policy, even in its limited application to the problem of south Leinster. By 1540 his view shows a further progression. He had abandoned the Skeffington policy of peaceful coexistence and emerged as the joint architect of a programme of general reformation, based on a new liberal formula which went much further than that proposed by the king in 1520.

The exchanges between the Irish administration and the English government on the subject of reform policy in the course of 1536 indicate that a different order of priorities operated on the two sides. Members of the Irish executive approached the subject on the basis of a predetermined political objective, the pacification of the island. In the light of that end they proceeded to consider means, turning finally to the question of cost. Government in England, on the other hand, considered the matter in the inverse order. They stressed the cost of military operations in Ireland and sought an augmentation of the revenues to offset them before committing the crown to deeper political involvement there. The financial consideration was to be crucial in determining the outcome of the debate.

When John Alen and Gerald Aylmer arrived back from court in June 1536 with the news that only £7,000 would be available

---

[59] *S.P. Henry VIII*, ii, p. 385. *L.P.*, viii, no. 973, x, no. 1143, xi, no. 1149, xii(i), no. 1027.

for payment of the army, it became clear that a final decision about the policy to be pursued in Ireland had been further deferred and that no substantial advance towards a general conquest could be made in the summer campaign of that year.[60] The reason for the deferment soon emerged. No sooner did news reach London of the passage of the sensitive legislation dealing with the religious Reformation and the attainder of the rebels of 1534 in the first session of the Irish Reformation parliament than Robert Cowley was dispatched with letters to the Irish council and to the lords and commons in parliament 'to devise how the charges, that his grace hath sustained, may be partly recompensed, and the like borne of the revenues there upon the ministration of semblable occasion, as hath lately chanced by the rebellion of Thomas Fitzgarrett, and his accomplices'.[61] Letters from the Irish council and others in June sidestepped the issue while continuing to appeal for money from England to enable the army to be paid and to embark upon the conquest.[62] It may have been to prevent evasion that William Body, a personal servant of Cromwell, was sent to Ireland at the end of June to represent the English government in the financial deliberations.[63] The specific proposal brought by Body was to obtain a further annual benevolence from parliament. The frustration he suffered at the hands of the Irish council in bringing consultation of the matter to a head confirmed the impression of evasiveness. They asked him to submit his proposal in writing, warned him about opposition from the Butlers, and eventually held over the question to the council meeting on 14 September, on the eve of the next session of parliament.[64]

In the event three money bills were put to the session. Two of these had for long been advocated by leading members of the Dublin executive, one for confiscating some small and for the most part derelict religious houses, and another for resuming to the crown the coquette custom traditionally retained by the port towns. The third, for the payment of an annual twentieth tax, was the result of the pressure from Cromwell and the king, and Body's persistent nagging. Bearing in mind the devastated condition of

---

[60] *S.P. Henry VIII*, ii, p. 318.

[61] *S.P. Henry VIII*, ii, pp. 315, 330, 380, *L.P.*, x, nos. 871, 1051, 1052.

[62] S.P. 60/3, fos. 79–82, 89–91. *S.P. Henry VIII*, ii, pp. 332, 337 (*L.P.*, x, nos. 1112, 1168, 1196, 1210).   [63] *S.P. Henry VIII*, ii, p. 330 (*L.P.*, x, no. 1051(2)).

[64] S.P. 60/3, fos. 121–2 (*L.P.*, xi, no. 259).

the Pale in the wake of rebellion, and the fact that at the previous session parliament had renewed the subsidy of 13s. 4d. in the ploughland, the Irish executive considered the further tax proposal as excessive. On the other hand the London administration seemed to think that parliament could be blackmailed by withholding the act granting a general pardon for complicity in the Kildare rebellion. The reaction in parliament vindicated the judgement of the local executive. The commons threw out all three financial measures.

The effect of this on the Irish administration was to provoke attempts to reformulate the conquest policy on a more modest scale in the hope that the English administration would agree to finance it.[65] The London government was not persuaded and determined to try again to coax an additional tax from parliament. The ground was prepared by further letters from the king to the lords and commons, broadly hinting that cooperation would elicit the much-desired general pardon, and drawing attention to the connection between the benevolence and the programme of reformation.[66] Neither argument could budge the commons, and the session in February produced stalemate. At this point London accepted defeat. The customs bill was dropped. The twentieth bill was modified to apply to the clergy alone and passed in this form as the Irish equivalent of the English clerical tenth. The monasteries bill also passed, the leaders of the opposition to it having been tacitly reassured that local vested interests would not be compromised in consequence.[67] The major casualty of the successful parliamentary opposition was the conquest policy.

A letter from Henry VIII on 25 February 1537 brought an end to the debate which began in mid-1535 when Cromwell posed the question of conquest or reformation. It provided a preliminary statement of the lines along which crown policy was to proceed henceforward. In doing so, it confirmed that the priorities of the one administration in the matter inverted those of the other. In England the determining factor was cost. The financial resources which the Lordship could muster were to determine the manner

---

[65] S.P. 60/3, no. 94 (*L.P.*, xi, no. 521). *S.P. Henry VIII*, ii, pp. 373, 380, 391.

[66] *S.P. Henry VIII*, ii, p. 403. The letter is misplaced in 1535 in *L.P.*, ix, no. 574.

[67] *Statutes of the realm (England)*, iii (London 1817), p. 493. On this whole episode see my 'The opposition to the ecclesiastical legislation at the Irish Reformation parliament', *I.H.S.*, xvi (1969), pp. 285–303. Also my *Dissolution of the religious orders*, pp. 47–65.

of its government and the objective of the policy to reform it. What is more, the letter indicated a radical switch in approach towards the question of reformation. Since the summer of 1536 London had been seeking a substantial augmentation of Irish revenues to offset substantial increases in expenditure, actual in the Kildare rebellion, and anticipated in the proposed conquest. Following upon the second rejection of the revenue proposals in parliament in January, the king's letter in February changed tack. The Irish Lordship was to be made self-supporting not by securing additional taxes, but chiefly by cutting the army to reduce expenditure.

This decision had profound implications for crown policy in Ireland. To cut the army to the measure of the Irish revenues entailed a reduction in the existing moderate force of about 700 to a permanent strength of something less than half that number. This, in turn, dictated its function. It could no longer be what the Irish executive wanted it to be, the vanguard of an army of conquest. So long as the military strength was limited to what the Irish revenues would bear it could not do more than provide for local defence. Henry VIII left no doubt that the flirtation with the policy of conquest was at an end. Simply by omitting to advert to them his letter indicated his lack of interest in the grandiose schemes for bringing the whole island into subjection which had been urged upon him so importunately by the Irish executive in the previous eighteen months. Instead he propounded as the first objective of government to balance the budget. The Irish council got the message. A separate rejoinder to Cromwell, written on the same day as their acknowledgement to the king, commented sourly, 'For these 200 years, and more, such hath been the miserable chance to this land, that whensoever the Prince was minded to the reformation hereof, having time and all things never so propitious thereto, some chance happed, which was the let thereof. . .so as, of likelihood, the time appointed by God for the reformation of this land is not yet come.'[68]

This assessed the English attitude accurately. The general reformation of the island was not definitively abandoned: it was

---

[68] *S. P. Henry VIII*, ii, pp. 422, 430 (*L.P.*, xii (i), no. 503). For two letters written earlier in the month by Lord Deputy Gray, which indicate that the king's decisions was by then anticipated in Ireland, see *S.P. Henry VIII*, ii, pp. 404, 419 (*L.P.*, xii (i), no. 343).

merely deferred. Henry VIII concluded his letter of 25 February 1537 by reaffirming his zeal 'to the advancement of the good of that country' and his purpose 'earnestly to devise for the reformation thereof, and the reducing of it to a perfect civility'. However, the council had read the situation correctly. Never again in the period of Cromwell's administration was the extension of the crown's sovereign jurisdistion to the disobedient territories seriously considered in England.

In one respect the outcome of the policy debate of 1535–6 was the same as that conducted between Henry VIII and Surrey in 1520–1. On both occasions the option of extending the crown's sovereign jurisdiction throughout the island was not taken up. The late medieval jurisdictional *status quo* was retained. There the correspondence between the two episodes ends. In its aftermath Surrey's expedition indeed belongs to the history of the medieval Lordship. It belongs to the category of those occasional, and largely futile, reforming visitations from England which punctuate the history of late medieval Ireland. Upon Surrey's departure the traditional method of providing for government was readopted – that is, by delegation of the function to one of the great local feudatories. The traditional consequence followed. The reforming initiative within the administration petered out. By the mid-1520s the link between the Lordship and its overlord was once more tenuous. The politics of the colony were once more dominated by a power struggle between the two great Anglo-Irish dynasties of Kildare and Ormond, a power struggle in which government became once more a pawn.

In 1537, in contrast, the English lord deputy and his entourage remained. The king's letter of February 1537 conveying the final decision intimated that this arrangement was to be permanent, and time proved it to be so. Earlier the same month Thomas Fitzgerald and his five uncles were executed in London. Although the family was reinstated in the reign of Mary it was never allowed to regain its political power. Meanwhile the strenuous efforts of the Butlers to capitalise on the downfall of their rivals were firmly resisted. New provisions were made to fill the power vacuum. On the administrative side the English bureaucrats also remained, and the internal reform, far from faltering, increased its momentum. Paradoxically, the king's letter of 25 February 1537, which ruled out a policy of conquest, at the same time brought down the curtain on the medieval lordship. If it deferred once more the project of establishing the crown's sovereignty throughout the island, it also set crown policy determinedly against reversion to the lordship of Anglo-Irish bastard feudalism. The policy which it represented superseded the latter without encompassing the former. This was the special characteristic of the Cromwellian settlement.

The Cromwellian settlement – the garrisoned Pale

Before analysing the settlement in detail, attention must be drawn to the context in which Cromwell considered the Irish question. It provides a better understanding of the considerations which led him to inaugurate a new phase in the history of crown government in Ireland, as well as of the orientation of the programme on which he embarked. Cromwell's approach to government was an integral one. From the beginning he related the problem of government in Ireland to the problem of governing the crown's dominions as a whole. The first of the many Cromwellian memoranda in which the Irish situation is noted for attention is the draft agenda prepared in the autumn of 1533 for the council in England with a view to obtaining endorsement for a mammoth programme designed to secure the crown's position in the aftermath of the royal divorce and the repudiation of papal jurisdiction. The draft included a number of provisions, corrected in Cromwell's own hand, for the government of Ireland and Wales. Although these items were deleted from the final agenda, for separate attention, they indicate the way in which Cromwell tended to view these areas as an extension of England itself for government purposes.[69]

With this in mind, the context in which the Irish settlement of 1537 must be set is immediately evident. It was part of a general scheme for the government of the outposts of the imperial kingdom which crystallised in 1536–7. The statutory basis for the programme was provided by a corpus of legislation enacted in 1536. The act 'for liberties and franchises' dealt with the re-organisation of government in those areas of England itself where feudal semi-autonomy still survived. Four acts provided for the

[69] S.P.6/3, no. 21 (*L.P.*, vi, no. 1487 (2)). Elton, *The Tudor revolution in government*, pp. 361–5.

assimilation of Wales. Finally, one monumental act was devoted to the reform of government in Calais. This spate of legislation was accompanied by an administrative offensive on the remote areas. The council in the north was substantially reorganised. The work of reform begun in Wales in 1534 was given a definite objective and a precise programme by the legislation of 1536. In Calais the act of 1536 provided the impetus for four years of intensive reform activity designed to modernise the garrison militarily and administratively.[70]

Examination of this background brings to light the fundamental principle on which the Irish policy was based – that of unitary sovereignty. In the history of Cromwellian reform the period 1536–7 complements in the secular sphere the work of 1532–4 in the ecclesiastical sphere. Both were devoted to giving statutory expression and administrative effect to the supremacy of the king's jurisdiction over all competing jurisdictions in his dominions. Examination of the background is equally important in so far as it brings to light the model on which the reorganisation of government in Ireland was based. That was the garrison at Calais. Although the king did not refer to the parallel case in announcing the policy in his letter of 25 February 1537, the replies of the Irish council to himself and to Cromwell make it explicit. They warn 'concerning the manner of the appointing of this garrison...if the soldiers should be after the order of Calais, or such like places, it will not be best, perchance, so here'.[71]

Recognition of the model employed in the reorganisation of the government of the Lordship is crucial to an understanding of the manner in which the Cromwellian principle of unitary sovereignty was applied to Irish reform. It might seem that the principle logically demanded the extension of royal government throughout the island. As we have seen, Cromwell did not draw this conclusion, for a reason indicated by the parallel with Calais. That outpost constituted the reality represented by the English

---

[70] P. T. J. Morgan, 'The government of Calais', unpublished D.Phil. thesis, Oxford, 1966, pp. 114–20, 159. J. A. Youings, 'The council of the west', *T.R.H.S.*, 5th ser., x (1960), pp. 41–59. P. Williams, *The council in the marches of Wales* (Cardiff 1958). F. W. Brooks 'The Council of the north' in J. Hurstfield (ed.), *The Historical Association book of the Tudors* (London 1973).

[71] *S.P. Henry VIII*, ii, p. 426. In a subsequent letter Gray, Brabazon, Alen and Aylmer developed the point at some length. *S.P. Henry VIII*, ii, p. 434. On Cromwellian policy and unitary sovereignty see G. R. Elton, *Reform and Reformation* (London 1977), pp. 168–229.

royal style of 'king of France'. It was no more incumbent upon the king, in virtue of unitary sovereignty, to proceed to the subjugation of the whole of Ireland than it was to undertake the subjugation of all of France. That principle enjoined, rather, the obligation to ensure that the existing community of the king's subjects were unilaterally governed under the crown's sovereign jurisdiction, without the insinuation of secondary jurisdictions. In its scope and in its concerns, therefore, the final Cromwellian settlement continues to bear comparison with the Anglo-Irish schemes of particular reformation. We have already seen that his scheme for the revival of crown government was much influenced by such reformist treatises. However, as we shall see, the principle of unitary sovereignty and the model of the Calais Pale caused him to depart radically from the Anglo-Irish concept.

The king's letter of 25 February 1537 did not provide a detailed programme of reform. It purported to be no more than a preliminary notification. It outlined the shape that the reorganisation of government would take, indicated matters calling for immediate attention, asked for comments, and announced the intention of sending 'a personage of reputation' from England to supervise the implementation of the full programme.[72] In the five months that intervened between the announcement of the king's letter and its fulfilment at the end of July the 'personage of reputation' had multiplied to a four-man administrative commission. As at Calais, a royal commission from London was to play the central role in the implementation of the programme of reform. But in contrast to the prestigious commission sent to Calais, which was composed of the duke of Norfolk and Sir William Fitzwilliam, the lord admiral, the Irish commission was more administrative and Cromwellian in character. The man who headed it deserves special mention since he was to return to Ireland as lord deputy in 1540 to join with Sir Thomas Cusack in launching another, and even more revolutionary, Irish policy. This was Sir Anthony St Leger, head of a rising Kentish gentry family who became increasingly involved in local administration under Cromwell.[73] He was accompanied by an auditor, Sir William Berners, a surveyor, Sir Thomas Moyle, and George Paulet, a loudmouth and trouble-maker whose inclusion may be

[72] *S.P. Henry VIII*, ii, p. 422 (*L.P.*, xii (i), no. 503).

[73] *L.P.*, vii, nos. 630, 788, viii, nos. 149(40), 314, ix, nos. 142, 236(3), 713, x, no. 562, xi, nos. 444, 580, xii(i), no. 1079.

attributed to the new promotion of his brother William as treasurer of the household. On to this group devolved the primary responsibility for implementing the new crown policy in Ireland. According to the powers delegated to them they virtually superseded the lord deputy, during the course of a stay which lasted from September 1537 to April 1538.[74]

It should be mentioned that this episode represents the high point of Cromwell's own involvement in Irish reform. In addition to the sheaf of letters and the comprehensive brief with which the commissioners were provided, a total of nineteen other letters from Cromwell to the commissioners survive in the period between their dispatch on 1 August 1537 and the king's letter recalling them on 17 January 1538, for which Cromwell was also responsible.[75] (We know of other letters from acknowledgements.) By this means Cromwell became for a period almost as closely involved in ordering the affairs of the Irish administration as those of the English one. In fact the nineteen surviving letters to the Irish commissioners represent more than half the total – thirty-six letters in all – of Cromwell's correspondence for the period. Never before and never again was he so preoccupied with Irish matters. Evidently Cromwell considered the policy the commissioners were sent to implement as definitive. In what follows the stress will be on what the commissioners set out to achieve rather than on what was actually accomplished, since the main purpose is to explore the nature of the Cromwellian concept of the reformed Irish Lordship.

At the centre of Cromwell's conception was the idea of the 'Englishry', the land of the king's obedient subjects, as a garrisoned and strongly fortified territory on the Calais model. The area he had in mind was not the late medieval Pale of four shires in the hinterland of Dublin but the territories of all those constitutionally bound to the crown by feudal tenure. In addition to the four shires about Dublin, these included the earldom of Kildare, the liberty of Wexford in the southeast, and the earldom and shires of Ormond. They also included one other area which had, however, virtually cut itself off from the colony since the mid fifteenth

---

[74] *S.P. Henry VIII*, ii, pp. 452, 464. *L.P.*, xii(ii), nos. 379, 382, 385.
[75] For the initial brief and letters to the commissioners see *S.P. Henry VIII*, ii, p. 452 (*L.P.*, xii(ii), nos. 375–8, 285–8). The letter of recall is calendared in *L.P.*, xiii(i), no. 89.

century: this was the area of the rebel earl of Desmond in the southwest and the feudal underlords of Munster under his control. It had been a major concern of Cromwell from the beginning to heal this schism, thereby restoring the colony to its constitutional and traditional dimensions. It had figured in the programme of 1534. The indenture subscribed by the Butler earl as part of the preliminaries before launching the programme included among its provisions a clause guaranteeing Butler cooperation with the lord deputy in any moves he might make to reform Desmond.[76] The tone was menacing, but it was immediately followed by a diplomatic initiative, through a local contact, Edmund Sexton of Limerick. The negotiations were brought to nothing in 1536 by the machinations of the Butlers, who could see only political disadvantage to themselves in the reinstatement of a powerful Desmond earl.[77] The question was reopened on the occasion of the visitation of the royal commission the following year, when Cromwell showed a lively interest in including Desmond and its shires in the reorganised Pale. The instructions provided for the royal commissioners contained a lengthy addendum on the subject. It was supplemented by a further series of directives from Cromwell, personally endeavouring to find a way round the difficulty that the incumbent's title was disputed by a politically weaker rival who, however, appeared to have a better claim in law. Eventually those negotiations also fell through, largely sabotaged by the bad faith of the Butlers.[78] Thereafter, until Cromwell's fall, the matter remained in abeyance.

Meanwhile a major reorganisation of the rest of the colony was put in train. The major innovation was the establishment of a permanent English garrison on whom primary responsibility for defence would henceforth devolve, rather than upon the retinues of the magnates, and the hosting of the shires. The garrison force was recruited from the English troops sent to Ireland to quell the Kildare rebellion. The king's original announcement of this decision specified that the size of the garrison would be proportionate to the capacity of the Irish revenues. In practice the details

---

[76] *S.P. Henry VIII*, ii, pp. 194–7 (*L.P.*, vii, no. 740).
[77] *L.P.*, vii, no. 1145, viii, nos. 115, 594, 621, x, nos. 1052, 1225, xi, nos. 199, 282, 1149. *S.P. Henry VIII*, ii, pp. 386, 395.
[78] *S.P. Henry VIII*, ii, pp. 467, 517, 536, 556. For the renewed dispute between the Butlers and the 'pretended' earl of Desmond see *S.P. Henry VIII*, ii, pp. 367 (recte in 1538), 517.

were worked out in England, and were included in the instructions to the commissioners before the investigation of the Irish revenues had taken place. The total strength of the garrison force was fixed at approximately 340, about half the force then in the country. Of these 140 were allotted as a retinue to the lord deputy, and a further 60 were made available to the vice-treasurer for security in undertaking hazardous survey work. The remainder were to be distributed in fortresses along the borders.[79]

Cromwell made one substantial modification in this design while the work of reorganisation was in progress. Pondering the economics of garrisoning the Ormond shires, he decided to take a chance on the Butlers. Lord James, the heir, went to court in the spring of 1537, with his brother Richard, and managed to give Cromwell a sufficient reassurance of their loyalty and amenability. Significantly, he was sent on a tour of the Calais Pale in the summer. He returned home in November with patents granting the family custody of a string of strategically placed crown castles in Carlow and Wexford, though a number of others were to be held by small English garrisons. He also brought back a patent for the Ormond title, long in dispute between the Butlers as heirs male and the Boleyns as absentee heirs general.[80] The pattern that finally emerged, therefore, left English troops garrisoning the border fortresses of the old Pale, the liberty of Wexford in the southeast, and a small number of fortresses on the Ormond borders. The Butlers retained major responsibility for the Ormond area, and for the area of north Co. Wexford bordering upon the Cavanaghs.[81]

Apart from the garrisoning of border fortresses, the major feature of the defence system was the cutting of passes through the heavily wooded countryside. This marks the first emphasis on a device already used in a small way by the earls of Kildare as deputies. The idea was to increase the speed and mobility of the army in defence of the border areas, enabling them to mount a permanent border patrol.[82] The work began in the spring of 1538, and by mid-April Lord Deputy Gray was able to report the

[79] *S.P. Henry VIII*, ii, p. 452. *L.P.*, xii(ii), nos. 786, 1097, 1318(2).
[80] *S.P. Henry VIII*, ii, p. 475. *L.P.* xii(ii), nos. 735, 763, 826, 1008(35).
[81] *S.P. Henry VIII*, ii, pp. 452, 475, 510, 517, 556. *L.P.*, xii(ii), nos. 591, 755, 826, 964(ii), 991, 1008(35), 1097, 1318(2), xiii(i), nos. 497, 537, xv, no. 558.
[82] John Alen suggested such a strategy to the commissioners, *S.P. Henry VIII*, ii, p. 486.

completion of five passes, some of them 'a mile in length cut, and so broad cut that four or five carts one by another, may easily pass'.[83] It is indicative of the most vulnerable point of the Pale's defences that all five passes were located along the border with O'Connor's territories in Offaly, 'the door whereby much war and mischief hath entered amongst the king's subjects'.[84] It is necessary to emphasise that the project of cutting passes originated as a function of the reorganisation of the Pale's defence system and not, as has been assumed, as part of the process of opening up the Gaelic areas to an English army of conquest. The work began at a time when conquest had been deliberately ruled out as an immediate object of crown policy. Subsequently Lord Deputy Gray, on his own initiative, went beyond the original scheme and proceeded to cut passes within the Gaelic lordships. However, the intention remained defensive, to enable his retinue and ordnance to penetrate the Gaelic territories on punitive expeditions. Nothing in the contemporary correspondence at this period associates the project with a policy of conquest.

The confiscation and redistribution of property formed an important aspect of Cromwell's programme of reform. There was, of course, a crucial difference between his scheme and the later projects of colonisation: it was designed to reinforce the colony within its existing boundaries, not to expand them by the expropriation of the Irishry. The early treatises of Anglo-Irish reformers emphasised the disintegration of the medieval network of landholdings in the colony. They drew attention to the abuse of absenteeism on the part of the great English feudatories, to the withdrawal of Anglo-Irish landowners from border properties, and to the general neglect of landlord responsibilities, particularly the failure to recruit and protect tenants of English stock, and the leasing of their lands instead to Gaelic immigrants.[85] The bill for the confiscation of the properties of absentees introduced at the first session of Cromwell's Irish parliament, 1536–7, showed his determination to tackle the problem despite the vested interests – Norfolk, Wiltshire, Shrewsbury, and some of the greatest

[83] *S.P. Henry VIII*, iii, p. 3 (*L.P.*, xiii(i), no. 770).
[84] S.P. Henry VIII, ii, p. 480 (*L.P.*, xii(ii), no. 729(4)). Gray's letter is the first reference to the commencement of the work, and it occurs after the commissioners had returned to England. But he was careful to point out in his report that the operation had been decided on in consultation with the commissioners before their departure.
[85] See my *Dissolution of the religious orders*, pp. 40–2.

English monasteries. The first, limited, Irish act for the dissolution of monasteries took up the problem, singling out run-down monasteries in border areas. At the same time, an extraneous development, the rebellion and attainder of the Fitzgeralds, added considerably to the land pool available for reallocation.[86] It was left to the commissioners of 1537 to deal with the redistribution of this property within the framework of the general objectives of their programme.

The policy governing the redistribution of the border lands was to allocate them to men of assured loyalty and military prowess. For the most part they were leased to the captains of the English garrisons, or to the local Anglo-Irish magnates, to provide them with a personal incentive to fulfil their role of defending the border area.[87] Thus William St Loe, appointed seneschal of the liberty of Wexford, got the property of two attainted rebels there as well as sharing in the spoils of the dissolved monastery of Tintern.[88] The Butlers got the confiscated monastic lands of Graiguenamanagh (Duiske) on the Wexford–Kilkenny border. On the southern borders of the four shires of the Pale, the local lord, Kilcullen, got the monastery of Baltinglass. Moving northwards along the border, the substantial Fitzgerald manor of Portlester, on the verge of O'Connor country, went – with grim appropriateness – to the English soldier Francis Herbert, in virtue of his distinguished service against the Geraldine rebels.[89] Lord Deputy Gray obtained two border monasteries, Grane in Co. Kildare and Ballyboggan in Co. Meath. Further north, in Westmeath, Vice-Treasurer Brabazon got a lease of the entire property of the English monastery of Llanthony. In this case the commissioners took it upon themselves to lay aside royal grants under patent because they would have had the effect of disposing of choice pieces of the property, leaving the border lands unleased. Brabazon got the lot because he undertook responsibility for the waste lands on the Westmeath borders, as well as for the more secure property further into the Pale.[90] Further down the social scale an interesting experiment was tried to stabilise the reorganisation of

---

[86] *Statutes at large, Ireland*, i (Dublin 1786), pp. 67, 84, 127. Bradshaw, *Dissolution of the religious orders*, pp. 40–3.

[87] See my *Dissolution of the religious orders*, pp. 40–5, 75–6.

[88] *L.P.*, xiii(i), no. 97.

[89] *L.P.*, xii(ii), nos. 389, 468, xiii(i), no. 559.

[90] *S.P. Henry VIII*, ii, p. 524. Cf. Bradshaw, *Dissolution of the religious orders*, pp. 75–7.

the colony, and to alleviate the consequence of depopulation in the border areas. This was to lease holdings to the soldiers of the garrison. It was hoped that the arrangement would provide them with an acceptable means of supplementing their wages, as well as encouraging them to regard themselves as permanent settlers, not as soldiers on foreign service.[91]

One other priority which operated in the redistribution of confiscated property stresses its place in the context of the scheme of Cromwellian reform. Here the consideration was Cromwell's desire to establish the nucleus of an efficient and loyal crown bureaucracy. Cromwellian administrators were handsomely rewarded with properties in the more secure areas of the old Pale, in contrast to the military personnel who were given lands in the border areas. Brabazon's semi-military role was recognised in the lease of the Westmeath property, but he was also granted the purchase of the site of the monastery of St Thomas Court within the city of Dublin. Sir John Alen, the master of the rolls, got leases in Co. Kildare within easy reach of Dublin. In addition to these, Englishmen who acted as their personal assistants were also rewarded: Alen's brother, Brabazon's servant Agard, Edward Beck, who was constantly employed as a courier, and Edward Basnet, the recently appointed dean of St Patrick's.

One rider must be added here. Ethnic background was not a necessary criterion in the redistribution of land. The patronage of Cromwell dominated the commissioners' allocations, and he did not hesitate to give preference to Anglo-Irishmen when it suited his purposes, even against the strong competition of English suitors. A case in point was Robert Cowley, who got a lease of the conveniently situated monastery of Holmpatrick in Co. Dublin against the suits of two Englishmen, one of whom had royal backing, and the other of whom happened to be the newly appointed archbishop of Dublin. Richard Butler provides another

---

[91] S.P. 60/5, no. 22 (*L.P.*, xii(ii), no. 786). *S.P. Henry VIII*, ii, p. 517. Although Patrick Barnewall referred to the idea of soldier–farmers in a letter to Cromwell as 'your lordship's device', its inspiration may have been Anglo–Irish. It seems to be an adaptation of the Gaelic system whereby the wages of the galloglasses were supplemented by the lease of farms on the lord's mensal lands. S.P. 60/5, no. 22 (*L.P.*, xii(ii), no. 786). G. A. Hayes-McCoy, *Scots mercenary forces in Ireland, 1565–1603* (Dublin 1937), pp. 54–8. Robert Cowley suggested the adaptation of the galloglass system in a submission to Cromwell in connection with the commissioners' programme, *S.P. Henry VIII*, ii, p. 445.

example: he beat off the competition of William St Loe, the seneschal, to secure leases in Co. Wexford.[92]

Nevertheless, it was by Cromwell's deliberate design, executed by the commissioners in 1537, that the new English established themselves as a permanent element within the loyal community in Ireland. Twice before in the Tudor period, under Poynings and Surrey, a shock force of English troops and bureaucrats had inaugurated government reform. But their achievements did not outlast the period of their visitations. One way in which Cromwell secured his own reform programme was by transforming another wave of transitory officials and army personnel into permanent settlers. For that reason his land reallocation scheme provides a landmark in the history of new English colonisation in Ireland as well as in the history of political reformation.

The scheme of land reallocation formed an aspect of a more general policy directed towards the reformation of the social structure of the obedient community. The other instrument of social engineering was parliamentary legislation. Three of the measures given force of law at the final session of Cromwell's Irish parliament, the session supervised by the royal commissioners, were directed to this end.

One links directly with the theme just discussed. It was 'for the defence to be kept upon the borders of the lands being in the king's obedience, by the lords marchers'. Its purpose was to revive the relevant statutes of Kilkenny 'and sundry other good statutes decrees and ordinances heretofore made' for the purpose of ensuring that the lords of the border lands would reside in their areas. According to the analysis provided in the preamble to the bill, the border problem was at source a social one. The disappearance of the landowning class from the border areas led to depopulation and cultural erosion. Anglo-Irish tenants were unwilling to remain without the protection of their lord, and they were replaced by an influx from the Gaelic areas, either of squatters or of hardier Gaelic tenants. This measure proposed to give the medieval legislation sharper teeth by the addition of a penal clause imposing a fine.[93]

---

[92] *L.P.*, xii(ii), no. 414, xiii(i), nos. 97, 537, xvi, no. 393. For a breakdown of the reallocation of monastic properties, see my *Dissolution of the religious orders*, pp. 233–6.

[93] *L.P.*, xii(ii), no. 384. Quinn (ed.), 'Bills and statutes of Henry VII and Henry VIII', pp. 150–1. Parliament was dissolved before this measure could be enacted, but it was promulgated by the commissioners in virtue of authority invested in them by parliament.

The two other measures for social reform dealt directly with the problem of Gaelicisation. One was 'for the Irish habit and tongue to be eschewed'. We have already seen that it is a serious mistake to regard such legislation as a symptom of racial antagonism.[94] The other was 'for restraining of alliance by marriage and fostering with Irishmen'. Again it will suffice to repeat the consensus of modern research that the purpose of such statutes from the Kilkenny legislation onwards was to ensure government control, not to provide a flat prohibition. That interpretation is patently the correct one for the 1537 enactment in view of the detailed arrangements it provides for making possible what it purports to prohibit.[95]

Two further observations are called for to set this legislation in its broader perspective. Its orientation towards the conservative concept of reform within the framework of coexisting communities is noteworthy. Its exclusive character, applying to 'the king's subjects within this land being' or to 'the lands being in the king's obedience', the analyses of the preambles echoing the Anglo-Irish reform treatises, and the frank reliance on a revival of the statutes of Kilkenny all serve to define Cromwell's Irish policy, in the parlance of the Anglo-Irish reform movement, as one of particular rather than of general reformation. At the same time the legislation serves to draw attention to the fact that Cromwell's Irish policy did not consist simply in implementing the Anglo-Irish programme of particular reformation. It formed part of a master plan for dealing with the outlying areas of the king's dominions. The process of social and cultural integration with the more dominant ethnic group taking place in the Irish colony was paralleled in the English Pale in France. Similar provisions to those of the Irish legislation were contained in the massive act for the reformation of Calais which passed in England in 1536.[96] Cromwell's use of Calais as a model for reform in Ireland did not necessitate a departure from the Anglo-Irish programme in the sphere of social reform. However, as we have already seen, that model provided a substantially new concept of the colony as a garrisoned English Pale. The difference between the Cromwellian concept and that

[94] Above, pp. 5–11, 40–2.
[95] *Statutes at large, Ireland*, i, p. 119(3). Quinn (ed.), 'Bills and statutes of Henry VII and Henry VIII', pp. 154–6.
[96] On this see P. T. J. Morgan's chapter on population in his unpublished thesis, 'Tudor Calais'.

of the Anglo-Irish reformers was to prove no less significant than their correspondence.

Cromwell and the Irishry

Although conquest had been ruled out as an immediate objective of crown policy, the final clause of the commissioners' instructions required them to canvass the opinions of men of wisdom and reputation about the means to be adopted towards achieving a general reformation 'when his majesty may take his time therefore meet and convenient'. That the question had any immediate relevance to the crown's concerns may be doubted. If the five surviving tracts produced in response to this instruction are any indication, the commissioners directed the thoughts of those from whom they canvassed opinions towards the particular rather than the general reformation. Only two of the five refer to the problem of the Irishry. One of the two devoted only one paragraph out of a lengthy treatise to the subject, though admittedly that paragraph contained the germ of a revolutionary new approach to the problem. It suggested proclaiming the English monarch in parliament as 'supreme governor of this dominion, by the name of the king of Ireland' and then to 'induce the Irish captains...to recognise the same', which, the author maintained, would be 'a great motive to bring them to due obedience'.[97] This idea was not taken up until after the fall of Cromwell. The other response was that of John Alen. His was a fuller treatment of the problem of governing the non-feudal lordships. Significantly, however, his proposals for doing so took for granted the continuance of the existing *status quo*. The task, as he stated at the outset, was to devise a system of government for 'this land being in several monarchies'.[98] Alen had reverted to the late medieval concept of coexisting communities. In his view, the basis for coping with the problem was provided by the 'old practice' of peace indentures. The scheme he outlined envisaged a policy of strong conservatism,

[97] *S.P. Henry VIII*, ii, p. 480 (*L.P.*, xii(ii), no. 729(4)). The tract is anonymous, but for the identification of the author see below, p. 194 note 4.
[98] *S.P. Henry VIII*, ii, p. 486 (*L.P.*, xii(ii), no. 1308). As well as the two treatises here discussed, submissions to the commissioners also survive from Lord Deputy Gray, *S.P. Henry VIII*, ii, p. 477; from Justice Luttrell, *S.P. Henry VIII*, ii, p. 502; and from David Sutton, *L.P.* xii(ii), no. 729(i).

although, emphasising the non-expansionist orientation of crown policy itself, it provided only for the restoration of the traditional colony and not for its enlargement by the assimilation of south Leinster.

The question is, having deferred the conquest, how did Cromwell himself envisage the crown's relationship with the Irishry? It must be said that the documents are strangely reticent in this regard. Like the *Ordinances for Ireland* in 1534, the 'Instructions to the Commissioners' in 1537 provide an elaborate blueprint for the organisation of the colony but have little to say about the Irishry. Apart from the final clause, which, of course, offered no guidance, only two other clauses referred to the disobedient areas. Both concerned the Gaelic lordships in the border areas. They indicated that policy was to continue along traditional lines. One provided for obtaining peace indentures from 'all such Irishmen as border upon the English pale'. They were to be persuaded 'by wisdom' to provide hostages in case they should feel disposed to 'make some trouble' when the army was reduced, 'as they have heretofore at such like changes been accustomed'.[99] This was complemented by an instruction to the commissioners to investigate the blackrents and 'such other acknowledgements' as the feudal lords received from 'Irish rebels'. They were to persuade the former to desist from the practice if possible, or else to report the matter to the king for further consideration. The purpose here was to place political relations with the Irishry under the control of the crown government and to restore the internal cohesion of the Englishry. The ultimate objective of both clauses was to promote political stability in the relationships of the two communities – the objective of the fourteenth-century policy of coexistence.

The act for 'restraining tributes to be given to Irishmen' must be set against this background. A high-sounding preamble referred to the presence of the 'army royal...whereby his grace's said subjects are highly animated and fortified, and the said Irish enemies greatly enfeeblished'. The act, passed in the autumn session of 1536, reflects something of the militancy of the majority of the Irish government in the debate about reformation policy that proceeded throughout that year. However, the effect of the act was not to prohibit the payment of blackrent but to rescind

[99] *S.P. Henry VIII*, ii, p. 452 (*L.P.*, xii(ii), no. 382).

any form of authoritative instruction to do so.[100] Whatever the intentions of those who formulated the measure, its application was dictated by the decision in the following year to cut the 'army royal' by half and to use it as an instrument of conservation rather than of conquest. The statute notwithstanding, a peace indenture with the bordering O'Tooles in 1537 provided for the continuation of such payments where they were customary over the previous forty years, and the exchequer accounts show that blackrents continued to be paid by the crown government itself between 1537 and 1540.[101]

As to the territories beyond the borders, Alen's scheme for the government of the Irishry by means of a framework of formal indentures between the crown and individual great lords probably corresponds to Cromwell's ideal for the disobedient territories as a whole. As early as 1533 a memorandum drawn up by him for the consideration of the English council had indicated some such *modus operandi*. It contained an item 'to draw combine and adhere towards the king as many of the great Irish rebels as is possible, and to practise to keep peace there and to withstand all other practices that might be practised there with others'.[102] The two lord deputies who headed the Irish executive in the course of Cromwell's administration seem to have proceeded on that basis. Sir William Skeffington (1535–6) was seen by subsequent advocates of the indenture procedure as its first modern exponent.[103] Lord Deputy Gray pursued the same policy with more determination than sense and with disastrous political consequences, as we shall see.

Cromwell's own practice suggests the tentative and the pragmatic, in contrast to his systematic and well-considered approach to the government of the colony. Indeed, the activities of the commissioners and the aftermath to their visit emphasise that Cromwell's most definite policy towards the Irishry was a negative one, to avoid embroilment in novel schemes in that quarter. Political events in the course of the commissioners' visit – notably the recalcitrance of O'Connor of Offaly – and personal observation served to persuade them of the desirability of making

100 *Statutes at large, Ireland*, i, p. 102.
101 *S.P. Henry VIII*, ii, p. 522. *L.P.*, xvi, no. 777 11(4).
102 S.P. 6/3, no. 21 (*L.P.*, vi, no. 1487(2)).
103 E.g. Archbishop Dowdall, T.C.D., MS 842, fo. 78.

special provision for the stabilisation of relationships with the greatest of the dynasts on the borders of the Pale. The proposal they supported was to grant status and title by patent to lords in such cases who were willing to accept English law and the crown's sovereign jurisdiction. Thus, when Brian O'Connor, chastened by a recent discomfiture by the lord deputy, and fearing a permanent alliance between the crown and his rival, Cahir, offered full submission in return for the grant of baronial status and a title of inheritance to his territories, the commissioners supported the council's suit to Cromwell for the acceptance of his terms.[104] They also supported Ossory's suit for similar terms for his son-in-law MacGillapatrick, and entered into an indenture with him in which the terms of submission were spelt out in detail.[105] A third Gaelic lord singled out for such exceptional treatment was O'More, another ally of Ossory.[106]

That the commissioners continued to lend support to this proposal is indicated by a submission to Wriothesley made by two of them in conjunction with Alen and Aylmer, some months after their return to England. Here proposals were outlined for capitalising on the progress made by the commissioners in reforming the Lordship. A second commission was suggested which should receive delegated authority, among other things, to negotiate with non-feudal lords for the grant to them of status and title under the crown. The scheme singled out especially for this purpose O'Connor, MacGillapatrick, his brother Cahir, and O'More.[107] Alen and Aylmer returned to Ireland in July 1538 with permission to pursue the question further with the three magnates. They reported on the favourable progress of negotiations in August, and subsequently pressed for authority to clinch the agreement. In September the scheme was extended to include the Gaelic Irish of South Leinster.[108] But, despite pressure from the lord deputy, from the Cromwellian group in the adminis-

---

[104] *S.P. Henry VIII*, ii, pp. 494, 534, 560, 561 (*L.P.*, xiii(i), nos. 437, 456).

[105] *S.P. Henry VIII*, ii, p. 514.

[106] *S.P. Henry VIII*, ii, p. 541, iii, p. 88.

[107] S.P. 60/6, no. 14 (*L.P.*, xii(i), no. 641), Cf. *L.P.*, xiii(ii), no. 937.

[108] *S.P. Henry VIII*, iii, pp. 71, 99, 111 (*L.P.*, xiii(ii), nos. 160, 569, xiv(i), no. 88). Cromwell's lack of interest was in schemes to assimilate the non-feudal areas. On the other hand he showed considerable interest in negotiations to reconcile the earl of Desmond, which, however, came to nothing, *S.P. Henry VIII*, ii, pp. 466, 467, 517, 519, 536, 548, iii, 15. *L.P.*, xii(ii), nos. 632, 698(i), 786, 943, 1096, 1189, xiii(i), nos. 114, 261, 606, 1136, xv, no. 314.

tration, from the Butlers, and from the erstwhile royal commissioners, none of these proposals came to fruition until after the fall of Cromwell in 1540 and of the beginning of a new phase of crown policy in Ireland.

Testimony to the consistency of Cromwell's attitude is provided by the episode of the Geraldine League, which marked the final eighteen months of Cromwell's administration. The invasion of the Pale by a powerful Gaelic combination, with the ostensible aim of reinstating the Fitzgerald heir in his earldom, produced a political crisis as great as the Kildare rebellion itself. That development, like the earlier crisis, called the policy of coexistence into question. One report to Cromwell in December 1539 stated that the opinion of wise men in Ireland was 'that without a general reformation the king's majesty shall vainly consume his treasure in this land'.[109] Members of the Irish administration once more began to urge that the reinforcements sent to preserve the colony should be used as the vanguard of an army of conquest.[110] In the autumn Henry VIII himself spoke of sending 'a main army, by sea and land, for the general reformation and winning of this land'. The Irish council responded in December with yet another scheme for a moderate radical programme.[111] However, in contrast to his dalliance with such proposals after the Kildare rebellion, Cromwell gave short shrift to the project. He wrote early in February with his own policy instructions, outlining a strategy within the framework of coexistence and making no allusion to the possibility of proceeding to a general conquest. Their hopes dwindling, and with obvious irritation, the council wrote immediately for clarification. Were they correct in taking Cromwell's letter to mean that the king's earlier promise had been no more than a piece of propaganda, to dismay the enemy, and hearten the colony in the crisis? If so, and if the army of conquest was not coming after all, they would have to change their tactics, which had been formulated on the basis of the imminent arrival of the great army.[112] If Cromwell replied the letter does not survive. However, no army of conquest arrived, and throughout the remaining three months of Cromwell's administration there is nothing to suggest

[109] *Cal. Car. MSS*, i, no. 138.
[110] *S.P. Henry VIII*, iii, pp. 145, 179 (*L.P.*, iv(ii), no. 137, xv, no. 142). *Cal. Car. MSS*, i, no. 137.
[111] *S.P. Henry VIII*, iii, p. 176 (*L.P.*, xv, no. 82).
[112] *S.P. Henry VIII*, iii, p. 187 (*L.P.*, xv, no. 328).

that he contemplated a departure from the settlement worked out in 1537.

The explanation for the lack of a clearly formulated policy for the disobedient area may simply be neglect. So much was initiated under Cromwell's personal direction in so many spheres that the work-load steadily outgrew even his gargantuan capacity. It may be, therefore, that he addressed himself in Ireland only to that problem that fell immediately within the compass of his master plan for the outposts of the imperial kingdom. As with the crown's claim to the kingdom of France, he may have given serious consideration only to that part of the problem that was most urgent, the securing of the English colony. His inclination to leave the situation in the Irishry to drift would have received support from an opinion prevalent in English government circles – although vehemently criticised by Anglo-Irish supporters of the policy of general reformation – that non-involvement in the politics of the Irishry was the crown's best guarantee of non-aggression. In this view Irish politics were dominated by the local power struggles of the dynasts to a degree that precluded joint action, unless crown government itself took the initiative in providing a focus for general opposition.[113] An analysis of Irish politics in the late medieval period provides much support for that viewpoint. However, the crisis of the Geraldine League gives grounds for believing that in the area of the Irishry also the late medieval phase had come to an end.

Whatever the obscurity of the evidence, it is clear at least that Cromwell never explicitly committed himself to a policy of conquest or to general reformation. Again, it is clear that if he had ambitions in that direction they were not strong enough to overbear considerations of cost. It is hardly necessary to add on the other side that Cromwell did not make a once-for-all decision against conquest. He allowed the late medieval arrangement to continue, which left the options open. It could be argued that in concentrating upon the particular reformation to the exclusion of the general one his purpose was to transform a crumbling last ditch into a bridgehead. In fact, this is what Cromwell achieved, as history was to show; but history will not permit us to say that it was what he proposed.

[113] B.L., Lansdowne MS 159, fo. 17 (*L.P.*, iv(ii), no. 2405).

Ireland and English foreign policy

The thesis just argued conflicts with the generally accepted view
of the effect of the Henrician Reformation on the crown's Irish
policy. It has been assumed that the royal ecclesiastical supremacy
committed Henry VIII to the extension of his sovereign jurisdiction
throughout Ireland, partly in order to make good his claim in
relation to the Irish Church, and partly because the Reformation
gave Ireland a new strategic importance in view of the increased
danger of a Counter-Reformation alliance between the Gaelic
lordships and the Catholic states of Europe. Plausible though this
reasoning is in theory, it does not correspond to the historical facts.
Why that was so needs some explanation. Cromwell's ecclesiastical
policy in Ireland will be discussed later. Here we are concerned
only with the way in which Ireland impinged upon his consideration of security and foreign policy. It can be said immediately
that at no stage in his career did Cromwell's attitude suggest that
Ireland constituted a grave or urgent security risk. In this respect
he showed much greater sensitivity to the strategic importance of
Wales and Scotland, and to the threat of a direct invasion of
England from the continent. A key to the understanding of his
attitude is provided by exploring the international significance of
the conflagrations in Ireland that coincided with the initial and the
terminal phases of his administration.

The Kildare rebellion occurred at the period of greatest tension
between Henry VIII and the emperor Charles V: it followed close
upon the king's divorce of the emperor's aunt, and his assertion,
in the process, of the royal ecclesiastical supremacy. The response
of the imperial party to the rebellion is well portrayed in the
correspondence of Chapuys, the imperial ambassador in London.
In a letter written at the outbreak of the rebellion Chapuys
outlined for the emperor his assessment of the place Ireland might
play in imperial diplomacy. He pointed out its strategic potential
in view of its proximity to Wales. However, he did not contemplate exploiting this by using Ireland as a stepping-stone to
England for an invading army. Rather, he assessed Irish trouble
in terms of its nuisance value. Local Gaelic leaders being 'such as
your majesty knows', i.e. shifting in their political allegiances, it
would be necessary, in order to maintain them in disaffection, to

send some aid or at least to hold out to them the prospect of aid.[114] What emerges clearly from subsequent correspondence is the peripheral place occupied by the Kildare rebellion in Chapuys' assessment of the English situation. In urging an invasion of England the ambassador was influenced not by the opportunity provided by trouble in Ireland but by the likelihood of English support, especially from powerful members of the nobility disaffected by the divorce and by the royal supremacy.[115] Similarly, his plan for an invasion of England was quite uninfluenced by the collapse of resistance in Ireland. In October 1535 he reported to Charles V that Silken Thomas had been committed to the Tower; yet in the same letter he made his strongest plea ever for an invasion of England, urging that the time was ripe and that the opportunity must not be lost.[116]

It is evident from the policy actually pursued by Charles V that he shared Chapuys' view. The only Spanish aid to arrive in Ireland as a result of the Kildare rebellion was a one-man diplomatic mission, who arrived in the winter of 1534–5, close on the heels of a similar emissary sent to Desmond in the spring of 1534. The purpose of both was to assess the political situation at first hand, to impress local dissident elements with the genuineness of the emperor's interest in their cause, and generally to stir up as much trouble as possible for the crown.[117] Similarly, the diplomatic mission by Silken Thomas to the emperor in the winter of 1534 was personally well received, but so far as tangible assistance was concerned it drew a blank.[118] The embassy to the Pope fared little better: it was granted a pardon for the execution of Archbishop Alen, a papal indulgence, and a hortatory address to the Irish faithful, the combined effect of which, in the event, proved considerably less than Skeffington's gigantic cannon.

Against this background Cromwell's attitude can be understood. The place of Ireland in continental diplomacy was well gauged in England, and consequently caused little perturbation. Henry VIII took the Spanish diplomatic mission to the rebels as an opportunity to bait the emperor's ambassador, rather than as an

[114] *L.P.*, vii, no. 957. [115] *L.P.*, vii, nos. 1095, 1206, 1368.
[116] *L.P.*, ix, no. 732.
[117] *S.P. Henry VIII*, ii, p. 201. *L.P.*, vii, nos. 437, 957, 1045, 1057, 1095, 1141, 1336, 1337, 1425, viii, no. 270. [118] *S.P. Henry VIII*, ii, pp. 217, 219.

occasion for serious diplomacy. In the course of one interview he taxed Chapuys with the presence in Ireland of a 'young little Spaniard' whom several Irishmen had offered to kill for him. The ambassador surmised that he was an outlaw from the emperor's dominions, and the king agreed, considering it unlikely that Charles V would want to become embroiled with the Fitzgeralds who, as he said, were now being forsaken by their allies.[119] When English merchants hesitated to trade with Spain, fearing reprisals in view of the known contact between the emperor and Irish rebels, they were assured by a member of the council that there was no fear of rupture between the two countries on that score.[120] Cromwell himself explained the English assessment of the diplomatic situation to Chapuys in an appropriate metaphor. He expressed incredulity that the emperor would embark on a project so fruitless and inconvenient as the usurpation of the king's power in Ireland, or that he would choose to launch his challenge to the king there, seeing that with his great power he had 'many better means of opening the ball with greater honour'.[121] Both sides were agreed that Ireland did not warrant being made a major issue in European power politics, or being allowed to exercise any real influence on the course of European diplomacy.

The European diplomatic situation had changed in one important respect by the time the crisis of the Geraldine League began to build up towards the end of 1538. By then the Counter-Reformation had become militantly active against Henry VIII under the inspiration of Cardinal Pole. Thus the Irish crisis coincided once more with a crisis in European diplomacy, precipitated on this occasion by the Counter-Reformation. In June 1539 the pope was instrumental in securing a ten-year truce between the emperor and the French king, from which the English monarch was excluded. In December he began preparations to promulgate the bull of excommunication against Henry VIII. At the end of the month Cardinal Pole set out from Rome to rally the Catholic powers, and in January the emperor and the French king entered into a form of compact that seemed to constitute a preliminary to joint offensive action.[122]

In Ireland also an incipient Counter-Reformation movement

---

[119] *L.P.*, viii, no. 189.   [120] *L.P.*, vii, no. 1193.
[121] *L.P.*, vii, no. 1297.   [122] Scarisbrick, *Henry VIII*, pp. 468–9.

appeared in the course of the late 1530s. From the close of 1538 onwards there is evidence of close collaboration between the papacy and the forces of clerical opposition to the royal supremacy in Ireland. This was reflected in widespread clerical support in the 'disobedient' areas for the developing political opposition to the crown. In the spring of 1539 the impending war of the Geraldine League against the king was preached as a holy crusade. At the same time, ecclesiastics were prominent in diplomatic activity in Scotland, France, Spain and Rome, soliciting aid for the League.[123]

Despite all of this, the place of Ireland in European diplomacy did not alter significantly. England's enemies encouraged disaffection in Ireland, but provided no material support. They displayed no special interest in the Irish situation beyond the desire to keep it agitated. The papacy alone showed a real disposition to help, but no capacity to do so beyond rewarding emissaries of the Irish insurgents with bishoprics, in the hope that they could be relied upon not to capitulate to the English supreme head.

Crown government for its part had the measure of the diplomatic situation. The Dublin administration showed some uneasiness in the spring of 1539 when Cardinal Pole's crusade seemed imminent and its destination was uncertain. Yet their correspondence even then gives no indication that they considered a foreign invasion likely. When the meeting of Charles V and Francis I sparked off further anxious speculation in England in December 1539, the Irish council dismissed excited talk among adherents of the Geraldine League concerning foreign assistance as a 'vain imagination'.[124]

The response of the English administration to the threat of a continental crusade in the spring of 1539 indicates the place occupied by Ireland in their calculations. There was near panic as frenzied preparations were made for the defence of England. The northern borders against Scotland, the western and southern seacoast, and the English outpost at Calais all came in for considerable attention.[125] But in the first half of 1539 nothing was done to guard against an invasion of Ireland, despite the ominousness

[123] *L.P.*, xiii(ii), nos. 559, 1087, 1164, xiv(i), nos. 1122, 1245, 1277, 1309, xiv(ii), nos. 95, 639. See my *Dissolution of the religious orders*, pp. 208–9.
[124] *S.P. Henry VIII*, iii, p. 176, (*L.P.*, xv, no. 82).
[125] Scarisbrick, *Henry VIII*, pp. 470–1.

of the local political situation at the same time. Cromwell did not take steps to deal with that situation until July, when the threat of a continental invasion had passed and he felt free to turn his attention to less urgent matters.[126]

Examination of the attitudes and reactions reflected in contemporary documents puts paid to the assumption that the Reformation and the consequent danger from the Counter-Reformation were the crucial factors in the new phase of crown government in Ireland that began in the 1530s. So far as Ireland's strategic importance was concerned, the ambiguity and flexibility of political relationships there rendered it a very slippery stepping-stone towards England. The continental powers knew this. And government in England knew that they knew it. It was not any new strategic importance attaching to Ireland, therefore, that dictated the crown's involvement with the Lordship in the 1530s, but the pressure for political reform mounted by the reforming milieu in Ireland itself and Thomas Cromwell's revolutionary concept of unitary sovereignty.

[126] *L.P.*, xiv(ii), no. 781, fos. 85b, 91b.

5

The Irish Lordship and the Cromwellian state

The tenet of unitary sovereignty postulated the king as the source of all authority within his dominions. Jurisdiction emanating from alternative centres was regarded as a usurpation of royal jurisdiction. This precluded acceptance, on the one hand, of an autonomous external source of spiritual jurisdiction, the papacy, and, on the other hand, of autonomous internal sources of temporal jurisdiction such as feudal liberties and other semi-independent franchises held by the great magnates. We have seen how the Cromwellian reform programme provided for the elimination of local autonomy within the area of the crown's sovereign jurisdiction in Ireland. In this chapter we shall consider the reform programme in relation to the Church. That discussion, however, must be preceded by consideration of yet another sphere in which unitary sovereignty caused the existing (medieval) situation to be superseded: the constitutional status of the Irish Lordship itself.

The principle of unitary sovereignty demanded a system of political organisation with one only source of sovereign juris-diction. Thus, just as it decreed the assimilation of the semi-autonomous local lordships within the framework of the crown's sovereign jurisdiction, so also it decreed the assimilation of the 'all but' autonomous Irish Lordship within the jurisdictional frame-work of the English kingdom. The historian is much assisted in examining the former process by the modification and redefinition of the magnates' political function that is authoritatively set out in the *Ordinances for Ireland* and in the indenture subscribed by the Butler earl in 1534. No similar source exists on which to base an examination of the transformation effected in the political institutions of the Lordship. Nevertheless, the process can be observed well enough in the practice of government.

Unitary sovereignty and central government in Ireland

Perhaps our study so far of the history of Cromwellian reform in Ireland gives the impression of an Irish executive, hand-picked by Cromwell, of one mind with him on the needs of Irish reform, and working in close harmony with him for the furtherance of his policy. The picture is true enough, so far as it goes. Yet a strong current of tension can be perceived in the relationship of Cromwell with his local collaborators right through the period of his administration. An indication of one source of tension is provided at the inauguration of the reform policy itself. The first evidence of the appointment of Sir William Skeffington as lord deputy – the event which ushered in the whole programme of reform – comes in two letters from Skeffington to Cromwell protesting about the way the latter had arrogated to himself the lord deputy's customary function in the disposal of offices within the Irish executive.[1] Another source of tension is revealed in the response of the Irish administration to the king's letter in February 1537, drawing the great debate about policy to a close: Lord Deputy Gray and three senior members of the Irish council wrote to Cromwell warning against the consequences of forcing decisions upon them by means of royal commands in this way, since it tended to stifle necessary comment. Replying to the king himself at the same time, they had the temerity to urge that the royal commission he proposed to dispatch to them would listen to the advice of those 'which know the land' – advice which had just been spurned on the basic question.[2] A lengthy list could be compiled of occasions in the course of Cromwell's administration when things were forced from England against the will of the local body, those who claimed to know the land. The two administrations differed on the issue of squeezing additional revenue from parliament in 1536–7, on withholding the general pardon after the Kildare rebellion, on the terms for the disposal of confiscated lands, on the reformation of the Wexford liberty, on financing the initial cost of the reform programme, and on the scope of the reform policy itself. On all of these issues the will of the English

---

[1] *S.P. Henry VIII*, ii, p. 193 (*L.P.* vii, nos. 704–5).
[2] *S.P. Henry VIII*, ii, pp. 426, 434.

government prevailed, at least unless it encountered a less controllable form of resistance than that of the Irish executive, namely that of parliament.

Paradoxically, it might seem, the effect of unitary sovereignty was to diminish not to augment the status of the central administration in Ireland. The fundamental fact of the relationship between the two executives under Thomas Cromwell was that real power was transferred from Dublin to London. More and more the London government took upon itself the function of decision-maker and handed down its decisions with scant regard for the expressed preferences of the Irish executive or for its constitutional status as the organ of government of the Irish Lordship. A corollary was the unprecedented degree of direction and surveillance to which the Irish executive was subjected from England.

One feature of this new style of government was the device of special commissions. Authorised representatives were sent from the English administration to act on its behalf in matters of special interest. An example was William Body, who came in 1536 to see to the introduction of Cromwell's financial legislation in parliament. Another was the royal commission of 1537 sent to launch the garrison policy. In each case the Irish executive had shown resistance to the measures devised in England. Each case illustrates, therefore, Cromwell's determination to ensure effective control of Irish policy for the English administration. The special commission represents an extraordinary device of the system developed under Cromwell for dominating the Irish executive from England. The ordinary method was by means of regular correspondence. For the first time correspondence between the two administrations became a regular feature of government. Cromwell insisted on semi-official reports from individual administrators, to augment the joint dispatches of the council. Negligence on this score earned rebukes for Gray, Brabazon, Alen and Archbishop Browne. A reprimand to the royal commissioners in 1537 underlines Cromwell's attitude. Reference in one of their dispatches to 'diverse things worthy reformation, much tedious to be written to you' elicited an immediate demand from Cromwell in the name of the king for a report on the matters in question 'notwithstanding any prolixity or tediousness'. He added an admonition, familiar to many members of the Irish executive, 'to advertise me, from time to time, of all manner occurrences there'.[3] Regular reports from a multiplicity of sources was the ordinary method devised by Cromwell for constant surveillance over government in Ireland. Similarly the regular dispatch was his ordinary method of exercising continual direction. The epistolary bombardment of the royal commissioners of 1537–8, referred to already, shows a more intensive application of a regular practice. It also shows how detailed Cromwell's supervision of Irish affairs could be. His directives to the commissioners descended to the minutiae – a neighbourly bicker at the Co. Wexford assizes, the distribution of minor offices and perquisites. They also extended to more substantial items of patronage – the disposal of confiscated properties, the selection of captains for the garrisons. At the same time they provided a flow of instructions on matters of major policy, the arrangements for the garrisoning of Ormond, the conduct of negotiations with James Fitz John, the claimant to the earldom of Desmond, the manner in which O'Connor was to be dealt with.[4] Admittedly the period of the royal commission of 1537–8 was exceptional. Nevertheless, correspondence was sufficiently frequent and detailed at other times to enable the London administration to exert a constant influence on the conduct of government in Ireland.

All of this represented a break with the past and a downgrading of the status of the Irish executive. The medieval pattern of intermittent intervention from crown government in England was replaced by regular direction and surveillance. The Irish executive was subordinated for the first time to the ordinary jurisdiction of its English counterpart. How, then, did Cromwell envisage the function of the reformed Irish executive? Here it is useful to advert once more to the broader context of Cromwellian reform. In discussing the internal reform of the Lordship in the previous chapter, attention was drawn to the place of that programme within the framework of Cromwell's general scheme for reform of the outlying areas of the king's dominions. The reform of the Lordship in its relationship to the centre of government in England must be set in the context of the same master plan. The functions of the Irish executive were now conceived in terms of the regional councils reorganised under Cromwell's aegis in the north and west

---

[3] *S.P. Henry VIII*, ii, pp. 517, 519.
[4] *L.P.*, xii(ii), nos. 414, 456–7, 485–6, 575, 591, 763, 826, 991, 1189, 1207.

of England, in Wales and in Calais.[5] This entailed a fundamental redefinition of its role. It was not for Cromwell a central government in its own right but a regional extension of the English one. Its function was to ensure the more effective jurisdiction of the latter in the Irish Lordship.

The downgrading in the status of the Irish executive is emphasised by consideration of another feature of Cromwell's method of conducting government in Ireland. This was the way in which he bypassed the central administration altogether in order to supervise affairs directly from London. The case of the liberty of Wexford provides a nice example. The liberty of Wexford was confiscated from the earl of Shrewsbury under the act of absentees in 1536.[6] In view of the general attack upon medieval franchises and the strong centralising emphasis of Cromwellian reform it would have seemed the obvious course to terminate the liberty at this point, thus bringing it within the jurisdiction of the Dublin government. On the contrary, the royal commissioners of 1537 brought with them a letter from Cromwell to the sheriff of Wexford assuring him of the continuance of the liberty, as well as a parliamentary bill to authorise the arrangement.[7] The virtue of this arrangement was that it gave London control of the administration of Wexford as part of the king's personal inheritance, without the interpolation of the Dublin executive. Thus, while the commissioners steered the relevant legislation through parliament in 1537, Cromwell himself attended to the staffing of its administration. The three key posts went to men in close contact with himself: William St Loe as seneschal, James White of Waterford as justice, and James Sherlock as receiver.[8] The anxiety of the Dublin administration to establish their jurisdiction in Wexford emphasises Cromwell's deliberate purpose in bypassing them. There had been previous attempts to encroach, and a Wexford correspondent warned the chief minister in 1537 of the need to make the new arrangement watertight against pressure

---

[5] On the reorganisation of the regional councils, see Youings, 'The council of the West', pp. 41–59. Williams, *The council in the marches of Wales*. Brooks, 'The council of the north'.

[6] *Statutes at large, Ireland*, i, p. 184.

[7] *L.P.*, xii(ii), nos. 375, 384. Quinn (ed.), 'Bills and statutes of Henry VII and Henry VIII', p. 156.

[8] *Cal. pat. rolls Ire.*, Henry VIII, p. 37, *S.P. Henry VIII*, ii, p. 561. *L.P.*, xii(ii), no. 735, xiii(i), nos. 537, 619.

from the 'learned men of Dublin'.[9] What Cromwell's collaborators in the Irish administration thought of the arrangement is indicated by their criticism of it to Cromwell throughout 1538–9, and their appeal to have it abolished, all of which Cromwell ignored.[10]

Another side of the policy of short-circuiting the Irish administration was the establishment of a network of direct links between the Irish localities and London. It is clear that Cromwell set about this as a complementary aspect of his appointments policy. For instance, on the same day as the patent issued for the appointment of Cromwell's servant Brabazon as vice treasurer in Ireland in October 1534, a patent also issued appointing Edmund Sexton as a sewer of the king's chamber and capacitating him and his family to hold public office in Ireland.[11] Sexton was a Gaelic merchant on the make who managed to attach himself to Kildare's entourage. He was recruited by Cromwell when he spent the winter of 1533–4 in London attendant upon Lady Kildare. He was used by Cromwell as an envoy to Silken Thomas and later as an agent in negotiations with the Desmond Fitzgeralds. Through Cromwell's patronage, he became mayor of his native Limerick in 1535, despite his Gaelic blood – which required the enabling patent of 1534. Throughout the latter half of the 1530s he acted as a special agent on Cromwell's behalf in the southwest, and made frequent visits to court in the process.[12] On the same day as Brabazon was appointed, yet another of Cromwell's local agents also makes his appearance. This was John Darcy, usher to the king. The grant of a royal manor at Rathwere in Co. Meath on that day brought him back to Co. Meath from where he reported to Cromwell about affairs in Westmeath.[13] Cromwell's contact deeper in the heart of the Pale was Thomas Agard, a former servant of the chief minister who came to Ireland with Vice-Treasurer Brabazon as clerk to the treasurer.[14] Along with these direct contacts in the Pale and in the southwest, Cromwell had two special agents in the southeast. One was William Wise, a

9 *L.P.*, xi, no. 200, xii(ii), nos. 173, 375.

10 *S.P. Henry VIII*, iii, pp. 111, 145. *L.P.*, xiii(ii), no. 1032, xiv(ii), nos. 51, 137.

11 *L.P.*, vii, no. 1122(5).

12 *Cal. Car. MSS*, i, nos. 84, 135. *L.P.*, vii, nos. 1122(5), 1144–5, viii, no. 58, x, no. 1052.

13 *L.P.*, vii, no. 1122(7), viii, no. 250. *Cal. Car. MSS*, i, no. 149.

14 On Agard as Cromwell's servant see S.P. 60/3, p. 103 (*L.P.*, x, no. 112). *L.P.*, xii(ii), no. 1280.

leading citizen of Waterford, with whom he maintained direct links from 1535 onwards.[15] The other was James Sherlock, also a Cromwellian servant, who was appointed receiver at Wexford in 1537. He was later used as a confidential agent to track the movements of Gerald Fitzgerald on the continent.[16]

By means of this network of personal servants the London administration was provided with an alternative route to the localities in Ireland other than through Dublin. It was now possible for London to interfere directly in local Irish politics, and Cromwell certainly did so. Of course, the Dublin executive was not entirely ignored for such purposes, but the creation of alternative possibilities helped to deprive it of the function and the status of a central government.

One episode has a special interest for the present discussion because it provides an insight into the attitudes of those who practised this new method of conducting the government of the Lordship. It relates to the formulation of legislation designed to alter the administrative structure of the Church in Ireland in accordance with the royal supremacy. The repudiation of papal jurisdiction entailed the establishment of machinery under the crown for the issue of ecclesiastical licences and dispensations, and for trying ecclesiastical causes. In 1535 the English lord chancellor, Audley, was deputed by Cromwell to draft bills for the Irish parliament to establish the necessary machinery. Letters from him to Cromwell explain the basis on which he proceeded. 'This way were honourable for the king', he declared, 'not to enable any primate of Ireland to grant...dispensations.'[17] Rather, they ought to be granted 'within this realm by the bishop of Canterbury'. Similarly, appellate jurisdiction in Irish ecclesiastical causes was to reside in England and to be exercised by means of delegated commissions there, 'like as subjects of England have in appeals'.[18] Accordingly, Audley suggested administrative arrangements for issuing ecclesiastical licences and for hearing appeals in ecclesiastical cases which bypassed both the Irish primate and the Irish central administration. The function was to be fulfilled by the Archbishop

[15] *Cal. Car. MSS*, vi, 470. *L.P.*, xiii(i), no. 872.

[16] *L.P.*, xii(ii), no. 735. R. Stanyhurst, 'The chronicles of Ireland' in *Holinshed's Chronicles*, vi (London 1808), pp. 305–6. For Sherlock's previous service to Cromwell, see Lambeth, MS 602, fo. 139 (*Cal. Car. MSS*, i, no. 84).

[17] *S.P. Henry VIII*, i, p. 438 (*L.P.*, ix, no. 41).

[18] *S.P. Henry VIII*, i, p. 439.

of Canterbury and the English chancery. Cromwell clearly approved, for this was the form in which the bills were transmitted to Ireland to be enacted by the Irish parliament. In fact the bills were amended in Ireland to provide the option of an alternative, locally based, administrative centre. However, Cromwell's reluctance to accept the amendment is evident from the fact that it took well over a year of constant pressure from the Irish council to prise from him the patents necessary to set up the local system.[19]

Against this background we can grasp more fully the implications of unitary sovereignty for the Irish Lordship. *A priori*, it might have been assumed that Cromwell's design was to restore the authority and influence of the Dublin executive as the hub of crown government in Ireland, ensuring its subordination in turn to the London administration. In this way the English government would exercise its jurisdiction in Ireland through Dublin as the local centre. This was not Cromwell's conception. For him unitary sovereignty permitted only one administrative focus throughout the king's dominions – the central administration in England. He showed no desire to maintain a monolithic structure of government in Ireland centred on Dublin. On the contrary, his policy was to ignore the Lordship as an administrative entity and to centralise its government at London rather than at Dublin. This, of course, had profound implications for the constitutional status of the Lordship itself, implications which were not lost either on the makers of policy in England or on the Anglo-Irish political community, as we shall see.

Unitary sovereignty and parliament in Ireland

Apart from the intrinsic importance of the legislation it enacted – the royal ecclesiastical supremacy, the attainder of the Fitzgeralds, etc. – Cromwell's Irish parliament is notable for two features. First, under Cromwell parliament in Ireland made a dramatic comeback as a legislative assembly. Six parliaments over

---

[19] The form in which the Irish bills for faculties and for ecclesiastical appeals were transmitted to Ireland, and their subsequent amendment, appear in W. Shaw Mason's 'Collation of the Irish statutes' in T.C.D., Add. MS W.8 (MS V, 2.7). Quinn (ed.), 'Bills and statutes of Henry VII and Henry VIII', pp. 153–4. The relevant acts are in *Statutes at large, Ireland*, i, 91, 141. The relevant commission to administer the system locally is in *Cal. pat. rolls Ire., Henry VIII*, p. 55 (*L.P.*, xiv(ii), app. no. 5). On this episode see my 'Opposition to the ecclesiastical legislation at the Irish Reformation parliament', 293–4.

the previous forty years leave a record of no more than 25 enactments; Cromwell's parliament produced 42 statutes in a life-span of less than two years.[20] Secondly, Cromwell's parliament was the occasion of the first suspension of the Poynings' Law procedure which had regulated the conduct of parliament in Ireland since 1494.

Both features seem anomalous in the light of the impact of unitary sovereignty upon the status of the Irish executive. Just as that principle led Cromwell to play down the role of the Irish executive as a central administration in its own right, and to treat it rather as a regional extension of the English administration, so he might have been expected to play down the role of the complementary institution, parliament, which also existed as an instrument of central government in its own right, distinct from its English counterpart. It seems equally remarkable that Cromwell's administration should have introduced the first bill for the suspension of Poynings' Law, the very device designed to ensure the control of the English administration over the legislation of parliament in Ireland.[21]

The explanation of these anomalies is found partly in a change of circumstances, and partly in a change of policy in England. The effect of Poynings' Law was to require prior licence under the great seal both for parliament in Ireland to convene and for the specific legislations to be placed before it. The purpose was to prevent the exploitation of parliament as an instrument of political subversion. The change of circumstances that diminished the necessity for such a safeguard was the downfall of the Fitzgeralds. The change of policy was necessitated by the exigencies of the Cromwellian reformation. The attitude of English government towards parliament in Ireland reflected in Poynings' Law is negative. It was designed to prevent abuse. The application of that policy resulted in an almost total ossification of the institution. Between 1495 and 1536 parliament met rarely and briefly, mainly for the purpose of renewing the subsidy.[22] Under

---

[20] The legislation of all these parliaments is set out in Quinn (ed.), 'Bills and statutes of Henry VII and Henry VIII', pp. 100–3, 108, 113–15, 123, 134–6, 154–6. In counting the statutes I have not included the conventional acts 'for confirming the liberties of the church' and 'for confirming liberties and franchises'.

[21] *Statutes at large, Ireland*, i, p. 89.

[22] Details of the sessions are tabulated in Quinn (ed.), 'Parliaments and Great Councils in Ireland, 1461–1586', *I.H.S.*, iii (1942–3).

Cromwell a new use for parliament emerged, to provide his programme of reform in Ireland with legislative underpinning.

The suspension of Poynings' Law under Cromwell, therefore, marks a new stage in the policy of English government towards parliament in Ireland. It was not to restore its lost autonomy to parliament itself, but to transform it into a positive instrument for the advance of English government. Ossory, indeed, recommended the suspension in 1535 in order to restore to parliament the capacity to initiate legislation. He urged that 'many acts right expedient, shall be devised...most of all at the assembly of the parliament, where every quarter and shire knoweth best their own mischief and remedy'.[23] The argument cannot have impressed the English administration. The result of the suspension was to produce not a great crop of private members' bills but a great increase in government legislation. The legislation of the first session in May 1536 was based entirely on a programme devised in England in the summer of 1535.[24] The legislation of the second session derived from the same source, with the addition of some later government money bills. The latter caused such a fuss that no further measures were passed until the final session. On this occasion also the interests of the English government predominated. The legislation consisted almost entirely of a programme newly devised in England and added to by the royal commissioners in the light of their first-hand experience of Ireland.[25] It is a testimony to the success of the English administration in controlling the legislation of parliament that 29 of the 42 acts inscribed on the statute roll were formally transmitted from England, even though the necessity for the procedure ceased with the suspension of Poynings' Law early in the first session. Most of the remaining 13 were also of English origin, either reenactments of English legislation or measures devised at the instigation of the royal commissioners.[26]

The suspension of Poynings' Law, therefore led not to a restoration of the legislative initiative of parliament itself, but to

---

[23] *S.P. Henry VIII*, ii, p. 255.

[24] *S.P. Henry VIII*, ii, pp. 245, 320, R. D. Edwards, 'The Irish Reformation parliament', *Historical Studies*, vi (1968), pp. 64–5.

[25] My 'Opposition to the ecclesiastical legislation in the Irish Reformation parliament', pp. 294–300. Edwards, 'The Irish Reformation Parliament', pp. 76–9.

[26] The record of transmisses derives from Shaw-Mason's MS 'Collation of the Irish statutes', cited above.

a transformation of the role of the English executive from the negative one of exercising a veto to the positive one of direction. This was dictated in turn by the exigencies of Cromwell's reform programme, in order to provide it with legislative underpinning. The restoration of parliament's legislative productivity took place within the framework of unitary sovereignty.

In order to explain precisely how Cromwell's purpose was served by suspending Poynings' Law, it is necessary to enter the lists of historiographical controversy. The received interpretation of the purpose of the suspension of Poynings' Law by government in the sixteenth century rests on a view of the relationship between the central administrations of both countries substantially at variance with the one presented here. This interpretation explains the suspension in terms of three factors. One relates to the law itself, the circuitous procedure it enjoined. Another relates to the purpose of the English government in seeking to suspend it. This was to speed up the legislative process. The third concerns the place of the Irish executive in the plan for speeding up the legislative procedure through the suspension of Poynings' Law. It is suggested that the advantage of suspending the law was that it enabled the Irish executive to act without reference to England in steering legislation through parliament. The intention of the English government in seeking a suspension of the law was, as one commentator explained, 'to strengthen the hand of the Dublin government' in the legislative process. This change of attitude towards the Irish executive is explained as the result of the reformation of that body in 1534, when it had been transformed from a Kildare clique into an agent of crown government that could be relied upon to act on behalf of the English administration.[27]

The trouble with this explanation is that it is partly true. Because it is no more than partly true it is necessary to correct it; but since it is partly true the task is all the more difficult. For instance, it is certainly true that the suspension of Poynings' Law made it possible for the Irish executive to deal with parliament without reference to England. That it was the intention of the English government 'to strengthen the hand of the Dublin govern-

---

[27] D. B. Quinn, 'The early interpretation of Poynings' Law, 1494–1534', *I.H.S.*, ii (1941–2), pp. 241–54. R. D. Edwards and T. W. Moody, 'The history of Poynings' Law: Part I, 1494–1615', *I.H.S.*, ii (1941–2), pp. 415–24.

ment' by this means is a different matter. The thesis presented here is that the intention of English government was rather to circumvent the function of the Irish executive in the legislative process in order to ensure for itself more effective control over parliament in Ireland. This view of the attitude of English government is in line with the general interpretation already presented of the relationship between the two executives under Cromwell's principle of unitary sovereignty.

The shortcomings of the received interpretation begin with an inadequate presentation of the operation of the law, and therefore of the effect of its suspension. Commentators have stressed the supervisory role it provided for the English administration in the Irish legislative process. The general view is that 'the two essential features of Poynings' Law were the obligation to get a licence under the great seal of England before a parliament could be called, and the injunction against placing before the Irish parliament any bills except those which had been transmitted from England under the great seal'.[28] In this view the essential feature of Poynings' Law was the procedure technically called transmission, whereby government in England formally communicated to the Irish executive licence to convene parliament and, then or subsequently, licence to present specific items of legislation. However, the crucial factor in understanding the purpose of suspending Poynings' Law is that it enjoined another formal procedure, referred to in the law itself as certification. This required government in Ireland to apply formally to England under its great seal for licence to convene parliament, and to submit formally for approval all proposed legislation for the parliament. The intention in framing this requirement originally had been to withdraw the function of initiating legislation from parliament, subjecting it instead to the prior approval of govern-ment. The consequence of the manner in which the law was formulated was that the capacity to originate legislation for parliament in Ireland was withdrawn also from the English administration. That body could transmit for presentation to parliament only such bills as were formally certified to it for licence in the first instance from the Irish council.[29]

---

[28] Quinn, cit., p. 247.
[29] Quinn adverts to the requirement of certification but is dismissive in his treatment of it. He suggests that it received little emphasis as a result of the 'flexibility in practice'

The preparatory stages for the parliament of 1536–7 show the awkwardness of such a stipulation in a situation where the English administration wished to use parliament in Ireland for the furtherance of its policies. It also shows that while the English administration took the view that Poynings' Law procedure enjoined only transmission, the Irish executive emphasised the requirement of certification. This was to be the pattern throughout the sixteenth century.

The programme of legislation formally certified by the Irish council in June 1535 had been laid aside, and Audley was well into a new draft programme under Cromwell's supervision in August, when representatives of the Irish administration drew their attention to the requirements of Poynings' Law. The source of one reminder was Walter Cowley, who came to London to present a long memorandum on Ossory's behalf which included proposals for the forthcoming parliament and a suggestion to suspend Poynings' Law.[30] The only remaining record of the other reminder is a bill for the suspension of the law which was drafted in Ireland for the parliament. It may have been presented by Alen and Aylmer, who brought the original certified bills from Ireland.[31] The line of argument presented in Ossory's memorandum and in the draft bill differs, but both focus attention on the same problem: the injunction which required all proposed legislation to be certified into England under the Irish great seal.

Cowley was still in England in August 1535 when Cromwell and Audley came to give serious consideration to the question. He was back and forth between them on a number of occasions and it can hardly be doubted that both questioned him closely in the matter.[32] Finally Audley, having studied the act himself, gave Cromwell his considered opinion. He did not 'take that act as they take it in Ireland'. Nevertheless, in effect admitting a legitimate doubt, he included with his draft programme a bill for the

---

introduced in operating the law, cit., pp. 247–50. However, the Irish executive defended its failure to introduce an English bill in the parliament of 1541 on the grounds that it was not certified in the first instance from Ireland 'so as if the same were passed without such certificate, it were to be taken for a void act', *S.P. Henry VIII*, iii, p. 404. Poynings' Law is reproduced verbatim in Quinn, cit., p. 242.

30 *S.P. Henry VIII*, ii, pp. 245, 249 (*L.P.*, viii, no. 881).
31 The bill is reproduced as an appendix to Edwards, 'The Irish reformation parliament', pp. 82–4.
32 *L.P.*, ix, nos. 147, 149, 164, 165, 229.

suspension of Poynings' law to safeguard the legislation of the parliament.[33]

The purpose of the suspension can be seen in the procedure which resulted from it. Government legislation continued to be formally transmitted from England, but the requirement of antecedent certification from Ireland of English transmisses was ignored. The purpose of the suspension, therefore, was to eliminate the function of the Irish executive in initiating parliamentary legislation, and to enable the English administration to assume that function instead.

Why this was done draws attention to the second shortcoming of the received interpretation, its view of the sixteenth-century Irish executive. In this view the Irish executive after 1534 constituted a 'permanent English administration...composed of English officials'.[34] It could, therefore, be relied upon to devise and initiate government legislation without reference to England, thus short-circuiting Poynings' Law procedure. That view of the Irish administration anticipates a state of affairs which did not emerge until the end of the century. Indeed, the key to the interpretation of the history of the law between the parliament of 1536–7 and that of 1611–13 is that the Dublin executive was neither the Kildare-dominated council of the earlier period nor the subservient agent of English government of the seventeenth century. Because it was not the former, the suspension of Poynings' Law was feasible; that it was not the latter provides the principal reason that rendered the suspension of Poynings' Law desirable.

In elucidating the nature of the problem posed for government by the role of the Irish executive under the law's procedure, the draft suspension bill already referred to is revealing. The bill's preamble justified the suspension on two grounds. First, it put forward the reason of delay in view of the scale of the government's proposed programme of legislation. The second reason is more instructive. It explained that Poynings' Law procedure considerably increased the opportunity for successful resistance to English legislative proposals, 'for that it resteth doubtful whether the body of the parliament here would assent to the same after the certificate thereof, they having knowledge and being instructed of the same

---

[33] *S.P. Henry VIII*, i, p. 439.
[34] Thus Quinn, 'The early interpretation of Poynings' Law', p. 241.

before as no doubt they should'. The expression of such a view in a bill intended to be presented to parliament indicates no little naivety on the part of the drafter. Nevertheless it draws attention to the limitations of the Irish executive as an instrument of English government at this stage. The process of formal certification by the Irish council entailed divulging English proposals to local administrators, and through their collusion provided an opportunity for organising parliamentary opposition to government measures inimical to local interests. Despite loyalty to the crown, and reformist proclivities, the professional administrators of the Pale who made up a large part of the Irish council could not be trusted to advance the English interest to the detriment of the locality.

These, then, were the circumstances which the first suspension of Poynings' Law were designed to meet. Its purpose was not to remove constraints upon the initiative of an Irish executive composed of permanent English officials. It was rather to circumvent the initiating function conferred upon the Irish executive by the law, precisely for the reason that that body did not then constitute a permanent English administration. Such an administration was eventually installed at the beginning of the seventeenth century, and this led to a dramatic reversal in the attitudes of English government and local community. Thereafter government in England resolutely upheld Poynings' Law procedure while the local community agitated for its suspension and total revocation.

To summarise, therefore. When the English administration under Cromwell wished to use parliament in Ireland as an active instrument of English government it found Poynings' Law a liability. The law gave English government only a negative power of jurisdiction, while it interposed the Irish executive between government in England and parliament in Ireland. This was undesirable, particularly since the Irish executive as a body could not be relied upon to act as a mere extension of English government. Consequently, in this sphere, as in the others already discussed, the exigencies of unitary sovereignty involved a derogation of the status of the Irish executive. With the suspension of the law it remained at the discretion of government in England to work through chosen agents within the Irish administration. This it not infrequently did as an alternative to exercising supervision directly by dispatching its own representatives to conduct parliament. However, the suspension of Poynings' Law was used to eliminate the necessary formal function of the Irish executive, as such, in the legislative process.

The suspension apart, the history of the parliament of 1536–7 provides another example of the manner in which the status and authority of the Dublin executive were diminished as a result of the direct involvement of the English administration in government in Ireland under unitary sovereignty. The initial programme of legislation devised by the Irish administration was scrapped when presented in London by Alen and Aylmer. A completely new one was devised by Audley under Cromwell's supervision.[35] At the second session of parliament the Irish council found themselves compelled to devise and sponsor the financial proposals forced upon them by Cromwell's agent William Body.[36] At the last session the presence of the special commissioners from England signalised the final humiliation of the Irish executive. Since they had failed to be effective in sponsoring the programme of the English administration, the function of representing the crown's interests in parliament was transferred to a group of English officials.

Unitary sovereignty and the Henrician religious Reformation in Ireland

It need hardly be said that the religious Reformation featured in Cromwell's Irish policy. Indeed, in this matter the danger is of allowing the tail to wag the dog. The concept on which the Cromwellian reform was based was unitary sovereignty, not royal ecclesiastical supremacy. The one contained the other.[37] Cromwell's Irish policy developed under different pressures from his English one, and it was not dominated by the religious issue to the same extent. In Ireland the challenge presented itself more urgently in the form of political autonomy, both local and central.

Nevertheless, the issue of ecclesiastical supremacy was too close to the heart of unitary sovereignty to be neglected, and

---

[35] *S.P. Henry VIII*, ii, pp. 245, 320. Edwards, 'The Irish Reformation parliament', pp. 64–5.

[36] *S.P. 60/3*, fos. 121–2. *S.P. Henry VIII*, ii, pp. 330, 345, 426. *L.P.*, x, no. 1051, xi, no. 259.

[37] Elton, *England under the Tudors*, pp. 162, 165. Idem, *Reform and Reformation*, pp. 196–229.

Cromwell's Irish policy did not do so. Both his comprehensive schemes for reformation in Ireland, those of 1534 and 1537, provided for the implementation of the religious Reformation. The *Ordinances* of 1534 instructed the lord deputy and the Irish council to arrange for the enactment of the ecclesiastical legislation. Meanwhile they were 'to resist the said bishop of Rome's provisions and other his pretended and usurped jurisdiction' on the basis of the English legislation. At the same time, the complementary indenture concluded between Ossory and the king contained a similar clause, binding the earl to resist papal jurisdiction within his own area.[38] Some attempt was made both by Lord Deputy Skeffington and by Ossory to launch a campaign in compliance with these directives in 1535.[39] In the same year, Lord Chancellor Audley drafted the necessary ecclesiastical bills for parliament under Cromwell's supervision. Meanwhile the vicegerent was attending to another need, finding a suitable agent to spearhead the religious campaign in Ireland and to fill the metropolitan see of Dublin. Friar George Browne arrived to take over the archiepiscopal office in July 1536, just over a month after the enactment of the royal supremacy in the Dublin parliament. However, nothing much came of all of this because of the creation of a number of obstacles.[40] It was left to Cromwell to revive the religious issue as part of the new programme launched by the royal commissioners in 1537. As a result of the activities of the latter in steering the second Act of Succession through parliament, and in rousing Archbishop Browne and Bishop Staples of Meath to action, the Henrician Reformation campaign was finally launched. To the religious Reformation in Ireland, as to the political one, Cromwell brought tenacity of purpose.[41]

The campaign conducted by Archbishop Browne in 1538 throws into sharp relief the nature of the religious Reformation dictated by unitary sovereignty. Its most striking feature is its correspondence in method and in content with the campaign

---

[38] *S.P. Henry VIII*, ii, pp. 194, 207 (*L.P.*, vii, nos. 740, 1419).

[39] *S.P. Henry VIII*, ii, p. 207 (*L.P.*, vii, no. 1419). A. Gwynn (ed.), 'Archbishop Cromer's Register', *County Louth Archaeological Journal*, x (1942–3), pp. 178–9.

[40] The circumstances that impeded the implementation of the religious Reformation are discussed in my unpublished M.A. thesis, 'George Browne, first Reformation archbishop of Dublin', University College, Dublin, 1966.

[41] My article 'George Browne, first Reformation archbishop of Dublin', *J.E.H.*, xxi (1970), pp. 310–12.

mounted in England. Browne's approach was strongly authoritarian. He sought to advance his cause by means of authoritative directives and looked to the penal clauses of the law and to the secular arm for support in securing conformity. His programme also was closely modelled on that implemented in England. It included the English liturgical reforms of 1534, the extrusion of the pope's name from the books of ritual, and the introduction of new bidding prayers. At the devotional level, English versions of the common prayers, *Pater*, creed and *Ave*, as well as of the Ten Commandments, were circulated, and the clergy were instructed to teach them to their flocks by rote as commanded by the Royal Injunctions of 1538. In preaching Browne adopted an evangelical style, 'moving questions of scripture', and struck the doctrinal poses favoured by official promulgations in England. He gave his flock the benefit of the teaching of the *Bishops' Book* of 1537 on Justification, and in line with that compilation and the Royal Injunctions he inveighed against indulgences, auricular confession, and images.[42]

The possible alternative to this approach was suggested by Bishop Staples of Meath, who was much less familiar than Browne with Cromwellian England, though much more familiar than he with pre-Cromwellian Ireland. In a letter written in the summer of 1538 to Sir Anthony St Leger, the former head of the royal commission of 1537, Staples was strongly critical of Browne's campaign. He condemned the archbishop's emphasis on authority and conformity. The common voice, he declared, was that 'the supremacy is maintained by power and not by reason and learning...Now all they do is for fear and ye know that is but a keeper of continuance.' He also condemned the novelty of the archbishop's programme, which he said was giving scandal. Staples' alternative approach contrasts with Browne's in two ways. In method he emphasised the importance of consent over conformity. In place of Browne's disciplinary approach, therefore, he advocated explanation, education, and the generating of popular enthusiasm. He suggested seminars for the clergy and, more spectacularly, the proclamation of Henry VIII as king of Ireland, which, he considered, would provide a wave of popular enthusiasm to carry the royal supremacy to shore. In contrast to

---

[42] Ibid., pp. 312–13. Also my unpublished thesis, 'George Browne, first Reformation archbishop of Dublin'.

Browne's close adaptation of the programme of the English Reformation, his proposal was to concentrate on securing acceptance of the one essential tenet, the royal ecclesiastical supremacy.[43]

Our interest in the dispute between the two ecclesiastics in 1538 is for the light it throws on Cromwell's own conception of a religious policy for Ireland. There can be no doubt that Browne more faithfully reflects his views. Staples was not close to the vicegerent. He was promoted to Meath in 1530 before Cromwell's advent. Their first contact was unfortunate: in 1534 the bishop, flying for his life from the rebellion, was rounded upon by Cromwell in London for cowardice. Subsequent evidence suggests that Cromwell did not choose to maintain the contact. A present from the bishop in 1537 went unacknowledged, and when he wished to gain a hearing in the dispute with Browne in 1538 he made his approach indirectly through St Leger.[44] On the other hand Browne was in constant touch with Cromwell throughout 1538. This was because he was a Cromwellian through and through. Cromwell picked him up as a likely man in 1533, and brought him into the thick of the official Reformation campaign in England as a propagandist and as a supervisor of the English friars on the government's behalf, in the period before their dissolution. He was promoted archbishop of Dublin in 1536 specifically to advance the religious Reformation in Ireland. He was in a better position than anyone else in the Dublin government, therefore, to know the vicegerent's mind about the religious Reformation and about its application to Ireland.[45]

One word sums up what Cromwell and Browne had in mind by way of ecclesiastical reform in Ireland. It was not simply royal ecclesiastical supremacy; it was Anglicanism. Just as in the political sphere unitary sovereignty dictated that the colony be governed as an extension of the realm of England, so in the ecclesiastical sphere it was to be treated as part of the *Ecclesia Anglicana*. The attempt of Audley and Cromwell in 1535 to bring the administrative structure of the church in Ireland within the jurisdictional ambit of Canterbury and the English chancery is complemented by Browne's programme in 1538 designed to

[43] *S.P. Henry VIII*, iii, pp. 1, 29. *L.P.*, xiii(ii), no. 64.
[44] *Fiants, Henry VIII*, no. 27. *S.P. Henry VIII*, iii, p. 29. *L.P.*, xiii(i), nos. 524, 1205.
[45] My 'George Browne', *J.E.H.*, pp. 305–10.

bring it within the Anglican ambit in liturgy, piety and doctrine. Cromwell's intentions are made finally clear by his dispatch to Ireland in the autumn of 1538 of a set of ecclesiastical injunctions. Although a copy does not survive, it is clear that they were based on the Royal Injunctions promulgated in England in that September. It seems that certain adaptations were made in the light of Irish conditions. For instance, no reference occurs to the injunction to provide an English bible in every parish church, a requirement that would have created a considerable problem of supply and that would have been of limited value in view of the widespread use of Irish, even in the Pale. However, the design obviously was that the local Church was to be brought into substantial uniformity with English practice.

The Irish act for the royal supremacy declared the king and his successors 'the only supreme head in earth of the whole Church of Ireland, called *Hibernica Ecclesia*'.[46] However, in practice there was to be no distinctive Church of Ireland. Just as there was only one shepherd, the king, and one flock, his faithful subjects, so there was only one Church, *Mater Ecclesia Anglicana*.

Since the supreme head based his title to ecclesiastical jurisdiction on a politico-constitutional criterion, it followed that the ambiguity of his jurisdictional relationship with the non-constitutional lordships in Ireland carried over into his jurisdictional relationship with the Church in those areas. Further, since the inhabitants of those areas lacked constitutional status under the crown in the political domain, their constitutional status ecclesiastically was open to question. If they were not subjects of the king, could they be members of the Christian community of which he was the head?

The religious policy is of a piece with Cromwell's Irish policy generally in its vagueness in relation to the area outside the crown's direct jurisdiction. There is no evidence of an explicit directive from him in this regard. The lord deputy seems to have taken the view that the royal ecclesiastical supremacy was not to be asserted outside the area of the crown's sovereign jurisdiction. He did not include a clause requiring recognition of the king's ecclesiastical claims in the indentures of submission which he negotiated with local lords, though such a clause was included in three exceptional

---

[46] *Statutes at large, Ireland*, i, p. 90.

cases where the form of submission was intended as a preliminary to a grant of full status and title under the crown. The lord deputy's attitude is illustrated in his spectacular journey into Munster and Connacht in the summer of 1538. His activities in the course of the journey are well attested by lengthy reports from himself and others, and by records of the submissions he obtained. All the evidence indicates that the only occasions on which he sought recognition of the royal ecclesiastical supremacy was in his visitation of the royal towns of Limerick and Galway.[47]

On the other hand, Cromwell's closest collaborators on the Irish council endeavoured to implement a policy with regard to the dioceses in the non-constitutional areas analogous to the policy regarding the lordships. This was to exert a form of external jurisdiction over them. They sought formal submission from local bishops by inviting them to subscribe to the oaths of supremacy and succession. They sought to have the royal authority recognised in the filling of episcopal vacancies. They tried to curtail resort to Rome from the Irishry for provisions and ecclesiastical faculties.[48] However, the reorganisation of the Church according to the Reformation programme was attempted only within the area of the crown's sovereign jurisdiction. The boundary of the new Anglicanism was coterminous with the boundary of the new Pale.

Cromwellian unionism

Few would dispute that the period of Thomas Cromwell's preeminence in government was not only a period of major administrative reform in England but one of constitutional innovation also, though the nature of the innovation and its author – king or minister – might be hotly disputed. It remains for us to consider, therefore, the constitutional implications of Cromwell's reform programme for the Irish Lordship.

It is hardly necessary to argue again here, since the point has already been treated extensively, that Cromwell did not aspire to alter the basic structural composition of the medieval Lordship.

---

[47] *S.P. Henry VIII*, iii, pp. 55, 57, 169, 248. *L.P.*, xiii(i), nos. 1283, 1381, 1447, xv, no. 830, xvi, no. 304. Gray plundered two religious houses in the course of the journey. This was not an attempt to implement the dissolution of the religious orders: both were intended as punitive measures against hostile local lords.

[48] *S.P. Henry VIII*, iii, pp. 111, 116. *L.P.*, xiii(ii), no. 1027. R. D. Edwards, 'The Irish bishops and the Anglican schism', *I.E.R.*, xlv (1935), pp. 42–6.

No attempt was made to extend the sovereign jurisdiction of the crown beyond the area occupied by the king's lawful subjects, or to establish proper constitutional ties with the disobedient Irishry. The constitutional and jurisdictional duality of the Lordship was allowed to continue as it had been formalised in the fourteenth century.

The question is, rather, what was the constitutional significance of enacting in parliament in Ireland that body of laws which established the royal supremacy in England, and of carrying through within the colonial area the same programme of political and religious reform which in England established the sovereign jurisdiction of the crown throughout the realm? If it can be argued that by this means the basis was laid for the early modern English constitution, founded on the twin concepts of national sovereignty and constitutional monarchy, what was the effect upon Ireland? In the first place it should be said that the supremacy legislation did nothing to enhance the constitutional status of Ireland as it did for England. It made no proud assertions about Ireland's sovereign status as an empire. All such claims referred to England. The Irish acts simply recited the English measures and transferred their legislative effect, in virtue of Ireland's union with the imperial crown of England.

Consideration of this aspect of Cromwell's Irish policy is illuminated, as others have been, by placing it in the more general context of his reform programme for the outlying areas as a whole. A historian who considers the constitutional implications of the Cromwellian reform programme from the perspective of the peripheries rather than from the centre is struck by the anomaly of describing its underlying principle as national sovereignty. The anomaly is highlighted by the example of Wales. The same principle which decreed the affirmation of England's sovereignty against any external interference decreed the abolition of Wales as a political entity and its absorption by the kingdom of England. True, in the process, the political status of the Welsh under the crown was actually enhanced. For the first time they became eligible to participate in government, to send members to parliament and to take public office. But the offices they accepted were those of the English administration centred at Westminster, and the parliament they attended was the English one. The point is that the principle which shaped Cromwell's reform was the sovereignty of the state, not the sovereignty of the nation. So far as the constitution of England was concerned, the two were synonymous. However, for those other dominions over which the king claimed jurisdiction the principle did not enhance their national sovereignty, but rather diminished it. So far as the king's sovereign jurisdiction extended, so far, jurisdictionally and constitutionally, extended the kingdom of England.

The concept of territorial union was made explicit in the acts for the union of Wales with England and for the reform of the English Pale in France. In the case of Ireland the situation was more complex politically. A constitutional union was not attempted by act of parliament. Indeed, the statutes enacting the royal ecclesiastical supremacy in Ireland expressed the constitutional position of the Irish Lordship in a way that could be endorsed by the local parliament: 'the king's land of Ireland, is his proper dominion, and a member appending and rightfully belonging to the imperial crown of the said realm of England, and united to the same'.[49] The notion of a personal union, in the imperial crown, of two distinct constitutional and jurisdictional entities – the kingdom of England and the Lordship of Ireland – is precisely what was was expressed by the Anglo-Irish separatist tradition of the fifteenth century.

However, as we have seen, this was not the constitutional concept which inspired Cromwell's programme of reform in Ireland. On the contrary, Cromwell's programme was designed to undermine the administrative and jurisdictional integrity of the government of the Irish Lordship, to shift its centre from Dublin to London, and to transform the Dublin administration from a central government into a regional council. Administratively the objective of his reform programme was clear, to reconstitute the colonial area in Ireland on the same basis as the Pale at Calais and to govern it, like Calais, as part of a political unity centred on London. It is clear also that the strategy was inspired not purely by a desire for efficient government, but by the concept of unitary sovereignty.

---

[49] *Statutes at large, Ireland*, i, p. 156. However, Sir John Davies attempted to argue, in his address as speaker of the Irish house of commons in 1613, that the phrase just quoted and others of a similar kind implied a union of the two kingdoms rather than a union of each to the English crown. The address is edited by H. Morley in *Ireland under Elizabeth* (London 1890), p. 394.

We do not have an explicit statement from Cromwell himself of the way in which he viewed the constitutional link between the kingdom and the Lordship. But the statements of two English administrators close to him may be taken as expressing his own attitude. One comes from Archbishop John Alen, Cromwell's former colleague in Wolsey's service, and his original contact within the Dublin administration. In a commentary on the jurisdictional status of his metropolitan see, in a register drawn up in the early 1530s, he speaks of it as a handmaid of the English Church. A further comment throws more light on his thought: there he explains the liberties of the Church in Ireland as deriving from the island's incorporation into the kingdom of England.[50] The significance of Alen's remarks is that for him the Irish Lordship is not linked directly to the crown of England but indirectly in a relationship of dependence upon the English kingdom. The second commentary brings the matter home in more senses than one. It is contained in Chancellor Audley's letter to Cromwell, already cited, in which he proposed that the centre of jurisdiction for judicial proceedings and the dispensation of faculties in the reformed Irish Church should be established not within Ireland but at Canterbury and at the English chancery. What Audley proposed was a union of jurisdictions under the royal ecclesiastical supremacy, by extending the English system to include the king's subjects in Ireland. The particular significance of Audley's proposal of administrative union is that he justified it not by considerations of administrative efficiency but on the basis of what he conceived to be the constitutional relationship of the Lordship to the kingdom, 'because England is the chief part of the crown and Ireland a member appendant to it'.[51] There is positive proof that Cromwell shared Audley's view of the appropriate administrative arrangement, and it must be taken as no less certain that he shared his view of the constitutional situation also. No doubt, the view of the Lordship as jurisdictionally subordinate to England was of long standing among English administrators; but the Cromwellian reform transformed it into a principle of constitutional union.

Though the Cromwellian constitutional concept was in general inimical to the notion of a constitutionally distinct Irish Lordship,

[50] C. McNeill (ed.), *Calendar of Archbishop Alen's Register* (Dublin 1950), pp. 281, 288.
[51] *S.P. Henry VIII*, i, p. 438.

it made one substantial contribution to the preservation of the Lordship as a distinct entity. This was in the revival of parliament. In Ireland, as in England, Cromwell's reform programme required a whole new body of legislation to carry it into effect. The result was to revitalise the institution of parliament in Ireland which the Poynings procedure had practically ossified. Ideally, unitary sovereignty would have entailed the discontinuance of a separate parliament for Ireland, and the attendance of members from the new Pale at the Westminster parliament. This would have been in line with Cromwell's arrangements for Wales and Calais which brought M.P.s from those areas to Westminster for the first time. However, the situation in Ireland was obviously not ripe for such an innovation in 1536. Cromwell's alternative, as we have seen, was not to reinstate parliament in Ireland completely: rather, he used it in such a way as to make it a positive instrument in the advancement of English government, mainly using it to endorse legislation already passed in England. With the notable exception of the parliament of 1541–3 the restored Irish parliament was never allowed to assume the role of 'partner in government' which the English institution became. Nevertheless the continued reliance upon statute as an instrument of government after Cromwell meant that parliament in Ireland continued to provide a focus and a forum for the Anglo-Irish separatist tradition.

6

Reform and reaction

The enduring importance of Cromwell's administration for Irish history lies not only in what it achieved – the ending of the hegemony of the Anglo-Irish magnates and the revival of crown government – but also in the hostile reaction it provoked. The liberal experiment of the 1540s must be examined in the light of the reaction to the Cromwellian settlement of the 1530s. In bringing down the curtain on the medieval Lordship, Cromwell set the scene for the establishment of the sovereign kingdom.

The settlement unsettled – Cromwellian reform and the loyal community

In examining the resistance to Cromwellian reform within the loyal Anglo-Irish community, attention tends to be concentrated on two episodes, the Kildare rebellion and the religious Reformation. But it can be said at once that as manifestations of popular reaction within the colony against Cromwell's Irish policy these have the least significance.

Although the Kildare rebellion occurred before the full Cromwellian programme was launched, it was precipitated by that series of events in 1533 and the spring of 1534 which prepared the way for the inauguration of the programme. It was essentially, therefore, a reaction to Cromwell's Irish policy.[1] The more closely the Kildare rebellion is observed, the more neatly it falls into the category of late medieval dynastic warfare. Silken Thomas was able to elicit the support of his father's Gaelic allies, and of most of his kinsmen, feudal underlords and tenants. He was able to bully many landholders in the Pale into neutrality or even support, by

[1] See my 'Cromwellian reform and the origins of the Kildare rebellion', pp. 69–93. Also above, pp. 90–8.

guaranteeing indemnity to their property. However, the ease with which the alliance disintegrated reflects the considerations of political expediency and local self-interest on which it was based. One thing is most certain: the Kildare rebellion was not the popular uprising which romantic nationalists fondly imagined. What mainly concerns us here is that as a reaction to Cromwellian policy it was purely a personal protest on the part of the greatest Anglo-Irish magnate family at the threat to their dominance. That protest received no general mandate from the loyal community of the Pale, even when broadened to include the religious issue, and much less as a simple act of defiance of the king.[2]

In dealing with the reaction to the religious Reformation it is necessary to repeat the warning already given in discussing its place in the Cromwellian programme. The tendency is to give it an exaggerated prominence in relation to its actual significance at this period. Three episodes provide evidence of opposition within the loyal community to the religious Reformation: the Kildare rebellion of 1534–5, the enactment of the royal supremacy in parliament in 1536, and Archbishop Browne's Reformation campaign of 1537–8. On each occasion the source of active opposition can be traced almost exclusively to the lower clergy. The evidence shows the response of the higher clergy as one of general submissiveness despite some prevarication. The laity displayed a general willingness to conform, if no enthusiasm.[3] Because of the limited nature of the protest the religious Reformation must be regarded as a less provocative aspect of the Cromwellian reform programme than those to be discussed later. However, one feature of the lay response to the religious issue has a special significance. This was the reluctance of Anglo-Irish government officials

---

[2] For an analysis of the response to the Kildare rebellion within the Anglo–Irish community, see S. G. Ellis, 'The Kildare rebellion', unpublished M.A. thesis, Manchester, 1974; idem, 'Tudor policy and the Kildare ascendancy'. My own study of the Kildare rebellion has benefited greatly from perusal of Mr Ellis's thesis and also of the unpublished M.A. thesis of Lawrence Corristine, 'The Kildare rebellion, 1534', University College, Dublin, 1975. I should add in fairness to them both that I here draw on their research rather than on their conclusions. For the response to the rebellion in the area of the Irishry, see below.

[3] In connection with the religious element in the Kildare rebellion I must again acknowledge my indebtedness to Mr Ellis, though with the qualification already mentioned. For the other episodes, see my 'Opposition to the ecclesiastical legislation in the Irish Reformation parliament', 285–303; also my unpublished thesis, 'George Browne'.

to operate the penal clauses of the ecclesiastical laws against local clerical dissidents.[4] In contrast to England, the movement of resistance in Ireland was not nipped in the bud by effective state action. This was a factor of no little importance in the gradual development of a widespread recusant movement among the loyal Anglo-Irish community.

So far as the local community was concerned, in the 1530s, the English garrison was a much more explosive issue than religion. At the early stages a free-for-all between Skeffington's soldiers and the apprentices of Dublin indicated the shape of things to come.[5] It may be that two such groups would have fought each other cheerfully for any cause or none. However, another Dublin riot at the close of the decade leaves no doubt about the reaction of the citizens generally to the continuing presence of the English army. The incident developed from a difference of opinion between a soldier and a municipal official. The city bell was rung, and the citizens poured into the streets to make a stand against the soldiery. The fact that one resultant fatality was that of a former municipal bailiff provides a further indication of the involvement of the more responsible elements of the city's community in the incident.[6]

The general unpopularity of the garrison gains heightened political significance when the causes of the resentment are analysed. One obvious cause was the abominable behaviour of the soldiers. Their indiscipline and harassment of the local population provoked a stream of complaints to Cromwell, the burden of which is indicated in a dispatch of 1539 which describes the retinue of William St Loe in Wexford as 'committing rather more oppressions and extortions to the people, than they do them good by any defence they make for them'.[7] As well as this social dimension, the resentment of the soldiery had also a strong economic aspect. The burden of their wages fell upon the English treasury, but they were underpaid, and frequently for long periods were left without any pay at all. Not unnaturally they turned to the source nearest to hand to make good their losses. Apart from bare-faced robbery there was also the legalised form, the system

---

4 *S.P. Henry VIII*, ii, pp. 512, 539, 563, iii, 6, 102, 103, 136. Cf. John Bale, 'The vocacyon, of Johan Bale', in *Harleian Miscellany*, vi, pp. 448, 449, 453.
5 Stanyhurst, 'The chronicles of Ireland' in *Holinshed's Chronicles*, vi, p. 285.
6 *S.P. Henry VIII*, iii, p. 235. *L.P.*, xvi, nos. 42, 43.
7 *S.P. Henry VIII*, iii, p. 111.

of cess by which the army could purvey victuals at a controlled price below market value. Furthermore the burden of victualling the army from the resources of an area where in any case food had to be imported to supply local needs led to scarcity and spiralling prices. The specifically political element in the resentment points to the danger – about which the Irish executive had warned – of equating the colony in Ireland with the Pale in France.[8] Apart from geographical factors which made the Calais Pale a more naturally defensible entity, the two areas were substantially different in social structure. Unlike Calais, the colony in Ireland was inhabited by a long-established and fully developed indigenous community. The abuses of bastard feudalism notwithstanding, the establishment of the garrison led to the usurpation by the English captains of status and functions which the Anglo-Irish nobility and gentry might legitimately regard as their own. Cromwell's collaborators in Ireland were soon complaining of the way the lord deputy distributed military command at general hostings, appointing 'light inexpert fellows to be conductors of the army, commanding the lords, the earl of Ossory's son, and other captains which came there to serve the king at their own charges to follow them'.[9] At this point opposition to the model for the Cromwellian reform programme, the garrisoned Pale, merged into opposition to the Cromwellian principle of unitary sovereignty.

The English garrison was a Cromwellian innovation that became a permanent feature of crown government in Ireland, as well as a major source of political tension down to the foundation of the free state, and indeed beyond. The other special feature of Cromwell's reform programme was no less enduring, and no less alienating, although here the Cromwellian episode marks not the origins, but the point of transition from medieval to modern. A new phase in the history of Anglo-Irish separatism begins with the response to Cromwellian unionism.

It was pointed out earlier that in seeking to use parliament as a positive instrument of English government in Ireland Cromwell revived the institution which had been the traditional forum of Anglo-Irish separatism.[10] Although the revival was strictly

[8] *S.P. Henry VIII*, ii, pp. 426, 434.
[9] *S.P. Henry VIII*, iii, p. 36 (*L.P.*, xiii(i), no. 1303).
[10] Above, pp. 162–3.

controlled, parliament could not be deprived of the capacity to repudiate government proposals, and the suspension of Poynings' Law gave it an undisputed power of amendment also, without further reference to the executive. Thus, if the members were deprived of the means of attack, at least they had the possibility of effective defence, and the greater the government's need for statute to carry through its programme the greater was the scope for local politicians to conduct a rearguard action. For this reason the emergence of a substantial movement of opposition at the parliament of 1536–7 is of special interest.

A modern study of the parliament argues that the spirit of 'independence and "Irishness"' characteristic of seventeenth-century parliaments had its 'real beginnings' here. The argument is based on the fact that, although the measures enacted were largely copied from England, parliament exercised its power of veto and amendment to impose an 'Irish slant' on business.[11] That is very true. The argument may be given further precision by looking more closely at the legislation affected.

In line with what has been said already it is necessary to refer in the first instance to the response to the legislation enacting the royal ecclesiastical supremacy. The corpus of acts enshrining that principle were passed at the first session of parliament. According to reports from the Irish executive no objection was raised except by the proctors of the lower clergy.[12] To say it again, the king's constitutional claim to jurisdiction over the Church was not generally disputed within the Anglo-Irish community in the 1530s.

It was a different matter when the same principle of unitary sovereignty on which the royal ecclesiastical supremacy was based was applied to the relationship between the English kingdom and the Irish Lordship. Although the claim of the king of England to be head of the Irish Church was allowed, the right to govern the Irish Church from England was disputed. As we have seen, this right was asserted in the bills drafted in England for faculties and for appeals in ecclesiastical causes. These proposed that the relevant processes should centre upon Canterbury and the English chancery, in virtue of Ireland's constitutional status as an appendage of the

---

[11] R. D. Edwards, 'The Irish Reformation parliament', p. 80.
[12] See my 'Opposition to the ecclesiastical legislation in the Irish Reformation parliament', pp. 290–2.

English crown. In both cases the English proposals were amended in Ireland to provide an alternative administrative procedure whereby the centre of jurisdiction under the acts would reside in the Irish executive.[13] To these may be added a third measure, applying the unionist principle in quite a different sphere: a bill to bring the Lordship into monetary uniformity with England by striking the sterling rate. Like the ecclesiastical proposals, it based itself on the constitutional principle that 'the land of Ireland is parcel of the crown of England'.[14] It was rejected out of hand.[15]

Thus, although details of the parliamentary debates do not survive, parliament's disapproval of the principle of unionism is clear. In the case of one of the measures concerned, some further light can be thrown on the local attitude. From 1536 onwards, members of the Irish administration emphasised the need for the establishment of an Irish-based commission for dispensing ecclesiastical faculties. They urged that this would cause Rome-runners to remain at home, and seek dispensations by crown patent. The insinuation was that the Canterbury office was not an acceptable alternative. Unfortunately records do not survive to show what happened after 1539, when Cromwell at last relented and delegated the authority to a special commission in Ireland. However, the Canterbury records for the period from 1536 onwards reveal very clearly its failure to attract Irish custom.[16]

Apart from these three measures, much of the government's legislative programme in 1536–7 was amended or totally resisted. As we saw in Chapter 4, the greatest storm of the parliament was caused by the introduction at the second session of the bills concerning certain customs duties, a tax of a twentieth, and the confiscation of certain monastic properties. It is reasonable to suppose that the tension generated by such proposals, regardless of the particular issues, and the vested interests concerned, received an added dimension in virtue of the fundamental constitutional challenge to the status of the Lordship posed by the Cromwellian programme of reform.[17]

---

[13] Above, pp. 145–6.

[14] Quinn (ed.), 'Bills and statutes of Henry VII and Henry VIII', p. 142.

[15] *L.P.*, xii(i), no. 1278.

[16] E.g., for 1536 only one out of some six hundred faculties issued by Canterbury was for an Irish diocese, and in 1538 only two from some seven hundred. D. S. Chambers (ed.), *Faculty office registers of Canterbury* (Oxford 1966).

[17] Above, pp. 113–14. Bradshaw, 'Opposition to the ecclesiastical legislation in the Irish Reformation parliament', pp. 295–8. Idem, *Dissolution of the religious orders*, p. 47–65.

The counterpart of the political tension generated by the Cromwellian programme was the racial antagonism which it served to heighten. Although, as we have insisted, Cromwell did not deliberately discriminate against the Anglo-Irish, his garrison policy resulted in an increased English presence of a most obnoxious kind. The misbehaviour of the soldiers served to discredit further their nationality as well as their profession in the eyes of a local population who already had no great opinion of either.

Here attention may be drawn also to the subject of race relations with the Gaelic Irish. The rebuff to the government bills against Gaelicisation introduced at the parliament of 1536–7 serves to underline the thesis argued earlier about attitudes to Gaelicisation within the loyal community. Although the bills drafted in England to curtail cultural Gaelicisation and social intercourse by marriage and fosterage do not survive, there is good reason to believe that the reason for the moderation of the acts as passed is their amendment by parliament in Ireland. It is known that the bills transmitted from England were drastically amended, but the nature of the amendments is not known, since the nineteenth-century collator from whom we derive our information regarded the amendments as so extensive in these two cases as to render collation impracticable. In any case, what emerged after parliament's handiwork was two bland decrees providing for the cultivation of English language and customs, and stipulating firmer conditions to ensure the political loyalty of marriage partners of Gaelic blood. Neither measure was allowed much bite in the way of penal clauses, and numerous loopholes were provided by, for instance, the qualification of injunctions with such phrases as 'to their ability' and 'as near as ever they can'.[18]

An incident in the town of Ross in July 1538 is worth mentioning for the light it throws on racial attitudes at this time. A number of Cahir McArt Cavanagh's galloglasses, who had come into the town for the celebrations on St Peter's Eve, were

---

[18] *Statutes at large, Ireland*, i, p. 118 (c.15), 3 (c.28). Quinn (ed.), 'Bills and statutes of Henry VII and Henry VIII', pp. 138, 153–4. For the background to the legislation, see *S.P. Henry VIII*, ii, pp. 445, 480, 502, iii, p. 218. In contrast to the Irish measures, the equivalent provisions in the 'Ordinances for Calais', passed by parliament in England in 1536, are less extensive but also less compromising, *Statutes of the realm (England)*, iii, p. 632.

set upon by a band of William St Loe's soldiers from Wexford, headed by his lieutenant, Watkin ap Powell. Most of them managed to get away with injuries, but Cahir's standard bearer was killed. The reaction of the townsmen is revealing. They were outraged. They regarded the galloglasses as friendly visitors, the retainers of a local lord with whom the town was on friendly terms. The sovereign of the town searched out the culprits, placed them in ward and reported the matter to Dublin. The incident sent Cahir McArt Cavanagh on the rampage, and Ormond wrote to Cromwell citing the case as an example of the political mischievousness of the army. As well as revealing how English gut reaction to the Gaelic Irish contrasted with Anglo-Irish tolerance and flexibility, the episode also draws attention to the tension between the English newcomers and the loyal Anglo-Irish community.[19]

In the light of all of this, the political tension within the loyal community in the second half of the 1530s assumes strong ideological overtones. Contrary to what might be supposed, these do not relate principally or immediately to the royal claim to ecclesiastical supremacy, still less to the constitutional status of the English crown in the secular sphere. The reaction of the Pale community to the crisis of the Geraldine League in 1539–40 reveals an attitude that was to remain generally characteristic so long as the old Anglo-Irish community retained a corporate identity, down to the end of the seventeenth century. Here they showed the imperviousness of their loyalty to the crown to the seduction of treason, whether for the sake of religion or politics. On the eve of the campaign by the Gaelic combination in 1539, John Alen expressed misgivings on this score. But both then and in 1540 such doubts were dispelled in the event.[20] The ideological implications of the tension generated in the loyal Anglo-Irish community by the Cromwellian reformation emerge against the background of the late medieval separatist tradition, and its corollary of anti-English racial sentiment. What primarily offended the susceptibilities of the Anglo-Irish was not the principle of royal ecclesiastical supremacy which the programme enshrined, but the

---

[19] *S.P. Henry VIII*, iii, pp. 36, 48, 63. *L.P.*, xiii(i), no. 1395.

[20] *S.P. Henry VIII*, iii, pp. 145, 223. H. Ellis, *Original letters* (2nd ser.), ii, (London 1827), p. 93.

concept of constitutional union associated with it. The two may have seemed synonymous in London, but the distinction was very evident from a more westerly perspective.

Crown government and the Irishry, 1534–40

The opening and closing phases of Cromwell's administration were marked by major political upheavals in Ireland. As the labels given to them by historians indicate, the Kildare rebellion of 1534–5 and the Geraldine League of 1539–40 were in one respect a Fitzgerald response to the ending of the dynasty's hegemony in Irish government. However, on both occasions the crisis was marked by the manifestation of substantial opposition to crown government within the Irishry. The political implications of this must be examined.

The rebellion of Silken Thomas has entered the canon of romantic nationalism beside the rebellions of Emmet and Pearse as a magnificent gesture of youthful idealism and defiance. Indeed, the combination of the great Anglo-Irish family with leading Gaelic septs, in a common gesture of defiance of the crown and the defence of the Catholic faith, has seemed to justify tracing the mainstream nationalist tradition back to this source.

When the Kildare rebellion is analysed in the national context, the appearance of a movement of solidarity based on nationalism and religion in defiance of the English crown soon breaks down. There is no indication that national consciousness, much less the concept of a national political community, exercised an influence on the course of events. The issues were thrown up by the rivalries of the great local dynasties, and by their concern for local status and political influence. Dynastic interests determined the nature of the alignments and dominated the course of the war. The traditional Kildare alliances immediately asserted themselves, centering on O'Neill in Ulster, O'Connor in Leinster, and O'Brien in Munster. The failure of the Butlers to rouse their traditional allies in West Munster, the McCarthys of Muskerry, in support of the crown illustrates the considerations of dynastic power politics that dominated the war. The latter had little interest in participating since their own great local rivals, the Desmond Fitzgeralds, did not participate on the other side, being embroiled in an internal dispute over the succession. The Butlers, in fact, had been able to exploit the Desmond dispute to neutralise this part of the Kildare alliance. In Thomond a marriage nexus enabled them to use Donough O'Brien, the lord's eldest son, as a thorn in the side of his father.[21] In the north O'Donnell came scurrying to Lord Deputy Skeffington, with his ally Maguire, to offer their services against Fitzgerald on the understanding that this would be reciprocated by government assistance with three of O'Donnell's pressing problems, the curbing of O'Neill, the recapture of Sligo Castle from the O'Connors of Connacht, and the chastisement of his disobedient son, Manus.[22]

In the same way the alliances dissolved in the course of 1535 in response to the exigencies of dynastic self-interest. Early in the summer O'Neill changed sides to offset the advantage of alliance with Skeffington gained by O'Donnell. After the fall of Maynooth in July, and with the prospects of a damaging summer campaign ahead, Kildare's Leinster allies opened up negotiations for peace. Finally, O'Connor, Fitzgerald's closest ally, made his peace in late August as the crown forces advanced into his territory.[23] Following the conventions of Irish dynastic warfare Silken Thomas himself also decided to retire from the struggle rather than fight to the finish. Although beaten in Leinster he might have joined his Munster ally O'Brien, who had already counselled him to hold out. This would have given him a respite at least, since the crown forces could not have reached him before that year's campaigning season closed, and if it came to the worst he could have slipped off to the continent. The Irish council enticed him in with the prospect of a generous pardon. The history of his family over the previous fifty years would have led him to expect a show of severity from the king at first, followed eventually by a restoration to favour. Tragically for himself, he discovered that times had changed.[24]

The Kildare rebellion of 1534–5, therefore, was conducted within the political framework and the conventions of Irish medieval dynastic warfare. This serves to underline the fact that the ideology of the Kildare alliance was particularist and dynastic,

[21] *S.P. Henry VIII*, ii, pp. 229, 230, 249. *L.P.*, viii, nos. 60, 114, 115, 881.
[22] *S.P. Henry VIII*, ii, pp. 205, 235, 243, 247, 273, 303. B. MacCarthy (ed.), *Annals of Ulster (Annála Uladh)*, iii (Dublin 1895), pp. 590–1, 602–3. *A.F.M.*, v, pp. 1406–7.
[23] *S.P. Henry VIII*, ii, pp. 249, 261, 263, 273.
[24] *S.P. Henry VIII*, ii, pp. 249, 273, 275.

despite the appeal to religion and the manifestations of xenophobia against the English which characterised it. There is the ring of truth in the incident, narrated by Stanyhurst, of the Fitzgerald bard delivering an ode of exhortation during the dramatic scene in St Mary's Abbey in Dublin in June 1534 when Silken Thomas renounced his fealty to the king before the Irish council.[25] It is the ideology of these odes, extolling the prowess and the lineage of the local dynasty, that the Kildare rebellion reflects, not the ideology of the nationalist poetry of the seventeenth century. Neither in the ideology which supported it nor in the politics which activated it can the Kildare rebellion be considered a nationalist uprising.

In the early autumn of 1539 the war of the Geraldine League burst upon the Pale in its first and most destructive phase. O'Donnell and O'Neill with their underlords swooped upon the Pale from the north, overrunning Louth and Meath as far as Tara, and sacking Ardee and the Navan on the way. That phase ended with the rout of Bellahoe in September, when Lord Deputy Gray caught the forces of the League by surprise as they withdrew from the Pale laden with booty.[26] The alliance regrouped in the course of the winter and spring, and in the summer of 1540 plunged the Pale into another crisis.[27] However, the League eventually succumbed, not to the military operations of the crown, but to the diplomacy of a new lord deputy, Sir Anthony St Leger, who arrived in the autumn of 1540.

The Geraldine League has received scant attention from historians. It is written up as a postscript to the Kildare rebellion, as an ineffectual coalition which ended ingloriously in the defeat of Bellahoe in September 1539 and the departure of Gerald Fitzgerald, the young heir, to continental exile. Unfortunately this is a case where historians have seen what they expected to see, not what actually happened. One false assumption – that the League was a Geraldine combination – has led to another – that it collapsed with the collapse of the Geraldine challenge. In fact, as we have noted, the combination reemerged in 1540 to provide as great a political crisis for the crown as in 1534 and, so it seemed within

[25] Stanyhurst, 'The chronicles of Ireland' in *Holinshed's Chronicles*, vi, p. 292.
[26] *A.F.M.*, v, pp. 1452–3. *Loch Cé*, ii, pp. 316–19.
[27] *S.P. Henry VIII*, iii, pp. 176, 179, 182, 187, 202, 206, 207, 223 (*L.P.*, xv, nos. 82, 142, 199, 328, 654, 684, 912).

the colony, a more menacing one in nature. Realisation that the Geraldine element was not essential to the survival of the League suggests that factors other than the Geraldine claim were at play in its origins.

The romantic account of how the nine-year-old Gerald Fitzgerald was whisked away from the clutches of the crown and into the protective arms of his aunt, Lady Eleanor McCarthy in West Cork, and of how the latter set out with the boy to marry Manus O'Donnell and rouse the north, is not quite the story of the formation of the Geraldine League. The documentary evidence indicates that the instigator of the League was not the Lady Eleanor but O'Donnell, the dazzling and audacious young prince of Donegal. A Geraldine alliance based on a marriage nexus with the widowed Eleanor McCarthy opened up attractive possibilities. It promised to extricate Manus from a diplomatic tangle with Con O'Neill, who had helped to install him as lord of Donegal but from whose tutelage he now wished to be free in view of the inevitable clash of interests between them as heads of the two dominant dynasties in Ulster.[28] The emergence of Manus at the head of a Geraldine alliance would spike O'Neill's guns, since the latter was the traditional Fitzgerald ally in the north. Further, the alliance represented an investment in the open market of Irish politics which offered the possibility of rich dividends not only in terms of status within the Irishry but in relation to the crown also. The situation which offered such possibilities for exploitation was created by the activities of crown government in the area of the Irishry in the aftermath of the Kildare rebellion. Here we return to the theme of Cromwellian reform.

Ironically, Cromwell, who resolutely set himself against a conquest policy in Ireland, must be held in no small way responsible for provoking the alliance that confronted the crown in the closing years of his administration. What has to be considered in this case is not the reaction to his policy but rather

---

[28] The best source on all of this is *A.F.M.*; Stanyhurst corroborates the Gaelic annals in presenting Manus O'Donnell as the initiator of the marriage proposal: to be sure, casting O'Donnell in this role suited Stanyhurst's purpose of exculpating the Fitzgeralds from involvement in political subversion, 'The Chronicles of Ireland' in *Holinshed's Chronicles*, vi, p. 305. Further corroboration is provided by a courtly love poem composed by Manus and addressed to 'the daughter of the earl', presumably the Lady Eleanor, in which Manus poses as the importunate suitor, T. F. O'Rahilly (ed.), *Dánta Gradha* (Dublin 1916), no. 4.

the reaction to his lack of one or, more accurately, the reaction in these circumstances to what his policy was construed to be.

If, as has been suggested, Cromwell was content to allow the situation in the Irishry to drift on the principle that the bees would sting only those who interfered with them, he seriously misread the situation. Such were the circumstances in the aftermath of the Kildare rebellion that the crown could not adopt a passive attitude. In putting down the rebellion it had enmeshed itself in the web of Irish dynastic politics, and extrication called for deft diplomacy. Cromwell's first lord deputy, Skeffington, might have managed it; but he died at the end of 1535, and his replacement, Lord Leonard Gray, was not the man for the moment. Impetuous, tempestuous and ruthless, his handling of the situation in the aftermath of rebellion kept tension at fever pitch instead of allowing it to cool. He continued Skeffington's policy of securing indentures from the non-feudal lords, but with an important change of emphasis. In the traditional manner Skeffington regarded the indentures primarily as treaties of peace, designed to secure political stability. However, Gray emphasised their character as formal submissions to the crown's overlordship. Accordingly he held out for the most stringent terms in the way of tribute and homage that the circumstances would allow. This provoked furious resentment.[29]

Here the approach towards the disobedient lordships urged by John Alen to the commissioners in 1537 may be noted. His scheme was designed to cope with existing realities: the limited military resources available under the new dispensation from England, the general state of political tension in the wake of the Kildare rebellion, the need for political stability to concentrate on the programme of internal reform. In view of these circumstances – the possibility of a general conquest having been ruled out – he urged a policy of peaceful coexistence. The Irishry were to have 'truth used to them that they might perceive that we desire more the weal and quiet, than their cattle or goods; for by peace they shall grow wealthy, and then they cannot endure war. I would have them, if I might, be put out of practice of war.'[30] Alen's proposal received no authoritative endorsement, and Gray's

---

[29] On this see St Leger's report of complaints form the Munster Gaelic about Gray's coercion, *S.P. Henry VIII*, iii, p. 362.

[30] *S.P. Henry VIII*, ii, p. 486.

arbitrary and aggressive conduct continued unchecked. The situation was further complicated by the fact that Ormond moved in to fill the dynastic power vacuum created by Kildare, and Gray considered that the most effective strategy to frustrate his design was to revive the old Kildare alliance with himself at its head. He became hopelessly embroiled in the internal politics of the Gaelic lordships in consequence, as well as in a bitter factional struggle with the Butlers.[31]

Despite the repeated warnings from the reform group in Dublin, Cromwell never came to grips with this situation. The result was catastrophe. Even though in reality a policy of conquest was not adopted at any stage in the course of Cromwell's administration, the appearance conveyed a different message to the disobedient Irishry. The apprehension caused by the ruthless treatment of the Fitzgeralds – the family was virtually liquidated, despite their collaboration with government forces during the rebellion and their conditional surrender – was intensified by Lord Deputy Gray's continued pressure on the lordships and by the continuing presence of an English army. The imagined threat of an impending conquest and the actual provocation of Gray and his army were major factors in precipitating the war of the Geraldine League, and in providing the colony with a political crisis more ominous in its implications than the Kildare rebellion. No doubt the Kildare rebellion sowed where the Geraldine League reaped, but the two movements had significantly different political connotations. The earlier movement was organised and led by the great Anglo-Irish dynasty. Although the later movement used the Fitzgerald heir as a figurehead, it was primarily a Gaelic phenomenon in sponsorship, in organisation, in control and in composition. Furthermore, as a Gaelic alliance it showed distinctly novel aspects. One was that it departed from the existing framework of Gaelic dynastic alignments. In this regard the alliance in Ulster indicated a particularly impressive breakthrough. It

---

[31] This was the reality behind the charge, relentlessly pressed by the Butlers, that Gray was the 'earl of Kildare newly born again', *S.P. Henry VIII*, iii, pp. 32, 77 (*L.P.*, xiii(i), no. 1224, xiii(ii), no. 160(4)). To bind Kildare's old allies to himself was a major objective of Gray's 'mysterious' expedition into Munster and Connacht in the summer of 1538. The presence on the expedition of two of Gray's Geraldine counsellors, Gerald Fitzgerald and Prior Walsh, as well as two of Kildare's major allies, O'Connor and O'Carroll, indicates the source in which the Munster journey originated and its purpose, *S.P. Henry VIII*, iii, pp. 46, 55, 57, 69, 71.

combined the three most formidable dynasties in the area – the O'Donnells of Tirconnell, the O'Neills of Tyrone, and the O'Connors of Connacht – as well as a host of lesser septs – Clandeboy, O'Rourke, McCoughlin, O'Kane, Maguire, McDermott – who, as Robert Cowley expressed it, 'never before was towards any of them'.[32] Cowley was not entirely accurate; but it was true that the three main protagonists were traditional rivals, that the lesser lords were shifting in their allegiances, and that the commitment of all of them to a common alliance was almost without precedent. The other novelty of this alliance was that it departed from the localised nature of Gaelic politics. O'Neill in Ulster took the Irish council aback in July 1540 by insisting on making provision for O'Connor in Leinster in his negotiations for a settlement with the crown. Two months earlier, O'Brien rebuffed Ormond's attempt to negotiate a truce in Munster so that government forces could concentrate on the Leinster situation, declaring that 'O'Neill, O'Connor and the O'Tooles are his Irishmen whom he intendeth to defend'.[33]

It need hardly be said that the League was not an all-embracing Gaelic alliance. The point is that it achieved a degree of unity at the national level despite the fragmented and localised nature of the Gaelic polity. Indeed it is remarkable, in contrast to the Kildare rebellion, that crown government managed to secure so few Gaelic allies in confronting the League. Of the greater dynasts only two, MacGillapatrick, and O'Byrne in Leinster, both Ormond allies, provided a measure of support. After the rout at Bellahoe, O'Reilly of Cavan, who was at odds with both O'Neill and O'Donnell over Fermanagh, also gave much-appreciated assistance in protecting Louth in the continuing crisis.[34]

The League cannot be dismissed, either, because analysis shows that its emergence was in fact heavily conditioned by dynastic politics. O'Donnell's marriage to Lady Eleanor McCarthy, the custodian of the Kildare heir, and his remarkable achievement in securing an alignment with O'Neill on the one side and Tadhg

---

[32] *S.P. Henry VIII*, iii, pp. 44, 52, 77, 145 (*L.P.*, xiii(i), nos. 1259, 1429, xiii(ii), no. 160(4), xiv(ii), no. 137. *Annals of Ulster*, iii, pp. 626–7. *A.F.M.*, v, pp. 1450–1. M. Carney (ed.), 'Agreement between Ó Domhnaill and Tadhg Ó Conchubhair concerning Sligo Castle', *I.H.S.*, iii (1942–3), pp. 282–97.

[33] *S.P. Henry VIII*, iii, pp. 207, 223 (*L.P.*, xv, nos. 672, 912).

[34] *S.P. Henry VIII*, iii, pp. 195, 197, 199, 207, 211, 225. *L.P.*, xv, nos. 387, 704. E. Curtis (ed.), *Calendar of Ormond deeds*, iv (Dublin 1937), no. 241.

O'Connor of Sligo on the other, seem less obviously the result of the subordination of local to national issues when his personal predicament in the context of Ulster dynastic politics is understood. The fact remains that the resultant alignment broke out of the traditional mould of dynastic politics and that it was bound together by a national purpose – resistance to crown government. Furthermore the alliance survived, however tenuously, throughout 1539–40, despite the considerable internal pressure from the dynastic rivalries of the participants, and Lord Deputy Gray's exploitation of them to subvert the movement.

Most especially in the summer of 1540 the uniqueness of the League becomes evident. By then it had been shorn of its Geraldine dimension. Gerald Fitzgerald had withdrawn to the continent, and James Fitzjohn, the Desmond Fitzgerald, had assumed a passive political stance. Freed of the last vestiges of the old Kildare dynastic alliance, the League now exhibited an impetus towards Gaelic political solidarity, generated from within the Gaelic community itself. The Geraldine League had transformed itself into a Gaelic one, a cohesive Gaelic movement of resistance to the crown.

Viewed against the background of medieval Gaelic Ireland, two features of the League made it a rare though not a unique phenomenon. The last appearance of something like a national Gaelic movement of resistance to the crown had been on the occasion of the first expedition of Richard II in 1394. In comparison the League seemed to represent a more developed movement, since it manifested at least a vague aspiration towards the establishment of an independent native polity. There was excited talk in O'Neill's camp of inaugurating their lord as high-king at Tara and of restoring the Kildare heir as his vassal. However shadowy, the concept of the high-kingship had reappeared in the sphere of practical politics.[35] In the spring of 1540 information reached the London administration from Scotland of a more realistic proposition, and one, it seems, of greater substance. This was a formal proposal, made by a combination of the great lords of Ireland to the Scottish king, to transfer their allegiance to him.[36] To find a precedent for a native movement at the national level

---

[35] *S.P. Henry VIII*, iii, p. 139 (*L.P.*, xiv(i), no. 1245(2)).
[36] *L.P.*, xv, nos. 570, 710.

with a constitutional, not merely narrowly political, dimension it is necessary to go back as far as the Bruce episode at the beginning of the fourteenth century.

However, one feature of the League distinguished it from both its medieval antecedents. This was its religious dimension. There is nothing to suggest that religion played a part in the Gaelic areas in the course of the Kildare rebellion, but it was very much to the fore in the course of the campaign of the League, for the purposes both of domestic propaganda and of foreign diplomacy. Underlying this was the sharp reaction among the local clergy to the inauguration of the Reformation campaign in the colony. The reaction was characterised by a tightening of the jurisdictional bonds between the papacy and the local Church: an uninterrupted flow of Rome-runners for papal provisions and faculties on the one side, and on the other the beginnings of a definite policy in Rome for the filling of episcopal vacancies with reliable native clergy, in particular members of the Observantine reform. In addition the religious reaction took on a directly political aspect. Resistance in arms to crown government received enthusiastic clerical support, both in propaganda to whip up local ardour and in diplomatic service in search of foreign allies. In all of this, in the tightening of the jurisdictional link with Rome, and in the attempt to provide religious opposition with political muscle, the beginnings of a Counter-Reformation ideology can be discerned.[37]

In discussing the late medieval ideological outlook of the Gaelic the significance was pointed out of the distinction between the Gaill (Anglo-Irish) and the Saxain (English).[38] That distinction is relevant in discussing the emergence of the new Counter-Reformation ideology. The Reformation was seen as a peculiarly English aberration, in the first place of the English king and then of the English nation. That is how it is presented in the annals, and responsibility for the attempt to spread it in Ireland, as well as for the alleged atrocities that accompanied the attempt, is laid at the door of the English. Precisely the same attitude is reflected in the propaganda of the League. According to information taken from a Gaelic messenger on a mission from Ulster to the O'Tooles

---

[37] See my *Dissolution of the religious orders*, pp. 210–11.
[38] Above, pp. 27–9.

in April 1539, 'O'Neill and O'Donnell, with James of Desmond and all their partakers, call all Englishmen heretics...and as for the king...they account him the most heretic and worst man in the world.'[39]

In one respect, therefore, the introduction of the Cromwellian reform programme produced a similar response both within the loyal community of the colony and in the Irishry. In both cases it seemed to exacerbate racial tension against the English. This xenophobia provided a common element in the ideology of Anglo-Irish separatism and of the incipient Gaelic nationalism in which resistance to Cromwell's Irish policy was given expression. However, the two movements were fundamentally different in their constitutional aspirations. The Gaelic movement was radical in its objective: repudiation of English dominance meant repudiation of the English king's overlordship in the first instance. Anglo-Irish separatism, on the other hand, carefully distinguished between the constitutional status in relation to Ireland of the English king and the English kingdom, allowing the jurisdiction of the one but not of the other. The difference between the aspirations of the two movements was related to the existing constitutional situation of the two communities from which they emerged. Within the loyal community, constitutional rights and validity of title were founded upon the individual's status as a subject of the crown. To the Gaelic Irish, on the other hand, the king's overlordship constituted an invalidation of their status and title. Thus the crown represented a threat at the constitutional level, apart from the political considerations. These circumstances predisposed to a different attitude towards the royal supremacy in the two areas. It could be seized upon by the non-feudal lords to undermine the king's constitutional title as overlord, particularly since the latter was based on a twelfth-century papal grant. On the other hand the deprivation of the king's title would have deprived the loyal Anglo-Irish also of the legal foundation for their own position. Unlike the 'Irishry', they had no political incentive to make an issue of the royal supremacy, but rather every incentive not to do so. The response to the religious Reformation in Ireland, therefore, was not such as to bring Gaelic and

---

[39] *S.P. Henry VIII*, iii, p. 139 (*L.P.*, xiv(i), no. 1245(2)). *Annals of Ulster*, iii, pp. 592, 608, 624. *Loch Cé*, ii, pp. 314–17. *A.F.M.*, v, pp. 1444–9.

Anglo-Irish together in common opposition. In a curious way it served to set them apart.

While it is possible to discern the beginnings of a new ideology of Gaelic nationalism in the League of 1539–40, it is necessary to question the extent of its practical impact. Unfortunately it is not possible to be clear even about the ostensible political objectives of the lords who participated in the alliance of 1539–40. The League has left nothing that could be construed as a manifesto. For a statement of its objectives it is necessary to rely in the first instance on dispatches of the Dublin executive interpreting the movement for the London administration. The letters of the Irish administration in 1539–40 presented the League as a movement for the overthrow of crown government in Ireland motivated by two considerations: the restoration of the Fitzgeralds and the vindication of the papacy. If that was the case, the League constituted a direct and absolute challenge to royal government and might be regarded as a fully fledged movement of Gaelic nationalism. However, allowance must be made for circumstances. The letters were written at a time of great crisis and were designed to impress government in England with the seriousness of the threat. Looking at it from the other side, the usefulness of such a programme to the League, for diplomatic and propaganda purposes, calls in question the sincerity with which it was proposed. If the confrontation was so absolute, it seems strange that neither O'Neill nor O'Donnell, the two most closely identified with the League, ever quite closed the door to negotiation with the crown. Furthermore (to anticipate), in the altered political circumstances of the 1540s these items proved highly dispensable so far as individual lords were concerned in concluding terms of peace with the crown. The English king's sovereignty was formally accepted; the pope's jurisdiction was formally rejected; and the plight of the Geraldine heir in continental exile caused not a ripple of concern.

A rather different impression of the motives of the League emerges from the only letter on record in which one of the leaders of the movement, O'Neill, presents his grievances to the king. It is worth bearing in mind that the letter dates from July 1540, a time when the Gaelic alliance seemed to be in the ascendant, and when the Gaelic leader was under no necessity to be unduly conciliatory. The letter denounced Lord Leonard Gray's aggressive style of government, his expeditions into the Gaelic lordships with English troops, and the demands for extortionate tributes. O'Neill rejected the possibility of securing peace and stability by this means. Instead he insisted that the crown's best interests were served, politically and economically, by governing the island, as hitherto, with the cooperation of the great magnates.[40] The letter suggests that the Geraldine League was less a response to the downfall of the Kildare dynasty than to the implications which that event assumed in the light of Lord Deputy Gray's aggressive style of government. Gray possessed neither the means nor the mandate to launch a conquest of the disobedient territories. However, he embarked upon a policy of forcefully asserting the crown's authority over local lords, and in particular of extracting indentures of submission containing exorbitant conditions for the payment of tribute.[41] The insecurity and resentment which the policy created conditioned the emergence of the Geraldine League. The preoccupations of the lords who participated in the movement, therefore, were the threat to local status and material interests constituted by the new regime in Dublin, rather than the more remote issues of the royal ecclesiastical supremacy or the constitutional status of the English crown. The success of the liberal experiment of the 1540s arose largely from the fact that its architects drew the correct inferences from the League.

The distinction between the ideology of the League and its practical political motivation is relevant, therefore, in explaining the ease with which it succumbed to the diplomacy of Lord Deputy St Leger. It is important for another reason also. The satisfaction of the local lords' limited aims did not satisfy those who had supplied the League with its ideological driving power, the element who constituted the hard core of resistance to the royal supremacy. Although the political leaders abandoned the movement, the ideology they had helped to create persisted to bedevil Irish politics throughout the early modern period.

The new political crisis in 1539–40 and the dispatch of military reinforcements from England provided an opportunity to reopen the question of a general reformation once more. The alacrity with which the opportunity was seized, jointly by the council and

---

[40] *S.P. Henry VIII*, iii, p. 223 (*L.P.*, xv, no. 897).
[41] Above, pp. 176–7.

individually, indicates a deepening conviction about the need for a national solution. The implication was that the emergence of the Geraldine League had proved the inadequacy of Cromwell's programme in failing to come to grips with the constitutional problem of the Irishry. William Wise informed him tactfully in December 1539 that men of wisdom in Ireland were of the opinion 'that without a general reformation the king's majesty shall vainly consume his treasure in this land', since the policy of punitive expeditions to keep the Irishry in check had proved futile.[42]

The response from within the Anglo-Irish reform movement at the time and subsequently makes it clear that the crisis of the League in 1539–40 was considered more menacing in its implications than the earlier Kildare rebellion. The later episode was taken as proof that a fear, never absent from the loyal community, had at last been realised, that a general alliance of Gaelic lords had been achieved for the purpose of the complete overthrow of crown government. The concern with which writers pointed to the unusual comprehensiveness and cohesion of the alliance manifests their conviction that Gaelic nationalism had now become a force to be reckoned with in Irish politics, and to be reckoned with as a matter of urgency.[43]

One incidental consequence of Cromwell's dramatic fall from power in the summer of 1540 was that appropriate action was taken. As noted earlier, Cromwell showed no signs of yielding to pressure for a general reformation in the spring of 1540. His removal in June brought Norfolk back to the centre of power in England – the man who had served in Ireland as lord lieutenant in 1520–1. By a strange set of circumstances it provided an opportunity also for a timely change at the head of the Irish administration. Cromwell's fall brought down not the administrators most closely associated with his reform programme, as might have been expected, but the turbulent lord deputy with whom they were at odds. The quick success of their final indictment of Lord Leonard Gray after years of frustration can be attributed to the fact that Norfolk had a *protégé* of his own to lead the Irish administration. He was Sir Anthony St Leger, who had

---

[42] *Cal. Car. MSS*, i, nos. 137, 138.
[43] *S.P. Henry VIII*, iii, pp. 145, 207, 223. S.P. 1/154, fo. 109 (*L.P.*, xiv(ii), no. 443). In 1558 Archbishop Dowdall maintained that the crisis of 1539–40 was more serious than that of 1534, S.P. 62/1, no. 61, S.P. 62/2, nos. 33, 44.

headed the Cromwellian commission to Ireland of 1537. Within two weeks of Gray's committal to the Tower, preparations were in hand for sending St Leger to Ireland as lord deputy.[44] When in Ireland in 1537, St Leger had even then shown an appreciation of the limitations of Cromwell's programme. He returned to Ireland in 1540 with definite views about how these were to be made good. His Irish policy was to be no less important in its historical significance than that of Cromwell.

[44] *L.P.*, xv, nos. 805, 942(26), xvi, no. 380, fos. 134v–139v.

PART III

The liberal revolution

Introduction

The mid-Tudor period is of epochal significance in Irish constitutional and political history. The early 1540s was the period when the crown at last embarked upon a policy of general reform in Ireland. It was also the period when the island's constitutional status was defined in terms of a sovereign kingdom, replacing the feudal notion of a lordship, and when the institutions of crown government began to be adapted to accord with a conception of the island's inhabitants as a single coherent political community. Within this constitutional framework the political history of early modern Ireland unfolds. All of these developments were associated with the promotion of the reform programme of commonwealth liberalism.

The reigns of Edward VI and Mary have their own unique significance. At the political level they saw, on the one hand, the disenchantment of the crown with the liberal experiment and its abandonment under Lord Deputy Sussex in 1556 and, on the other hand, the increasing commitment of the Anglo-Irish political establishment to it. This political tension was sharpened when the ideology of commonwealth liberalism – whose upholders were fated to become increasingly alienated from crown government – cross-fertilised with two other elements already present in the mental atmosphere of Anglo-Ireland. One was the traditional ideology of separatism, resistance to English domination; the other was a new sentiment of patriotism. In the opposition of commonwealth reformers to the new radical policies of the crown, the gestation of a new tradition of constitutional nationalism took place.

The launching of the liberal experiment, fraught with such epochal consequences, was the work of two men who have received less than their due from historians of sixteenth-century

Ireland. One was an English lord deputy, Sir Anthony St Leger, who replaced Lord Deputy Gray in 1540. The other was Sir Thomas Cusack, a member of the Anglo-Irish reforming milieu. Their backgrounds differed, but in such a way as to endow them with complementary qualities suited to their historic mission. In contrast to his two predecessors, St Leger's previous experience in government was administrative rather than military. Cromwell had given him considerable employment in local government as head of a rising Kentish family.[1] More important, however, his early career provided him with an education on Irish affairs unusual in one of his kind. Probably his schooling began when he was a member of Norfolk's household, in view of the latter's Irish sojourn in 1520–1 and his continuing contact subsequently.[2] This background, in turn, may have prompted his appointment to head the royal commission to Ireland in 1537. That visit provided him not only with over six months of first-hand experience, but with a mentor on the problems of government in Ireland, Thomas Cusack.

Cusack has made a number of fleeting appearances in this study already, as a secondary figure in politics and government. His close association with the effort of political reformers in 1533–4 to break the Fitzgeralds' grip on government seemed to promise high office under Cromwell. But he incurred the chief minister's displeasure in 1535, and his career never quite picked up again.[3] His main contribution in the following five years was made as deputy to Brabazon in the complicated business of administering the crown's confiscated properties.[4] The diligence of Cusack's service in this capacity, despite the rebuff from on high, earned the commendation of Brabazon and of his assistant, Agard. His unflinching devotion to duty was commended by Sir William Brereton in the crisis of 1539–40, and subsequently by St Leger himself.[5] It was the hallmark of a long though chequered career in government administration, lasting to the end of the 1560s. In the light of his career as a whole it would show excessive scepticism to put this down merely to the drive of an ambitious careerist. No doubt

---

[1] *L.P.*, vii, nos. 630, 788, viii, nos. 149(40), 314, ix, nos. 142, 236(3), x, no. 562, xi, nos. 444, 580, xii(i), no. 1079.   [2] *S.P. Henry VIII*, iii, p. 267.
[3] *L.P.*, xii(i), no. 1027.
[4] Ibid. See my *Dissolution of the religious orders*, pp. 58, 81, 116.
[5] *S.P. Henry VIII*, ii, p. 567, iii, p. 204. *L.P.*, xii(i), no. 1027, xiii(i), no. 677, xv, no. 683.

Cusack was interested in preferment. His service for Brabazon earned him a lease of the nunnery at Lismullen, beside his estate at Cosingston in Co. Meath, and the patronage of St Leger was to bring handsome rewards, including eventually the office of lord chancellor.[6] But there was more to the man than that. His English legal training at the Inner Temple and his link by marriage with Sir William Darcy draw our attention to an Anglo-Irish tradition in which government administration was looked upon not merely as a professional career but as a public service, and to a class of public servants who were both politically active and politically reflective.[7] Cusack was a worthy representative of the class and of the tradition. First and last he was a politician with a mission.

What these two men shared in the first instance in their approach to Irish policy was a capacity for a sympathetic appreciation of the political perspective of the Irishry. No doubt St Leger's conciliatory approach was largely conditioned by temperament and by a liberal humanist background. An early biographical note assures us that his education took him to Cambridge, Gray's Inn and Italy.[8] A reference by Roper indicates a connection with the More circle.[9] This would explain a breadth of vision evident in him singularly lacking in his predecessor. Cusack's attitude, on the other hand, was primarily determined by personal involvement. He lived in the remoter areas of the Pale and so was brought into personal contact with the Gaelic borderers. He spoke their language and understood their mentality. Whether in conception or in execution, it would be invidious to single out the contribution of either of these over the other. Obviously, the programme owed much in conception to Cusack's grasp of local politics, and in execution to his contacts among the Irishry. Yet St Leger must be credited with no less political acumen, if only for recognising the validity of Cusack's analysis. His contribution to the policy in execution was highly important also. After the resentment and suspicion generated by his predecessor, he scored a great personal triumph in gaining the confidence of the local lords, essential to the implementation of the liberal

---

[6] *Fiants, Henry VIII*, nos. 91, 309.

[7] On Cusack's legal training and his marriage, see the *D.N.B.*

[8] *D.N.B.*

[9] William Roper, *The Life of Sir Thomas More, Knight*, ed. E. E. Reynolds (London 1963), p. 47.

programme. At the same time, his contact with men in high places in England and a friendly relationship with the king, dating from his period as a courtier, enabled him to win and retain the support of the English administration despite opposing factions in Ireland and Henry VIII's own considerable reservations.[10] The liberal enterprise of the 1540s was the brainchild of two highly gifted politicians whose different backgrounds happily complemented each other in equipping them for the role of parenthood.

[10] As well as his association with Norfolk, St Leger was on intimate terms with Paget, the clerk of the council, and was a kinsman of Moyle, the general surveyor, *L.P.*, xvi, no. 272, xx(ii), no. 30. On his friendship with Henry VIII, see the *D.N.B.*

7

The reform of the Irishry

The liberal formula

The visit of the royal commission headed by St Leger in 1537 marks the real beginnings of the liberal policy of the 1540s. Already the mind of the future lord deputy can be observed groping towards the formula for the liberal programme. Having witnessed the transitory nature of the victory gained by the crown forces over O'Connor in Offaly, he drew the conclusion for Cromwell that 'the same country is much easier won than kept, for whensoever the king's pleasure be to win the same again it will be done without great difficulty, but the keeping thereof will be both chargeable and dificil'.[1] Nevertheless he was obviously convinced that the problem of the Gaelic borderers had to be faced. The solution he supported is significant. He returned from Ireland in 1538 with indentures concluded with three of the border lords, including O'Connor, in which they offered total submission to the crown's sovereign jurisdiction in return for noble status and hereditary tenure of their lordships by letters patent.[2]

One other idea floated in the course of the visit of 1537 assumes major significance in retrospect. It came from a treatise on political reform devised by Bishop Staples of Meath, whom we have already met as the critic of Archbishop Browne's Reformation campaign in 1538.[3] At the request of St Leger, Staples set down his ideas on political reform. For the most part the resultant treatise was given over to the needs of the four shires of the old Pale. That aspect need not concern us here, except to note that it demonstrates Staples's moderate and liberal attitude in politics as well as in

---

[1] *S.P. Henry VIII*, ii, p. 534.   [2] Above, pp. 130–2.
[3] Above, pp. 156–7.

religion. However, the treatise opened with a novel proposal. It pointed out that the Gaelic Irish traditionally regarded the pope as possessing sovereign jurisdiction in Ireland, and the English king as holding the island by an inferior jurisdiction as his vassal. To disabuse them of this notion he suggested changing the English monarch's title in Ireland from lord to king, and then persuading the Gaelic lords to swear fealty to him as sovereign. This, he felt, would be 'a great motive to bring them to due obedience'. The following summer Staples wrote to St Leger reminding him of 'the instructions that I wrote concerning this country by your commandment, and especially to have our master recognised king of Ireland and... to have all Ireland then sworn to due obedience'. He again urged that to set forth the king's sovereignty plainly would much improve the obedience of the Irishry.[4] Events would prove that St Leger had not forgotten: the proclamation of the kingly title, and the grant of tenure and titles of nobility to the Irishry, were to provide the pivots of the liberal programme of the 1540s.

Meanwhile St Leger had come in contact with Cusack in the course of the 1537 visit also. He was obviously impressed, because he brought the inconsequential official back with him to England for a prolonged stay at court.[5] It cannot be said for certain if already at that stage Cusack had begun to advocate the idea of a general reformation based on a conciliatory formula. We saw that in 1535–6 he was closely associated with Skeffington's conservative policy.[6] In the light of later developments, this does not necessarily imply that he was then committed to the retention of the *status quo*; on the other hand, it does show that he was firmly convinced of the need for a conciliatory approach.

---

[4] *S.P. Henry VIII*, ii, p. 480, iii, p. 29. (*L.P.*, xii(ii), no. 729(4), xiii(i), no. 1205). The treatise survives only in an unascribed copy in the handwriting of John Alen, which has caused confusion about its authorship. In view of the later letter the authorship can hardly be doubted. It can be said with equal certainty that the general ascription of the treatise to Alen, on the basis of the handwriting, must be mistaken. It is preserved with four other treatises presented to the royal commissioners in 1537, S.P. 60/5, pp. 23–59. Three of the five are in Alen's handwriting. One of these is headed 'the lord deputes boke'. The second is headed 'presented by the master of the rolles'. It seems clear that Alen was requested to make copies of the submissions of Gray and Staples. It should be added that the unascribed copy in Alen's handwriting and Alen's own compilation are altogether unalike in content. It would be difficult to conceive of both as compilations by the same author.

[5] *S.P. Henry VIII*, iii, p. 65. *L.P.*, xiii(i), no. 772, xiii(ii), no. 40.

[6] Above, pp. 111–12.

The final fruition was facilitated by two extraneous events already noted. One was the crisis in Ireland provoked by the activities of the Geraldine League. This called the wisdom of Cromwell's passive attitude towards the disobedient lordships seriously in question, while at the same time it discredited Lord Deputy Gray's administration. The other was the power struggle within the English administration which removed Cromwell from the scene and, incidentally, Lord Deputy Gray also. Thus the way was open for St Leger's return to Ireland as head of the administration.

St Leger arrived in Ireland as lord deputy late in July 1540. It soon became clear that the nature and pace of Irish policy was no longer determined by government in England, as under Cromwell, but within the Irish executive. It soon became clear also that those who dominated the Irish executive under Cromwell had lost ground, and that a new political lobby had come to the fore. Thomas Cusack became St Leger's right-hand man straight away.[7] The impression given by St Leger's administration from the beginning – of a new departure, a sense of direction, and a route systematically plotted – was the result of the continuous contact between the two men from 1537 onwards.

The policy launched in the autumn of 1540 addresssed itself to that fundamental problem which the dual system of government devised in the fourteenth century was designed to circumvent but not to solve. This was the problem of the non-constitutional lordships of the Irishry, and the resultant anomaly of the existence of obedient and disobedient territories within the one Lordship under the crown.

The overall concept of the liberal formula was to transform the island's political infrastructure while leaving its superstructure intact. It was designed to assimilate the non-constitutional lordships to the polity of the crown, constitutionally, jurisdictionally and socially, but without disturbing the existing framework of local leadership or of landownership. This required a process of political engineering at two levels. At the local level the non-constitutional lordships had to be stripped of the features of the Gaelic political system, reorganised on the English model, and provided with

---

[7] St Leger commended Cusack to the king in October 1541 as 'a man that hath taken more pains with me, sith my repair to serve your highness here, than any other', *S.P. Henry VIII*, iii, p. 318.

constitutional status. At the national level the concept of the island's inhabitants as an integral political community under the sovereignty of the crown, rather than an English colony and an alien Irishry, had to be given expression constitutionally, and in the institutions and practice of government.

The objective of the liberal programme was not fundamentally different from the one to which the moderate radical programmes for general reform aspired. What made the liberal formula unique was its strategy of conciliation. Where the moderate radicals proposed to achieve the assimilation of the Irishry by compulsion, the liberals envisaged achieving it by consent. Furthermore, the basis on which they were prepared to conciliate sharply distinguished their policy, as we shall see, from that proposed by Henry VIII in 1520.

The reform of tenure – surrender and regrant

The pivot of the liberal programme at the local level was the formula employed to resolve the crux between the crown and the dynastic lords on the issue of tenure, the formula that has come to be known as 'surrender and regrant'.[8] The formula prescribed that the lord should apply for a grant of tenure under royal patent. By this gesture he surrendered at one and the same time his own rights of sovereign jurisdiction and the allodial (absolute) tenure under which he held the possession of the lordship. Reciprocally the issue of the letters patent regranted title in perpetuity under the sovereignty of the crown. Surrender and regrant was conceived by the reformers not only as a means for stabilising relationships between the crown and the local lords, but also as a means of promoting internal stability within the lordships themselves. The effect of the grant of title under royal patent was to replace the Gaelic tenurial system with the English one. By this means it was hoped to eliminate one major source of instability within the lordships, conflicts over rights of inheritance.

The Gaelic system envisaged tenure corporately. Radical possession was held by the kin group, the sept, the membership of which was normally constituted by kinship to the fourth gener-

[8] The phrase was coined in a pioneering study of Tudor land policy over sixty years ago, W. F. T. Butler, 'The policy of surrender and regrant', *Jour. R.S.A.I.*, ser. VI, iii (1913), pp. 47–65, 99–128.

ation in the male line (i.e. second cousins). The individual held on the basis of a life interest, and at his death the property reverted to the sept. The inheritance was disposed of either by partition among the sept, or where the inheritance was not partible, e.g. the succession to the lordly title, by selection from the corporate group. In contrast, feudal tenure was invested in the individual, and inheritance was decided on the basis of primogeniture, i.e. the principle of direct descent by seniority in the male line. The effect of the change from Gaelic to English tenure, therefore, was twofold. Radical possession was transferred from the sept to the individual; secondly, and in consequence, the right of inheritance was invested in the legitimate male heir of the current holder of the life interest under Gaelic tenure.

Granted the *bona fides* of the reformers, little time need be lost on hoary nationalist arguments about the morality of perpetrating such a change. The charge is that the effect was to exclude from the inheritance an indefinite number of male kin, to the degree of second cousins, who were potential beneficiaries. In practice most of them would not have benefited at all, or at best only slightly. The title and endowments of the lord were not partible. The effect of the introduction of English tenure was simply to provide another system for deciding the individual successor. In other cases, since the Gaelic system allowed for partition of the inheritance, the extent of the deprivation of any individual beneficiary was minimised. In any case, Gaelic custom had a system of its own for limiting the group of beneficiaries when the number strictly entitled began to expand beyond practicable limits.[9] On the other side of the scale were the interests of peace and stability. The rigidity of primogeniture was not always an advantage. Nevertheless, the looseness and complexity of the Gaelic system lent itself to interminable disputation, and because of the weakness of Gaelic legal institutions might was usually the criterion of right.

The ultimate objective of surrender and regrant, therefore, was not change but stability. That formula was intended to initiate a process by which the Gaelic lordship would be transformed, more or less as it stood, into a feudal one. The enfeoffment of the lord through surrender and regrant was to be followed by the

[9] For a discussion of the Gaelic tenurial system see Nicholls, *Gaelic and Gaelicised Ireland*, pp. 37–9, 57–67.

subinfeudation of the lordship, again with the object of stabilising
the structure. Thus, the Irish council is found putting forward for
consideration to the king in January 1542 a list of 'those Irishmen
thought by us meet to be at O'Neill's leading...for that they be
of his kin, and within the precinct of those lands he now hath in
possession, after such rate as the earls of Ormond and Desmond
have the rule in their quarters'. In addition to O'Neill's own
kinsmen the list included his hereditary galloglasses, the McDonnells, and his traditional underlords, McLoughlin and O'Kane.
It is important to note, as a reflection of the impartiality of the
liberals, that it also included the major rivals of O'Neill within
his own kin, Niall Conallach and Feidhlim Rua, who had rendered
service to the crown against him since 1535.[10]

Of course the impartiality of the crown was intended to operate
to protect the rights of the underlords also. Commissions, under
the leadership of the lord deputy, were to arbitrate on the division
of landholdings so that, as the lord deputy explained in the case
of Cavan, 'every gentleman may have a reasonable living to them
and to their heirs, as likewise the said O'Reilly hath to him and
to his heirs'.[11]

Later, in the Elizabethan period, some Gaelic magnates attempted to assert undue claims on their underlords in virtue of patents
obtained by surrender and regrant. The possibility arose because
of the arrest of the liberal enterprise before the process of
reconstitution had been completed. Thus Hugh O'Neill could
claim at the end of the century that O'Kane held from him as a
tenant at will. Although, in the event, surrender and regrant made
such claims possible, it was not the intention of those who
launched the liberal programme that it should be so. Their
intention was to eliminate political tension by stabilising the
existing framework.

Just as surrender and regrant assimilated the lordship to the
English tenurial system, the indenture, to which the lord subscribed
in conjunction with the grant of a patent, provided for the
assimilation of the lordship jurisdictionally and socially within the
polity of the crown.[12]

---

[10] *S.P. Henry VIII*, iii, p. 355.

[11] *S.P. Henry VIII*, iii, p. 306. For a statement of the same policy in the case of the
O'Tooles, see *S.P. Henry VIII*, iii, p. 266.

[12] The indenture relating to the grant of a patent to Turlough O'Toole in 1541 was
devised as a prototype. *Cal. pat. rolls. Ire., Henry VIII*, p. 81. *S.P. Henry VIII*, iii,

The change in the jurisdictional status of the lord and his lordship was emphasised in the first instance by the clause which required the signatory to renounce his Gaelic noble title – the use of the patronymic alone – accepting instead a title designated by the king. In the change of noble title, as in the change of tenure, the absolute quality which characterised the Gaelic version was lost. Henceforth the lord's status derived from the crown, not from the sept. By the change, also, the internal sovereignty which the Gaelic title designated was lost. The local lordship was brought within the scope of the ordinary jurisdiction of the crown.

The implications of this were spelt out in a series of provisions designed to put the relationship between crown government and the lordships on the same basis as those envisaged in the Cromwellian reform for the feudal lordships of the colony. The lord acknowledged the jurisdiction of the crown's judicial machinery, its laws, its writs, and its courts, and undertook to ensure obedience to it throughout his lordship. He also accepted the control of the central administration over his military organisation. On the financial side the indentures specified the extent of the lord's obligations as a vassal of the crown, by way of chief rent and military service. He was required to desist from the exaction of blackrent, and his exactions upon his own lordship were subjected to the supervision of the central administration. However, no specific provision was made for the collection of the crown's extraordinary revenues, the subsidy and special taxes: this was to be left over until good government created conditions in which such demands could be met.

The provisions for the assimilation of the lordship jurisdictionally were complemented by provisions for its social assimilation. Two projects of social engineering were envisaged. One was the familiar scheme for cultural anglicisation. The grantee undertook to eschew Gaelic forms in dress, social conventions generally, and, to his ability, in speech. The other also echoes earlier reform treatises. The lord undertook to reorganise the socio-economic structure of his territories, replacing the predominantly pastoral system with an agricultural one. The necessity to build houses in order to establish settled rural communities on the English style was

p. 297. That the prototype was adhered to is evident from the indentures issued in similar circumstances to McWilliam Burke, *L.P.*, xviii(i), no. 636(3); O'Brien, ibid., no. 636(5), (*Cal. pat. rolls Ire.*, *Henry VIII*, p. 87); MacGillapatrick, *S.P. Henry VIII*, iii, p. 291 (*L.P.*, xviii(i), no. 636(4)); O'Neill, *S.P.* 60/10, no. 82 (*L.P.*, xvii, no. 832).

especially emphasised. Behind this scheme lay a conviction that the Gaelic socio-economic system, particularly the practice of transhumance, the migration of the community with their flocks to summer pastures, was a major source of social and political instability. Indeed, it was seen, with justification, as an ancillary of the dynastic military system. It provided a large reservoir of men who could be transferrred without difficulty from herding to soldiery. Secondly, foodstocks on the hoof were mobile and, therefore, less vulnerable to destruction by the enemy. Like the process of Anglicisation in the narrowly cultural sphere, the Anglicisation of the socio-economic system was prompted not by purely chauvinistic ideological considerations but by the practical exigencies of political reform.

Thus the formula of surrender and regrant and the accompanying indentures of submission provided the legal basis for a scheme of general reform. In broad outline, the programme of reform envisaged had been anticipated in the treatises devised by the moderate radicals over the previous two decades. What had not been anticipated was that such a programme could be implemented without an initial conquest. It was the genuineness of the attempt to provide an acceptable basis for conciliation that distinguished the liberal programme of the 1540s from anything devised before.

The liberal policy of conciliation

The overthrow of the Fitzgeralds and the aggressive militarism of Lord Deputy Gray undoubtedly alarmed the leaders of the non-constitutional lordships. But the events of 1539–40 serve as a corrective to the view that the effect was to cow them into submission. That was not how the new lord deputy assessed their mood on his arrival in the autumn of 1540. He felt they could be persuaded to come to terms, but they would have to be met halfway. In this conviction the liberal strategy of conciliation was moulded.

The uniqueness of the conciliatory approach of the 1540s is highlighted by contrasting it with the king's own formula for a conciliatory settlement. The great pioneers in the study of Henrician policy in Ireland, Dunlop and Butler, assumed that the programme of the 1540s represented the policy formulated by

Henry VIII himself in accordance with the dictum enunciated by him in the 1520s of 'sober ways, politic drifts and amiable persuasions founded in law and reason'. Their assumption has been followed without question ever since.[13]

The fundamental difference between the two formulas centred on the issue of tenure, precisely the problem that constituted the crux of the political and constitutional question. As we have seen, the king proposed the principle of legality as the basis for conciliation on this issue. The policy of conquest and general expropriation was to be repudiated, but the lords would be expected to concede the validity of ancient feudal titles, especially where these had since reverted to the crown.[14] He continued to adhere to this principle in 1540. In indicating general consent to St Leger's proposal to grant tenure to the non-constitutional lords, he stipulated that 'special regard' was to be had 'that by such gifts we do not, in any wise, in clouds depart with any of our said inheritance, to such as both have disloyally behaved themselves towards us, and our most noble progenitors, and therewithal have encroached upon us, and so prescribed of that which justly, and by special title, belongeth unto us'.[15]

St Leger and Cusack, on the other hand, regarded legality as an unrealistic basis on which to build a policy of conciliation. The revival of claims of ancient title would seriously disadvantage most of the non-constitutional lords, for, as they put it, 'as far as we can perceive, there be few or none of the disobeisants of this land which have any possessions, but the same of right appertaineth to your majesty by one of the means premised'.[16] Furthermore, on the moral issue, the Irish council pointed out to the king without much varnishing that the appeal to the principle of legality involved the application of a double standard. The justification on which that principle rested, the original Anglo-Norman conquest, was scarcely distinguishable from the justification which the lords of the Irishry provided for their opposing claims, 'long usurpation by strength of the sword, which they take for as just a title as your highness' subjects do to hold their lands from the conquest'.[17]

---

[13] Butler, cit., pp. 47–65, 99–128. R. Dunlop, 'Some aspects of Henry VIII's Irish policy', in T. F. Tout and J. T. Tait (eds.), *Historical Essays* (London 1902), pp. 279–305.

[14] Above, pp. 63–4.   [15] *S.P. Henry VIII*, iii, p. 302.

[16] *S.P. Henry VIII*, iii, p. 306.

[17] *S.P. Henry VIII*, iii, pp. 324, 339 (*L.P.*, xvi, no. 1284).

The alternative criterion, which the promoters of the programme of the 1540s insisted upon, was acceptance of the *status quo*.

The difference, in practice, between the two was enormous. In reminding St Leger of his legitimate claims the king mentioned explicitly the defunct earldom of Ulster, the abandoned lands of English magnates appropriated by the crown under the recent act of absentees, and the possessions of the attainted Fitzgeralds.[18] The vindication of the crown's rights in these instances would have entailed large-scale recovery from O'Neill, McWilliam of south Connacht, O'Connor, and the disaffected earl of Desmond. In fact the king was persuaded to relent, and the crown's claims were not allowed to become an obstacle to the conclusion of settlements in any of these cases. One other example worth adding to these, to illustrate the lengths to which conciliation could go in the 1540s in pursuit of a permanent settlement, is provided by the O'Tooles of south Dublin. These had been ousted from the royal manor of Powerscourt by Kildare in the early 1520s. Possession was bitterly disputed by them throughout the 1530s, but the government held on grimly. The castle was reedified by Sir William Brabazon in 1536–7. Subsequently a local Anglo-Irishman, Pierce Talbot, was granted a portion of the manor by royal patent. Nevertheless, in the first of the projects of surrender and regrant to reach the stage of finalisation, St Leger included Powerscourt as part of the O'Toole territory of Fercullen, 'which his ancestors heretofore had, till they were expulsed by the earls of Kildare'.[19]

The second discrepancy between the conciliatory formula proposed by Henry VIII and that applied by St Leger and his adherents arose on the sensitive issue of revenue. It seemed reasonable to the king that the grant of full constitutional status should carry with it the full financial responsibilities of a subject. Again St Leger and his associates regarded this as an unrealistic basis for conciliation. They agreed that the king's argument was 'invincible' except, they ventured to suggest, that it was 'grounded of experience of civil countries'. Ireland had to be treated as an exceptional case. It would be politically alienating to demand full payment of taxes from a community that was neither accustomed to nor capable of paying them. Before making such demands a

---

[18] *S.P. Henry VIII*, iii, p. 302.
[19] *S.P. Henry VIII*, iii, pp. 266, 270, 279. *L.P.*, xi, nos. 257, 266, 282, xii(ii), nos. 762, 1097.

process of political conditioning must first of all take place by the creation of a stable, ordered and prosperous society. When the programme of political reformation had taken effect, 'the profits of the prince and king must needs daily increase both in revenues and other profits'. Meanwhile the cost of undertaking the reform was to be regarded in large part as an investment for the future. It took eight months of dogged resistance to wear down the king on this one, but at last he relented in the late spring of 1542.[20]

The alternative criterion applied by St Leger and his group in negotiating the financial side of the agreements with local lords was to demand what they judged could be conveniently paid and what would be willingly paid, bearing the circumstances of each case in mind. Thus, in fixing the dues of the lord to the crown the obligation of military service was usually heavy, whereas the rent was usually light, to take account of the socio-economic structure of the lordships, which provided easier access to men than to money.[21] Originally it was not intended to make any demand for extraordinary revenue (royal taxation). However, as a concession to the king, minimal contributions were sought by way of payment of the subsidy. Even the terms agreed upon were subject to further mitigation in practice. Remission of rents was granted, and the loss of revenue entailed to the lord by the waiving of customary exactions such as blackrents was offset by the grant of crown pensions.

The difference between the conciliatory policy of the king and that of the liberals of 1540 is emphasised in one other sphere, that of motive. The cynicism of the king's attitude in 1520 has been commented on already.[22] This had not changed by the 1540s. Before consenting to the formula of surrender and regrant, he first sought a reassurance from the privy council in England that the grant of title would not preclude the possibility of the expropriation of the grantees should a conquest become feasible in the future.[23] The same cynicism is reflected in the guidelines he provided for the Irish council to govern their negotiation of terms with the lords. The object was to extract maximum benefit for

---

[20] *S.P. Henry VIII*, iii, pp. 313, 323, 326, 330, 339, 362, 366, 394. S.P. 60/10, nos. 35, 36.
[21] *S.P. Henry VIII*, iii, pp. 340, 362.
[22] Above, p. 61.
[23] *S.P. Henry VIII*, i, p. 668. L.P., xvi, nos. 1058, 1085.

the crown by exploiting its bargaining position to the full. A distinction was to be made between the lordships 'lying upon the danger of our power', and those more remote, beyond the effective striking range of the royal army. The latter were to be coaxed, but the former were to be milked for as much as they could yield. One of the suggestions made by the king for raising additional revenue is particularly worth mentioning. It was to be put to the lords that in return for the confirmation of their own titles by patent they should agree to give the crown possession of the lands of the 'meaner gentlemen', at least in chief, but if possible in freehold. Thus, in return for the confirmation of their own titles, the lords were to be asked to connive at the reduction of local landholders to the status of tenants.[24]

Such tactics were rejected by St Leger. He pointed out to the king that it would be inexpedient to forfeit the good will of the bordering lords, since the government was dependent on it in order to penetrate as far as the more remote magnates. Consequently he advocated a 'meaner way' which was to concentrate in the first instance on winning the whole-hearted support of the local lords, in which case the king's profits would in time be found to look after themselves.[25]

The contrast in outlook between Henry VIII and the liberals of the 1540s towards the policy of reform is highlighted in an exchange of letters in the second half of 1541. The enthusiastic reports from the lord deputy and council about the response to their conciliatory initiative produced an irritated rejoinder from the king. He was little impressed by 'the discreet training of the Irishmen to their due obedience' at the cost of waiving the ancient land titles of the crown, and without exacting terms for rents and taxes which would balance the Irish budget. St Leger's reply, in which he associated the council for support, was suitably apologetic but firm. To appreciate their sense of satisfaction, St Leger pointed out, the present state of the country had to be seen in the context of what had immediately preceded it, 'violent insurrections and rebellions... first as well by the traitor Thomas Fitzgerald... as the entry after made by the young Gerald with the assistance of O'Neill and O'Donnell, and since the universal combination of

---

[24] *S.P. Henry VIII*, iii, pp. 323, 330. P.R.O., S.P., 60/10, no. 36.
[25] *S.P. Henry VIII*, iii, pp. 339, 362.

all the Irishmen...which most wise and expert men here feared would not have been pacified in many years'. Peace had been restored, but the task of political reform remained. The king must reconcile himself, therefore, to further heavy expenditure. Indeed, the lord deputy insinuated, this was a moral obligation, since Ireland's poverty and backwardness was the result of English neglect and bad government. Finally he declared unwavering commitment to his own formula for reconciliation 'upon some reasonable conditions, being yet such as they may perform, to make them gifts of the lands and possessions that they now possess'.[26]

In the difference of attitude and concerns reflected in this exchange of letters lies the difference between the royal liberalism of Henry VIII and the commonwealth liberalism of St Leger, Cusack and their adherents. Undoubtedly neither party would have admitted to a conflict of interests between king and commonwealth. But in practice their attitudes indicated different underlying priorities. The king emphasised the rights of the crown, and assessed the programme of reform in terms of what it contributed to the king's power and prosperity. St Leger and his group, in contrast, emphasised the needs of the community and the duties of the crown in its government. This political attitude hearkens back to the commonwealth treatise of the second decade of the century, and looks forward to the self-styled 'commonwealth party' of the Elizabethan period. It provides a link in the chain of tradition of Anglo-Irish political reform.

In contrast to the conciliatory terms of the settlements concerning political status, land titles, and financial exactions, the terms relating to judicial and social reform might seem unreasonably demanding. However, they were intended to be implemented with discretion and moderation. They provided a strong medicine, but the dosage was to be diluted and sweetened so as not to upset sensitive and unaccustomed constitutions.

The conciliatory approach of the commonwealth liberals in this area did not provide a source of tension with the king, since his material interests were not touched. Indeed, he himself led the way in 1520 in outlining the manner in which the crown's judicial system might be adapted so as to make it acceptable locally.

[26] *S.P. Henry VIII*, iii, pp. 330, 337, 339.

English laws and judicial institutions were not to be imposed peremptorily. Rather, the local lords were to be consulted, and in conjunction with them a legal code was to be devised for use in the lordships that would absorb the acceptable elements of Gaelic law. This proposal was taken in hand by the liberals twenty years later. A set of ordinances were devised 'for the reformation of the inhabitants of this kingdom...who are not as yet so acquainted with the laws as to be able to live and be governed according to them'.[27] Here the characteristic features of the Irish legal system are retained, while English elements are introduced. Thus the devices of kincogish (joint responsibility) and the eric (fine and compensation) are retained for dealing with homicide and theft, but the severe penalties of English criminal law, mutilation or death, are imposed in more serious cases, e.g. highway robbery and rape. Similarly, the much-denounced coyne and livery was not abolished, but the limits within which it could be demanded were clearly specified. In the social sphere the English concept of vagabondage was applied to curtail the floating population of professional soldiers without, however, attempting to abolish the class. The intention was that these ordinances would be eventually displaced by a revised code of Irish penal legislation. In July 1542 the Irish council wrote to the king explaining that the matter had been raised in parliamant. They asked for permission to undertake the task, abrogating those laws which they found not to be beneficial and putting the others in print, 'for these of the Irishry, which newly have submitted themselves, be in great doubt of such uncertain and unknown laws'. The task was to take more than three decades to complete.[28]

In the sphere of social reform there were no sweeping innovations either. The emphasis was rather on constructive assistance and encouragement. A formal agreement concluded with the Cavanaghs in September 1543 illustrates the attitude of benign paternalism. The Cavanaghs undertook to proceed to the habitation and cultivation of waste lands in their territories the following year. The government for its part remitted all financial dues on the waste lands for the first three years, and guaranteed loans for the purchase of horses and farm implements.[29]

[27] Lambeth, MS 603, pp. 23Aff., 28ff. (*Cal. Car. MSS*, i, no. 157).

[28] *S.P. Henry VIII*, iii, p. 398 (*L.P.*, xvii, no. 491).

[29] *Cal. pat. rolls Ire., Henry VIII*, pp. 43–5.

In the cultural sphere, similarly, the emphasis was on incentives rather than constraints. Gifts of English costume were liberally bestowed on the lords, and highly expensive parliamentary robes were presented to those who received noble titles. However, the main hope was to Anglicise the next generation of leaders by persuading the lord to entrust his heir to the government to have him brought up in an English environment, either in a suitable Anglo-Irish household or at court. Some attempt was made to tackle the problem at a more general level also by sponsoring the teaching of English. But these were pilot schemes, and it is clear that the Anglicisation of the masses was envisaged as a very gradual – and gentle – process.

One of the most remarkable achievements of St Leger and his collaborators was their ability to win the confidence of the local lords. This has to be seen against the background of six years of political tension in which the crown had become associated in the disobedient areas with duplicity, ruthlessness, and latterly heresy. There had been the shock of the betrayal of the Fitzgeralds' trust and of their execution; the exemplary massacres perpetrated by Skeffington and Gray in stamping out resistance in 1535–6; this followed by Gray's tyrannical regime, and Archbishop Browne's aggressive Reformation campaign in the Pale. The two years of open hostility and political crisis in 1539–40 gave expression to the mood of resentment, insecurity and suspicion which the policy of the crown and its agents had generated in the lordships.

In dissipating this mood the strategy of the liberals in government was quite as important as their conciliatory programme. Here St Leger's deployment of the military force provides a revealing contrast with what had gone before. If he was optimistic enough to adopt a policy of conciliation he was realistic enough to see a place in his policy for force as a tactic of persuasion. However, it was applied judiciously and with a constructive design. Military operations were conceived as an instrument of a policy of appeasement. Two of his major campaigns will serve to illustrate the point.

One was his initial campaign in south Leinster, to which he first turned his attention on arrival. He prosecuted a sharp ten-day war against the Cavanaghs, with the object of bringing their leaders to talk of peace. The ensuing negotiations provided an opportunity to impress on them – and to announce to the disobedient lords as a whole – that his mission was one of reconciliation, not retribution. It gave him his first opportunity to explain the source of tension between the crown and the disobedient lords, and to unveil his own formula for resolving it. The king's quarrel with them, he explained, sprang not from greed for their lands, but from a desire to have his rightful claim to supreme sovereignty acknowledged. Submission to the crown would not undermine but secure their position, since it would be reciprocated by the confirmation of their titles. In a subsequent report to the king he describes how he treated the Cavanaghs 'very gently, not taking from them any part of their lands nor goods, but only of such as would not condescend to...reasonable submission, which part so taken we again gave one of themselves, which we saw most conformable to the said honest submission...alleging that it was neither their lands nor goods that your majesty so much esteemed, as their due obedience to the same, which at length they should well perceive should redound most to their own profit'.[30]

The novelty of the strategy on which St Leger embarked from the beginning is highlighted by contrasting it with the strategy being worked out for him at the same time in England. While he was engaged with the Cavanaghs, Henry VIII and the privy council, on Norfolk's advice and at the instigation of the moderate radicals of the Irish executive, had come to quite different conclusions about the strategy for government in Ireland. A peace was to be patched up with the magnates of the remote areas, but the Leinster lords were to be singled out for exemplary punishment. By the time the instruction arrived St Leger was too far advanced to be deflected from the path of exemplary conciliation.[31] Before Christmas he had completed the preliminary negotiations for the grant of title by patent to the most troublesome of the Leinster lords, those of south Leinster and O'Connor.[32]

Just as the campaign against the Cavanaghs in the autumn of 1540 played an important part in advancing the conciliatory policy among the Gaelic Irish of Leinster, so the campaign against O'Neill the following autumn was crucial in winning over the great magnates. St Leger's initial diplomatic advances to the lord of Tyrone the previous March, and again in May, had been repulsed.

---

[30] *S.P. Henry VIII*, iii, p. 235 (*L.P.*, xvi, no. 42).
[31] *S.P. Henry VIII*, iii, p. 223, 232, 234, *L.P.*, xv, no. 912, xvi, nos. 2, 9, 14.
[32] *S.P. Henry VIII*, iii, pp. 235, 241, 263, 266, 267, 272.

It seems that O'Neill still hankered after a Gaelic League with himself at its head. Accordingly the lord deputy began preparations for more forceful persuasion by isolating him diplomatically. In May he ingratiated himself with the Magennises, important O'Neill allies. In July O'Donnell committed himself to applying for a royal patent, and to assisting in overcoming O'Neill's resistance. Shortly afterwards the McMahons, on O'Neill's southern flank, also submitted.[33] None of this succeeded in budging the great lord. Accordingly it was necessary to resort to force, and to the rare tactic of a winter campaign, before O'Neill could be brought finally to heel.[34]

Our interest is less in the campaign than in its sequel, for the way it illustrates the liberal strategy. Despite the recalcitrance and the costly military campaign, St Leger set himself against retribution. Nothing more was demanded of O'Neill than what O'Donnell had already agreed to without a war. At the beginning of January 1542 he subscribed to the stereotyped form of preliminary agreement, in which he undertook to apply for title under royal patent, and to live as a subject on the same basis as the earls of Ormond and Desmond – not exactly a humiliating prospect.[35] The subsequent reports to the king reveal St Leger's attitude. Elaborate explanations were made as to the impracticality of taking a harsher line. Besides the practical considerations, however, the lord deputy explained that O'Neill's was a test case, 'for, in effect, all the great men of the Irishry hearkened what end should be taken with him'. The banishment of O'Neill 'should cause all other Irishmen to judge that the same should at length be done to them which might be occasion of universal rebellion'. He reiterated to the king his conviction that the solution of the problem of the disobedient territories was not in the expulsion of the dissidents but 'by policy or strength to cause those inhabitants that be there now to be true and faithful subjects'.[36]

For St Leger, therefore, the military campaign provided an opportunity for exemplary conciliation rather than exemplary punishment. Brandishing the submission of O'Neill, he returned

[33] *Cal. Car. MSS*, i, nos. 154, 160. *S.P. Henry VIII*, iii, pp. 302, 313, 318. *A.F:M.*, v, pp. 1462–3.
[34] *S.P. Henry VIII*, iii, pp. 311, 313, 318, 337, 339, 350, 355.
[35] *S.P. Henry VIII*, iii, p. 352, *L.P.*, xvi, no. 335. *Cal. Car. MSS*, i, no. 167.
[36] *S.P. Henry VIII*, iii, pp. 350, 355.

southwards to overcome the hesitation of O'Brien and McWilliam of Clanrickard. With the penitence of a sinner touched by mercy, O'Neill turned up in Dublin of his own volition in the summer to make the journey to court for the final act of reconciliation.[37]

In contrast with Lord Leonard Gray, St Leger's military campaigns reveal that his outlook was that of a statesman. He employed force as an instrument of a political strategy and resorted to it only when political means failed. His political methods also deserve some scrutiny. They reveal the style of government that won a response to the crown which was never again to be repeated. His main reliance was on straightforward negotiation; but he backed this up by a strong support programme of public relations.

St Leger understood the value of the great public occasion as a means of moulding public opinion. Important events were carefully staged with a view to their propaganda value. The sessions of parliament, and in particular the proclamation of the kingship in June 1541, provided, of course, the most obvious occasion for this. But the reconciliation of the earl of Desmond in January 1541 had already provided an impressive curtain-raiser. Eighty years of estrangement between the crown and the Desmond earls was brought to an end by the formal recognition of James Fitzjohn's title to the earldom and the latter's subscription to an indenture agreeing to the revival of crown government in his territories, closely patterned on the agreement between Ormond and the crown in 1534.[38] This was the first great triumph of the liberal policy, and St Leger ensured that the significance of the event would not be lost on the disobedient lords in general. He managed to secure the attendance of some 200 'Irish gentlemen', including O'Connor and McWilliam, at the public act of reconciliation in the castle of Sir Thomas Butler of Cahir. To ensure an impressive spectacle he had the metropolitans of Dublin and Cashel in attendance, four royal commissioners on a visit from England, and a bevy of councillors from Dublin, all despite the snow of a January that was the worst within living memory.[39] The immediate aftermath shows how closely the public-relations campaign was allied to the main programme of political nego-

[37] *S.P. Henry VIII*, iii, pp. 359, 362, 366.
[38] *S.P. Henry VIII*, iii, p. 285. *L.P.*, xvi, no. 459. *Cal. Car. MSS*, i, no. 153. *Cal. Orm. Deeds*, iv, no. 253.   [39] Cit.; *A.F.M.*, v, pp. 1460–1.

tiation. The lord deputy pressed southwards with Desmond, indifferent to the wretched conditions. A week later, Limerick was favoured with the first visit of a Desmond earl to a royal town since the mid fifteenth century. The object was less to impress the citizens than to open negotiations, through Desmond's mediation, with McWilliam and O'Brien of Thomond.[40]

Ultimately, of course, the success of the liberal programme depended on the success of such negotiations, not on grand demonstrations. At this level also, in relations with individual lords, St Leger conducted his campaign with unusual flair and imagination. He explained his technique in a letter to the king some six months after taking up duty: 'I perceive them [the Gaelic lords] to be men of such nature, that they will much sooner be brought to honest conformity by small gifts, honest persuasions, and nothing taking of them, then by great rigour.'[41]

'Technique' may be the wrong word to use in describing this approach. St Leger understood that the dissipation of political tension demanded not only a conciliatory policy on the part of the crown, but one that was seen to be so by the disobedient lords. The gestures, therefore, were not empty, hypocritical, or in any way artificial. Behind them lay magnanimity, integrity, and respect. The correspondence of public image and real attitude goes far towards explaining the charismatic quality of his relationship with the leadership of the Irishry, and the speed with which he dispelled their distrust. It need only be added that in the rapport which he managed to establish with local lords he stands apart from his immediate predecessor and from a long line of successors.

The other part of the explanation lies in the group he associated with himself as co-workers. His advent brought a new group to the fore in crown service in Ireland who were distinguished by two characteristics. One was a conciliatory attitude; the other was personal contact with the disobedient areas. Thomas Cusack may be regarded as the archetypal figure here. Another member we have already met was Bishop Staples of Meath. Staples lived at Trim on the outskirts of the Pale, and this brought him into contact with the Gaelic borderers. The obscurity of both in the course of Cromwell's administration now turned out to be an advantage. It meant that their credentials with the Irishry were not

---

[40] *S.P. Henry VIII*, iii, p. 285 (*L.P.*, xvi, no. 552).   [41] Ibid.

tarnished by close association with Gray's regime. St Leger's advent led to the return of two others from the political wilderness who soon came to play a prominent part in advancing his political programme. One was George Dowdall, the late prior of Ardee Crutched Friars, one of the few religious who offered resistance to the dissolution of his community. He reemerged in 1541–2, working for the reconciliation of O'Neill, and went on to become, under St Leger's patronage, archbishop of Armagh, and a major figure in the history of both political and religious reform.[42] The other was Sir Patrick Gernon, a Geraldine supporter who had been so compromised by the rebellion that he subsequently took refuge with O'Neill. In 1541 he was deputed as an arbitrator on the crown's behalf in St Leger's negotiations with the Magennises, and the following year he received a royal pardon.[43] A fifth name must be added to these, that of the newly reconciled earl of Desmond. It is clear that the earl also had reflected on the need for political reform in Ireland. In the course of conversations on the subject with the lord deputy in the period following his reconciliation, he had responded enthusiastically to St Leger's ideas. The lord deputy swore him a member of the Irish council and commented later to the king that 'since my repair into this your land, I have not heard better counsel of no man for the reformation of the same, then of the said earl of Desmond, who undoubted is a very wise and a discreet gentleman'.[44] Thenceforward, until his death in 1558, the active support of this good man and powerful earl was thrown behind the liberal policy.

This was the nucleus of the team that gathered around Lord Deputy St Leger and worked enthusiastically for the advancement of the liberal programme. The emergence of a group of supporters of the lord deputy whose credentials in the lordships had already been established served to enhance the credibility of the new policy. It strengthened the impression of a new approach on the part of crown government, an impression that was well founded. In this atmosphere local lords were willing to trust the lord deputy not to turn the strings that were attached to acceptance of status under the crown into a whip to flail them.

42 See my *Dissolution of the religious orders*, pp. 126–7.
43 *Cal. Car. MSS*, i, no. 154.
44 *S.P. Henry VIII*, iii, p. 285 (*L.P.*, xvi, no. 552).

The progress of assimilation

The assimilation of a dynastic lordship to the polity of the crown entailed three separate stages. These could dovetail, or even overlap. But it is necessary to distinguish between them in order to assess the progress made by the policy before its suspension at the end of 1543.

The first stage was one of preliminary negotiation between the lord and the crown's representative. The entitlements of the potential patentee as to lands, area of jurisdiction, and special dues were generally agreed upon. Some formula was sought for an equable agreement where rights were in dispute, e.g. between McWilliam and O'Donnell for the customs of Sligo. This stage was formally concluded when the lord subscribed to a preliminary indenture in which he bound himself to undertake to apply for tenure and a title of dignity under the crown, meanwhile to attend parliament and to resist papal jurisdiction.[45]

Once the crown and the lord managed to find a general basis for agreement over terms, the major obstacle in the way of proceeding to the second phase – the process of surrender and regrant proper – was the question of the succession. St Leger and his assistants were fully alive to the dangers of committing the crown to upholding primogeniture in the second generation if to do so would embroil the government in a major succession dispute. Where the succession was already being contested they endeavoured to have the issue settled either by compensating the challenger, as in the case of O'Neill's nephew, Niall Conallach, or by persuading the holder to concede the right of succession, as in the case of O'Brien.[46] Inability to resolve this difficulty within the period probably provides the main explanation for the fact that many of the negotiations for a patent, where the dynastic lord seemed anxious to conclude, had not passed beyond the preliminary stage when the policy was suspended at the end of 1543.[47]

---

[45] As the process was brought nearest to completion in the case of the Tyrone lordship, I confine myself in this study to documenting the various stages in the reconciliation of Conn O'Neill. For the first stage in his case, see *S.P. Henry VIII*, iii, p. 352. *L.P.*, xvi, no. 335. *Cal. Car. MSS*, i, no. 167.

[46] *S.P. Henry VIII*, iii, p. 432.

[47] See, for instance, the case of O'Connor. *S.P. Henry VIII*, iii, p. 517. The O'Tooles present another case in point. Although Turlough O'Toole secured a promise of a patent from the king as a result of a personal visit to court in the winter of 1540–1,

The procedure for the second phase was laid down by the king himself. At least in the case of the greater magnates, the final formalities of reconciliation were to take place at court. The lord was to journey thither to make formal suit for the king's pardon to present his claims for ratification, to do homage, and to be invested with a noble dignity.[48] The king's insistence on the journey to court serves as a minor illustration of the difference in outlook between himself and the lord deputy. St Leger's letters reveal a livelier sense of the inconveniences of the system than its benefits. Absence from his territory was politically risky for the lord. The journey was expensive, and the lord deputy usually had to find most of the money to finance the outward trip. Finally, there was the danger that the intensely proud Gaelic lords might be offended by court boorishness – as they were when King John visited Ireland in 1204 – and St Leger's careful diplomacy thus brought to naught. Fears on this last score did not materialise: the strange visitors from Ireland were well treated, St Leger having drawn attention to the dangers in advance.[49]

A special word must be said about the indentures which characterised these stages of assimilation. Two kinds were involved, which must be distinguished from each other, and from the traditional indentures associated with the simple submissions of fealty and peace. Failure to do this in the past has led to hopeless confusion about the policies pursued in the later Henrician period.

The preliminary indenture which completed the initial phase of negotiation resembled the traditional indentures of fealty and peace in so far as it implied only an external relationship between the crown and the signatory. The difference between the two consisted in three additional provisions. One extended the crown's jurisdiction to the ecclesiastical as well as the secular sphere. The signatory renounced papal supremacy and undertook to resist it within his territory. Under the second, the Lord undertook to attend parliament. The special character of this kind of indenture was found in a third provision, under which the signatory definitely committed himself to submit to the formula

he was assassinated before the patent could issue, and the proposal to grant the patent to his heir was also stymied by the assassination of the latter in 1542, *S.P. Henry VIII*, iii, pp. 235, 241, 266, 267, 366, 456.

48 *S.P. Henry VIII*, iii, p. 293 (*L.P.*, xvi, no. 656).

49 For the grant of a patent to O'Neill and his investiture at court as earl of Tyrone, see S.P. 60/10, nos. 77, 82. B. L., Cotton MS Titus B. XI, p. 381. *S.P. Henry VIII*, iii, pp. 410, 416, 427. *L.P.*, xvii, nos. 780, 806, 832, 833, 884, 890, 897, 924. *Cal. Car. MSS*, i, nos. 173, 174, *Cal. pat. rolls Ire.*, *Henry VIII*, i, p. 85.

of surrender and regrant proper. He promised to apply for a royal pardon, to abide by the conditions attached to it (i.e. to accept the internal jurisdiction of the crown), and to accept tenure and a title of dignity by royal patent.

When, in fact, the process reached that later stage, the formal grant of tenure and title under patent, another indenture was subscribed. Its terms need not be discussed here, since they have already been described.[50] It will suffice simply to emphasise that the difference between this and the preliminary indenture was that it bound the signatory and his lordship to the crown's internal jurisdiction, to royal writs, to the crown's judicial machinery, etc. That point is emphasised in a negative way by the apparently strange omission, in the later form of indenture, of two of the earlier clauses – the undertaking to attend parliament, and the repudiation of papal jurisdiction. Neither was now required. Once the patent had been issued, the lord enjoyed full constitutional status. He was summoned to parliament in virtue of his noble title. Similarly, the royal ecclesiastical supremacy was exercised in his lordship as an area of the crown's internal jurisdiction.

It is possible, therefore, to distinguish three different common forms in the indentures concluded between the crown and the dynasts in the later Henrician period. It is also important to do so, for they reflect different relationships between the crown and the signatory, and different policies towards the disobedient lordships. Failure to distinguish the traditional indentures of fealty from those associated with surrender and regrant has led to the monumentally absurd supposition that St Leger simply continued a process begun by his predecessors, Skeffington and Gray.[51] On the other hand, failure to distinguish between the preliminary and final indentures associated with the grant of title and tenure has caused considerable confusion and vagueness about how far the policy of surrender and regrant actually got. For instance, although Manus O'Donnell was the first of the great magnates outside Leinster to subscribe to a preliminary indenture, he never actually applied for a patent, and the lords of Donegal remained without constitutional status under the crown until 1603.[52] As we shall see,

[50] Above, pp. 196–200.

[51] Of course, not all the indentures concluded by St Leger were associated with surrender and regrant. He continued to negotiate the traditional indentures of fealty and peace where the situation was not yet ripe for embarking upon surrender and regrant.

[52] *S.P. Henry VIII*, iii, pp. 313, 318 (*L.P.*, xvi, nos. 119, 1127). *A.F.M.*, v, pp. 1462–3.

only in relatively few cases did the preliminary indenture reach its intended consummation.[53]

The final phase of the process provides the counterpart, in respect of local political relationships, of the procedure of surrender and regrant through which the relationship between lord and crown were redefined. Two tasks were involved. One concerned subinfeudation, the organisation of the internal structure of the lordship on the English model. The rights and obligations of the magnate and his underlords were arbitrated upon and defined in indentures which were mutually subscribed, the crown acting as guarantor of the settlement. The other task was to regulate the external relations of the magnate. Here the objective was to transform autonomous dynasts on the Gaelic model into local nobility within the framework of a centralised state under the government of the crown. One major task was to arbitrate on long-standing disputes between rival dynasts, enshrining the final agreement in legal indentures, as the basis for a permanent solution. The other was to dissolve the dynastic alliances, formed under the Gaelic system of clientship, by which the magnates sought to make local lesser lords their satellites. It is not proper to regard this last project as an attempt to undermine the power of the magnates. Like the process of subinfeudation, it formed part of an attempt to reformulate local political relationships in accordance with the English system. If the dissolution of dynastic alliances diminished the magnate's external power, the process of subinfeudation served to strengthen his internal control, and the liberals pursued both objectives impartially. Thus, for instance, while Maguire of Fermanagh was released from O'Neill's claims of clientship, O'Neill's internal rivals, and erstwhile allies of the crown against him, were bound to him as vassals. In both cases the objective was the same: the reformation of the localities.[54]

[53] For examples of the simple fealty submissions associated with the policies of Skeffington and Gray, see *Cal. Car. MSS*, i, nos. 56, 72, 76, 78, 79, 80, 90, 110, 122, 124, 136, 139. For examples of preliminary surrender and regrant submissions, see ibid., nos. 116, 159, 160, 163, 164, 165, 167, 170, 171. For a discussion of the final surrender and regrant submissions, see above, pp. 196–200.

[54] *S.P. Henry VIII*, iii, pp. 381, 383, 385, 394, 398, 404, 407, 478. *Cal. Car. MSS*, i, nos. 169, 177, 180, 181. In recommending terms for O'Neill's final submission in 1542, St Leger advised deferring a final decision on the extent of his jurisdiction as overlord 'till his highness see further proof of him', *S.P. Henry VIII*, iii, p. 416. However, the intention was quite clear, to grant him the jurisdictional rights of an earl in relation to his traditional underlords. *S.P. Henry VIII*, iii, p. 355.

Criticism of the liberal programme of the 1540s as either deluding or deluded does not take into account the sensitivity which its promoters showed at all stages to the local political situation, and the attention they paid to ensuring that the settlement would hold. This was illustrated by their concern both to eliminate internal tensions over leadership and succession, and to act as the honest broker in finding an equable solution to external disputes between rival magnate dynasties. Similarly, it is not proper to interpret St Leger's activities in the localities as a game of power politics. There was a radical departure from the traditional crown tactic of playing off one dynast against another, and of exploiting jealousies within the sept to undermine the dynast's power. On only one issue did he eschew the role of arbitrator and honest broker. That was in breaking up the great dynastic alliances. But here also he acted without fear or favour towards one rather than another. In this, as in all else, he was pursuing not the narrow advantage of the crown but local political stability and genuine political reform.

Having equipped ourselves with the necessary technical knowledge of the workings of the system, we can now follow the progress of the campaign. The battle over whether the royal or the commonwealth formula was to be applied in the conciliatory offer to the dynasts ended in April 1542 with a letter from the king to the Irish council in which he conceded victory, though with characteristic huffing and puffing. He took their 'discreet considerations and regards to the estate of that realm in good part', assured them of his desire to reduce it 'to order and civility without extremity or rigour', contemplated the dread prospect should he be 'irritate[d]...too much against the offendors', and warned that if the lords would 'grate too much of us, or too precisely indent with us at their submissions, our honour may not sustain it, but shall enforce us to look upon them in such sort as shall be to the example of all others'. Having made this dutiful obeisance to his own magnanimity and might, he descended to particulars, in which he displayed great docility to the lord deputy's promptings. Most importantly, he indicated acceptance of the preliminary indentures concluded with O'Brien and O'Neill, and his readiness to grant them patents and titles of nobility on that basis – though he drew the line at O'Neill's suggestion that he be granted the title of earl of Ulster, 'being one of the great earldoms of christendom, and our proper inheritance'. O'Neill had to be satisfied to take the title of Tyrone. But the way was at least clear to take the conciliatory policy to the next stage, that of surrender and regrant.[55]

The end of the wrangle was followed in June by the first of a series of visits to court by great lords of the disobedient territories for the purpose of finalising their reconciliation with the crown. Despite the high diplomatic activity at court with which they coincided in the prelude to the invasion of France, the historic importance of the visits, and the curious origins of the visitors, made the episode something of a sensation.

Desmond was first to make the visit, his case being a simple matter of reconciliation, without the necessity for surrender and regrant. He was heralded at court by an anxious dispatch from the lord deputy, emphasising the importance of the occasion as a pioneer venture, 'as the same might be hereafter example to other in these confines'. He urged that the earl be treated with 'princely clemency', rewarded with 'kingly bounty', and dispatched 'with as short return as may be for defence of his parts'.[56] The point was well taken. Though Desmond and his entourage were delayed and could not present themselves in court until late evening, the king himself saw to it that a decent show was made at their reception by forbidding those attending that day to leave until after the presentation of the Irish visitors. The visit was not protracted beyond a week, and they were dismissed with handsome rewards of clothes and of money.[57]

O'Neill's arrival in mid-September caused an even bigger stir than Desmond's. The name was tinged with an aura of wild romance, as is suggested in the report of the French ambassador to his master that the greatest lord of the savages who all his life had made war on the English had come to do homage. Meanwhile St Leger impressed on the English administration the historic nature of the event 'forasmuch as it cannot be known that ever any O'Neill repaired in person before this into England'. Copies of O'Neill's form of submission, beautifully printed under a royal

---

[55] *S.P. Henry VIII*, iii, p. 366 (*L.P.*, xvii, no. 249). The king's capitulation was completed in a following letter on 5 July, *S.P. Henry VIII*, iii, p. 394 (*L.P.*, xvii, no. 460).

[56] *S.P. Henry VIII*, iii, p. 385 (*L.P.*, xiii, no. 367).

[57] *S.P. Henry VIII*, iii, pp. 394, 410, *L.P.*, xvii, nos. 453, 460, 468, 688, 880, app. B no. 21, *Addenda* vol. no. 1548.

patent, survive to show how the propaganda possibilities of the occasion were exploited.[58] O'Neill was accompanied by the two Magennises, who were knighted in conjunction with his investiture as the first earl of Tyrone, but they did not receive a patent for their lands, as the preliminary negotiations had not yet been completed in Ireland.[59]

The expedition of the western contingent to court took place early the following June. If it lacked the novelty of the first two, it compensated by quantity. Two new earls were created, Thomond (O'Brien), and Clanrickard (McWilliam). Donough O'Brien was made baron of Ibracken with right of succession to the earldom. MacGillapatrick, who by exception had been created baron of Upper Ossory without visiting the king, came now to fulfil the obligation. He was knighted with four others of the attendant party. Three of them were minor lords of Thomond, McNamara, O'Grady, and O'Shaughnessy; the fourth was William Wise of Waterford.[60]

This proved to be the last such expedition, a fitting climax to a unique and historic enterprise. While the privy council concluded the terms of their patents with the Irish lords and arranged for the ceremony of ennoblement, the air at court was already electric with the excitement of impending war. The king was committed inextricably to a project to annex Scotland, and was deep in preparations for the invasion of France. One of the incidental consequences of these foreign commitments was the suspension of the liberal policy in Ireland. It never regained its initial momentum.

The privy council, writing to Harvel, the English agent in Venice, while this last Irish contingent was still at court, rather exaggerated what had been achieved. They claimed that all the Irish lords of consequence had now submitted, so that never had there been so great a conquest of Ireland.[61] Unfortunately that claim needed an important qualification. By the summer of 1543 all the dynastic lords of consequence had committed themselves positively to surrender and regrant. Many had subscribed a

---

[58] For the relevant documents see above p. 214 note 49.

[59] *S.P. Henry VIII*, iii, p. 427 (*L.P.*, xvii, no. 924).

[60] *S.P. Henry VIII*, iii, pp. 345, 450, 451, 453, 455, 463, 464, 473. *L.P.*, xviii(i), nos. 550, 630, 632, 633, 634, 636, 981 (1, 2, 3), xviii(ii), no. 231(10), *Cal. Car. MSS*, i, no. 178.

[61] *L.P.* xviii(i), no. 707.

preliminary submission of external jurisdiction. However, the roll of those who had to be brought from this preliminary stage was longer by far than the roll of those who had completed the process by the surrender of internal sovereignty and the grant of title and tenure under the crown. The latter list included all the Gaelic magnates of Leinster except MacGillapatrick, all the Gaelic magnates of Ulster except O'Neill, and all the Gaelic magnates of Munster and Connacht except O'Brien. Had surrender and regrant already progressed as far as the privy council claimed in the summer of 1543, the history of modern Ireland must have shaped very differently.

From the moment the king indicated his willingness to go ahead with the second stage of the process, the grant of tenure and noble title by patent, St Leger energetically moved forward to the third, the complementary stage of reformulating political relationships in the locality.

He turned first to the knotty problems of Ulster. The internal problems of Tyrone were tackled in the course of the parliamentary session at Trim in June 1542. There the lord deputy and the council arbitrated in the feud between O'Neill, his nephew and tánaiste (successor-elect), Niall Conallach, the head of the rival branch of the sept, Phelim Roe, and his hereditary galloglasses, the McDonnells.[62] His progress to external problems was signalised by an agreement in the summer of 1543 over the rights to the estuary of the Bann, a rich fishing ground. This had been the object of fierce contention between O'Neill's client McQuillin and O'Donnell's client O'Kane. St Leger's solution was to remove the flashpoint by getting both lords to renounce their claims in return for crown pensions. The rights were transferred to John Travers, the master of the ordnance, with a view to the greater security of the fishermen.[63] The climax of all these activities was a ten-day session in July 1543 when St Leger managed to get O'Neill and O'Donnell to come to Dublin to submit their differences to the arbitration of the council and to conclude a formal legal settlement.[64]

O'Donnell's visit to Dublin in July was used also to sort out

---

[62] *S.P. Henry VIII*, iii, pp. 381, 383, 385, 394, *Cal. Car. MSS*, i, no. 169 (*L.P.*, xvii, no. 422). *A.F.M.*, v, pp. 1466–7.

[63] *S.P. Henry VIII*, iii, pp. 398, 404, 407, *Cal. Car. MSS*, i, no. 177. *A.F.M.*, v, pp. 1468–75.

[64] *S.P. Henry VIII*, iii, 478 (*L.P.*, xviii(i), no. 885).

the tangled succession dispute in Donegal which was obstructing the finalisation of surrender and regrant there. The lord deputy felt sufficiently confident of progress to propose O'Donnell's visit to court for the following spring.[65] However, time was now running out. In September he completed the paperwork stage of the reformation of south Leinster. This was to be dealt with rather differently from the rest so as to bring the septs more directly under the jurisdiction of the Dublin administration.[66] Having concluded an indenture with the Cavanaghs, the lord deputy set out with members of the council for Limerick and Galway, as he informed the king, 'to establish some good order in those parts, whereunto we have been specially required by the earls of Thomond and Clanrickard'.[67] We know of what took place from an account in the *Annals of Loch Cé*. They record a meeting of the 'council of Ireland', attended by most of the Gaelic and Anglo-Irish lords of Connacht. Of the council's deliberations the annalist records only the grant of some monastic property to his patron, McDermot.[68] No doubt the overall purpose of the trip was to advance the assimilation of the area in line with what had been already accomplished in Ulster.

The lord deputy was back in Dublin by the beginning of November for the final session of his great parliament. The close of that session on 19 November may be regarded also as the end of the liberal programme as a dynamic crown policy. Licence had come enabling St Leger to visit England, a well-earned break after more than three years of incessant activity. He departed at the end of January. By the time he returned to Ireland the following June, England's foreign wars dictated a policy of passivity in Ireland. Between then and the king's death in January 1547 no substantial progress could be made in advancing political reform. The project of surrender and regrant never got much further than it was in the winter of 1543–4 – well begun.

---

[65] *S.P. Henry VIII*, iii, pp. 470, 478, 481, *Cal. Car. MSS*, i, nos. 180, 182 (*L.P.*, xviii(i), nos. 885, 889). *A.F.M.*, v, pp. 1458–9, 1478–81.

[66] *S.P. Henry VIII*, iii. pp. 398, 456. *Cal. Car. MSS*, i, no. 170, *Cal. pat. rolls Ire.*, Henry VIII, p. 43 (*L.P.*, xviii(ii), no. 124).

[67] *S.P. Henry VIII*, iii, p. 484. (*L.P.*, xviii(i), no. 165).

[68] *Loch Cé*, ii, pp. 338–9.

The dynasts and the reconstitution of the lordships

So far the liberal formula for the assimilation of the local lordships
has been examined from the central perspective, from the point
of view of the crown and of the liberal reformers within
government. To conclude this study it is necessary to consider the
reform of the lordships from the local perspective. What were the
considerations that governed the response of the dynasts?

An earlier generation of nationalist historians used the word
'bribery' to explain the appeal of the policy of surrender and
regrant. They alleged that the government aimed to win over the
great Gaelic lords by aggrandising them and their immediate
families at the expense of other inhabitants of the lordship. The
charge is that the grant of a royal patent involved a double
swindle. It invested the lord with the freehold of all the lands of
the lordship, thereby reducing other landholders to the status of
tenants at will. At the same time it invested the succession in his
immediate family, thereby depriving the rest of the kin group.

So far as the first part of the charge is concerned, we have seen
that the liberal scheme envisaged the subinfeudation of the
lordship, following upon the grant of tenure to the lord himself.
The liberals regarded this process as just as essential as the grant
of tenure to the lord himself. The importance of the point is
stressed in a letter to the king regarding the O'Toole territories:
'lest that the whole being granted to the brothers [the O'Tooles]
. . . the others having nothing should be driven to be as those men
have been'.[69] They would not have wanted the grantees to be
under any illusion in the matter either. Thus, the lord deputy and
the council are found asking the king in 1541 to write to O'Reilly
granting his application for a patent, and also informing him of
the appointment of a commission under the lord deputy to
supervise the subinfeudation of the lordship.[70] The liberals had
no intention of solving one problem by creating another.

Primogeniture is a rather different matter. It was certainly the
intention in granting tenure to substitute succession in the direct
male line for the Gaelic system. However, it may be doubted if
primogeniture was regarded as a major incentive by either side
in negotiating surrender and regrant. It is true that the occupant

---

[69] *S.P. Henry VIII*, iii, p. 266.   [70] *S.P. Henry VIII*, iii, p. 306.

of the lordly dignity would have wished to keep the title in the family. But the accounts of succession disputes which abound in the annals suggest that holders of the title would have reacted with mixed feelings to primogeniture. In existing circumstances they usually had the opportunity of grooming a successor from among all their male children. Even though that system did not guarantee the succession, the prospect of a rigid law of inheritance cannot have been attractive. In any case, it is clear that the promoters of surrender and regrant moved warily on the whole question of inheritance. Here also they had no desire to solve one problem by creating another. Their hope was that by the third generation the principle of promogeniture would become operative. Meanwhile the policy was to underwrite the strongest candidate for the succession under the Gaelic system in order to ensure a smooth transition. Thus in Thomond, the ruler, Murrough O'Brien, was persuaded to concede right of succession to his brother Donough.

Finally the history of the negotiations themselves do not suggest either that the agents of the crown were doing an underhand deal with the lords against their followers, or that the lords themselves were snapping up an attractive bargain. Neither O'Brien nor McWilliam felt able to commit himself in his initial negotiations in January 1541. O'Brien explained that he would have to consult with the members of his sept and others under his rule, 'for as much as he was but one man, although he were captain of his nation'.[71] Terms were finally concluded with both the following year only after a further prolonged period of negotiation. Again, O'Neill's long-drawn-out resistance, from the spring of 1541 until the end of the year, succumbing eventually only after a major military campaign, does not suggest a man with an itching palm for what the crown had to offer.

The evidence suggests that the magnates realised the implications of the proposition made to them. They recognised that it would effect a novel and permanent alteration in their situation, a change that offered advantages, but also disadvantages. Accordingly, they accepted the deal only after serious deliberation.

In considering this matter historians have paid little attention to what those Anglo-Irish politicians who were closest to the problem had to say. These might be expected to have as sharp a

---

[71] *S.P. Henry VIII*, iii, p. 285.

perception of the motives of the lords of the Irishry as twentieth-century scholars. Sir Thomas Cusack explained the matter thus to the council in England: 'for as much as the Irishmen in Ireland be in opinion amongst themselves, that Englishmen one day will banish them, and put them from their lands forever, so that they never were in assurance of themselves, and also considering that they won their lands by encroachment, as well upon the king's majesty's most noble progenitors as otherwise, and especially the earldom of Ulster; which causeth them, when opportunity serve them, to persevere in war and mischief, and now they having their lands of the king's majesty, by his grace's letters patents, whereby they may stand in assurance of their lands, and being accepted as subjects, where before they were taken as Irish enemies, which is the chiefest mean, by good wisdom, to continue them in peace and obedience.'[72]

According to Cusack's analysis, the tension between the crown and the disobedient lordships sprang from the ambiguity of the crown's attitude. This could only be resolved by granting the lords security of tenure, and in the process transforming their constitutional status from 'Irish enemies' to subjects of the crown. The effect would be doubly reassuring to them. It would eliminate once and for all the threat of the revival of the twelfth-century racial conquest; more than that, it would remove the threat to lands held in violation of feudal titles.

The examination of political attitudes in the 'disobedient' lordships in the late medieval period, undertaken earlier, substantiates Cusack's diagnosis of a continuing sense of insecurity arising from the dispute over tenure.[73] As we saw also, the experience of the six critical years beginning with the Kildare rebellion had brought that tension to the surface once more. That period had witnessed the appearance of an English standing army, and a sustained aggressive militarist stance on the part of crown government. These were the conditions in which the crisis of the Geraldine–Gaelic League developed.[74] So far as the liberal policy of conciliation was concerned, that crisis could well be regarded as a *felix culpa*. It served not only to prepare the way for the sponsorship of the liberal formula by government, but also to create an atmosphere propitious to it in the lordships. The

[72] *S.P. Henry VIII*, iii, p. 326.   [73] Above, pp. 11–12, 27–8.
[74] Above, pp. 175–8.

campaign of 1539–40 served to bring home to the magnates two major flaws in the notion of a Gaelic alliance. One was the difficulty of giving cohesion to such a gangling structure, and of achieving the concerted action necessary to smash the forces of the crown. The other was the insubstantiality of the expectation of assistance from England's European enemies.[75] Paradoxically, the exceptional bellicosity of the disobedient lords in 1539–40, and their exceptional conciliatoriness in the succeeding six years, both reflect a sharpened awareness on their part of the vulnerability of their position. There was, then, a strong element of self-interest in the appeal of surrender and regrant for the magnates. However, the appeal was related to a desire for security, rather than to avarice.

The liberal offer, of course, was a package deal. With surrender and regrant went reform. The patent granting tenure was complemented by the indenture of submission through which the patentee bound himself to the reform of his lordship politically and socially. The response of the local lords to this aspect of the liberal programme remains to be considered. Was surrender and regrant the sugar coating on the pill of reform? Is it possible that the non-constitutional lords could have responded positively to the liberal concept of a reform of government?

The weight of two very different historiographical traditions combines to crush the proposition of a positive response to the reform programme. One is the Celtic nationalist tradition, most formidably represented in the scholarly writings of Eoin MacNeill. He defended the viability of the Gaelic polity and of Gaelic political institutions. He could not admit that crown government had anything to offer the Gaelic communities, except bondage. The conciliatory policy could appeal to Gaelic lords only on the grounds of base advantage, by offering a means of transforming the corporate rights of the sept into a personal proprietorship held by themselves – the bribery thesis already discussed.[76] The Celtic

---

[75] Above, pp. 136–8.

[76] MacNeill spent so much time demolishing interpretations which conflict with his own that it is difficult to find a positive presentation of his main thesis, but see his *Phases of Irish history* (Dublin 1919), pp. 349–56. He admitted, by way of exception, that primogeniture had practical advantages over the Gaelic system of succession, though he argued that the Gaelic system was conceptually superior, and that it began to adapt to a form of primogeniture in the later medieval period, *Early Irish laws and institutions* (Dublin 1935), pp. 149–5

nationalist view directly confronts what may be called the 'West Britain' tradition of Irish historiography, represented for the medieval period by MacNeill's great opponent, Professor Orpen of Trinity College, Dublin. The tradition found a scholarly exponent for the sixteenth century in Bishop David Mathew, though he looked to Oxford rather than to Trinity College, Dublin, for a mentor. He built his *Celtic peoples and renaissance Europe* on the interpretation of European cultural history presented in Christopher Dawson's *The making of Europe*. According to this interpretation the extension of English rule to the Gaelic lordships in the sixteenth century marks the stage at which European civilisation finally came to grips with an older barbaric culture under the impetus of renaissance and Reformation. The result was inevitable death for the older, declining species which proved incapable either of resisting or adapting – doomed in accordance with the law of evolution by natural selection at work in the historical process. This interpretation could not, any more than the Celtic nationalist one, admit the possibility of a positive response from the autonomous lords to a political initiative from the crown. It represented the situation in the lordships in the sixteenth century as one of rudimentary and decaying social and political institutions, presided over by a warrior class incapable of perceiving the need for political reform or of sharing the concerns and the values of the crown officials whose mission was to provide the island with modern and effective government.[77]

Recent Irish scholarship suggests that the truth about late medieval Gaelic Ireland strikes a balance between these two historiographical traditions. Taking a more sceptical look than MacNeill at the Celtic heritage, it emphasises the inadequacies of its social and political organisation.[78] However, the reaction against MacNeill's idealised and idyllic presentation does not lend substance to Mathew's equally conceptualised and predetermined view. On the contrary, the work of recent scholars serves to show that for all its archaism Gaelic society in the later medieval period was dynamic, and that its social and political institutions had a

---

[77] C. Dawson, *The making of Europe* (London, 1932), pp. 67–78. D. Matthew, *The Celtic peoples and renaissance Europe* (London, 1933), passim but see especially pp. viii, xii–xvii, 263–75, 289–92, 378–82, 448–54.

[78] Binchy, 'Secular Institutions' in Dillon (ed.), *Early Irish Society*, pp. 52–65. Nicholls, *Gaelic and Gaelicised Ireland*, pp. 26, 31–40, 50–2.

capacity for change and adaptation in practice, though overlaid with a veneer of immutability.[79]

This provides the context in which the functioning of the dynasts in the Gaelic system in late medieval Ireland must be examined. In Mathew's view, one of the concomitants of the onset of *rigor mortis* in Gaelic society was the moribundity of its political leaders. He conceived of these as so totally dominated by the image of the heroic warrior as to put the idea of political reform beyond their capacity to comprehend, or at least beyond the range of their interests. If that was the case, what is to be made of the growing personal involvement of the great lords in civil government which was a feature of the development of the great dynastic lordships in the late medieval period? They issued ordinances for the government of their lordships, came to participate directly in judicial proceedings, saw to the execution of justice, and offered protection against arbitrary exactions by lesser lords.[80]

In attempting to understand the role of the lord in the Gaelic system at this period, it is instructive to analyse the composition of the obituary notices provided for Gaelic leaders in the annals. They referred to the leader's functions as a war lord, and his ability to defend his territories and to maintain others under tribute. They also alluded to his position as patron of learning and the arts. Our special interest is the third sphere to which the conventional notice drew attention. This was the lord's function in civil government. An excerpt from an obituary for Hugh Dubh O'Donnell, lord of Tirconnell, who died in 1537, will illustrate the general line followed: 'A repressor of evil deeds and evil customs, the destroyer and banisher of rebels and thieves, an enforcer of the laws and ordinances after the justest manner; a man in whose reign the seasons were favourable, so that sea and land were productive; a man who established every one in his country in his proper hereditary possessions, that no one of them might bear enmity towards another.'[81] The idealised image of the leader presented

[79] MacNeill, *Early Irish Laws and institutions*, pp. 147–9. Idem, *Phases of Irish history*, pp. 295, 323–56. Hayes-McCoy, 'Gaelic society in Ireland in the late sixteenth century', pp. 45–61. Ó Corráin, *Ireland before the Normans*, pp. 74–9. Nicholls, *Gaelic and Gaelicised Ireland*, pp. 44–6. Seán Ó Tauma, 'The new love poetry' in Brian Ó Cuív (ed.), *Seven centuries of Irish learning* (Dublin 1971), pp. 87–102. Seán MacAirt, 'The development of early modern Irish prose' in ibid., pp. 103–15.
[80] Lydon, *Ireland in the later middle ages*, p. 143; Nicholls, *Gaelic and Gaelicised Ireland*, pp. 42–3, 44–6, 53–6.   [81] *A.F.M.*, v, pp. 1438–9.

in the annals, therefore, is not merely that of the war lord. He was a civil ruler also, endowed with political ability, whose government brought justice, peace and prosperity to the community. The same theme occurs in encomiastic verse, exemplified in the sixteenth century in the work of one of the last great masters of the form, Tadhg Dall Ó Huiginn.[82] It is reasonable to assume that the lords themselves were influenced to a greater or less degree, according to personal capacity and temperament, by the image of the beneficent ruler, just as they were by the image of the warrior–hero, and that they aspired to fulfil the conventional expectation in both roles.

A second source from which the lord derived a sense of responsibility towards civil government was that of the clergy. Chapuys relayed to his imperial master in 1534 reports in England about the extraordinary hold of the Observant friars over the Gaelic Irish generally, and especially over their lords. The report gave an exaggerated impression. Then as now it seems that the myth of the priest-ridden Irish was cherished in England. Nevertheless, there is evidence to show that the friars actively exerted themselves as a moral influence upon local lords.[83] The lords were susceptible to clerical influence in another way also, because of their dependence on clerics for administrative and diplomatic purposes. The clerical influence must have helped to keep the lord's responsibilities in civil government to the fore, and to draw his attention to the social needs of the community under his jurisdiction.

Against this background we can return to St Leger and the liberal group in 1540 to note their assessment of the prospects of the reform programme in the localities. Quite frequently they declare themselves impressed by the political sagacity displayed by the lords in negotiation, and by their receptiveness to the notion of political reform. O'Connor much lamented 'the miserable estate that he and other of his sect liveth in'. O'Brien was found to be 'of such sobriety and towardness that there is a great hope that both he and his will continue in their obedience'. O'Donnell was 'a sober man and one that in his words much desireth civil order'. McWilliam was commended for the 'wisdom and policy'

---

[82] For examples see E. Knott (ed.), *The bardic poems of Tadhg Dall Ó Huiginn* (London 1922), i, pp. 41, 67, 229.
[83] See my *Dissolution of the religious orders*, pp. 11, 13.

by which he reduced his territories 'to much better civility and obedience than they have been of many years past'. The highest accolade went to Desmond, in respect of whom St Leger declared that he had 'heard better counsel of no man for the reformation of [Ireland]'.[84] Although Desmond's subsequent contribution as a political reformer shows him to have been a political leader of rather special calibre, he must be seen, at the same time, as the product of the same milieu as the dynasts of the Irishry in whom also a concern for political and social reform was noted.

The receptiveness of the local leadership to the notion of political reform is suggested in another way also. This was the alacrity with which they began to avail themselves of a facility provided by the new system where Gaelic institutions were seriously deficient. A report by St Leger after he had spent his first three months in Ireland attending to the reform of Leinster describes how he spent the Christmas at Carlow Castle, whither the Leinster septs resorted in the vacation period for the redress of wrongs, and how he and the lord chancellor made such order in these matters as redounded to the king's honour and the quiet of the country.[85] The council, and parliament when in session, provided central institutions for arbitrating in the disputes of the dynasts themselves, and these readily and widely availed themselves of the facility both in the internal disputes of the septs and in their external relations.

In 1555, after the initial campaign for general reform had been in abeyance for over a decade, a liberal treatise advocated a fresh start. The author felt confident that the campaign would meet with a favourable response in the Gaelic lordships because, as he said, 'of the experience I have of their sharp wits in politic causes'.[86] The foregoing review serves to show that the author's confidence was not without a sound basis. That is not to say that statesmanlike considerations were uppermost in dictating the response of local lords to the liberal programme. However, it is clear that common political and social concerns existed between them and the commonwealth liberals, which provided a basis for ecumenical endeavour. No doubt it would be naive to suppose that the lords would have willingly conceded their functions in

---

[84] *S.P. Henry VIII*, iii, pp. 264, 285, 362, 398, 455, 478.
[85] *S.P. Henry VIII*, iii, p. 285 (*L.P.*, xvi, no. 552).
[86] Hatfield, Salisbury MS C.P. 201/116.

civil government to crown administrators for the sake of the programme of reform. But that is not what the liberals envisaged. The existing lords were to retain the status and function of leadership in the localities, and local government was to be operated through their agency. Not surprisingly, later pro-grammes of reform which brought new English officials into the localities to usurp the place of the local leader were sharply resented. This does not prove the unwillingness, much less the inability, of the local leadership to adapt. Though it salved the conscience of sixteenth-century colonisers to think so – and twentieth-century historians also, perhaps – the tragic fate of the great Gaelic and Gaelicised nobility in the early modern period may not be shrugged off as the necessary price of progress.

8

The transformation of the Lordship

Concomitantly with the programme for assimilating the dynastic lordships to the polity of the crown, the programme designed to abolish the duality of the medieval Lordships at the national level was proceeded with. What follows attempts to show the inter-relationship between the two programmes, and how the liberals proposed to reconstitute the island as a political entity, like the local lordships, by changing the infrastructure, constitutionally and politically, while leaving the superstructure intact.

The act for the kingly title, June 1541

Just as surrender and regrant was the pivot for the programme of reconstitution in the dynastic lordships, so the act 'that the king of England, his heirs and successors be kings of Ireland' provided the pivot on which the programme for the reconstitution of the state revolved. In fact, the two have always been regarded as the most significant developments in the last phase of Henry VIII's reign in Ireland. Yet the relationship between them has not been satisfactorily demonstrated – not surprisingly, since the significance of each in itself has not been adequately grasped.

The received historiography has blurred the significance of the act for the kingly title by setting it in the wrong context. It has been mistakenly regarded as a manifestation of the king's own political ambitions in Ireland, an earnest of his determination to subjugate the whole island. In addition, its relationship to the religious Reformation tends to be misconceived. In establishing the context to which the act relates, the first misconception to be cleared up is that concerning the source of the proposal. It did not come from Henry VIII or the English administration. It does not reflect the revived bellicosity of the king in the 1540s which was soon to plunge England into a war of conquest in Scotland and an invasion of France. As a matter of fact, as we shall see, the king subsequently berated his councillors in Ireland for urging the title upon him, precisely because it carried a moral commitment to subjugate the island. The initiative for the change of the royal style came from within the Irish executive. It has already been noted that the proposal was put forward originally by Bishop Staples of Meath to St Leger and his fellow commissioners in 1537, and was reiterated in a personal letter from the bishop to St Leger in the summer of 1538.[1] It reemerged as a formal proposition from the Irish council to the king after three months of St Leger's administration as lord deputy.[2]

Close attention to the context in which the proposal was put forward on these occasions will dispel the second misconception about the provenance of the act. In so far as historians have related it to reform, they have set it in the context of the religious Reformation. Its purpose is seen as the removal of the anomaly, created by the repudiation of papal supremacy, of the derivation of the king's title as lord of Ireland from a twelfth-century papal grant. Certainly in putting forward the proposal Staples, and later the Irish council, referred to the papal grant; but the issue was not papal ecclesiastical supremacy. In fact, Staples clearly separated the two. He first put forward the proposal for the kingship as a means 'to induce the Irish captains...to due obedience'. He then went on to propose separately a scheme to secure recognition of the king's ecclesiastical jurisdiction by the administration of the oath under the act of supremacy 'to every of the king's subjects'.[3] The formal proposal on the part of the Irish executive was put forward in precisely the same context, reasoning that 'they that be of the Irishry would more gladder obey your highness by name of king of this your land, than by the name of lord thereof'.[4]

The matter at issue in the act for the kingly title was the political aspect of sovereignty – the 'regal estate' of Ireland, as Staples put it – not the island's ecclesiastical constitution. Of course, in the Cromwellian concept of national sovereignty, both were intrinsically related. However, they were distinct, and the distinction

[1] Above, pp. 193–4.
[2] *S.P. Henry VIII*, iii, p. 277 (*L.P.*, xvi, no. 367).
[3] *S.P. Henry VIII*, ii, p. 480 (*L.P.*, xii(ii), no. 729(4)).
[4] *S.P. Henry VIII*, iii, p. 277 (*L.P.*, xvi, no. 367).

is important. The background against which the act for the kingly title emerges is Irish political reform, not the English Reformation. This is borne out by events in the Marian restoration. At that time the royal-supremacy legislation was rescinded, but the 'regal estate' of the queen in Ireland was reaffirmed with papal approval.

Finally, the act must be set in context against the background of the movement for political reform in Ireland. What needs to be emphasised here is that the proposal came from within the liberal lobby, not the radical one. The source of the original proposal, Bishop Staples, indicates this. The circumstances in which the proposal was put forward by the Irish council confirm it. The occasion was the meeting of the council assembled by the lord deputy at Christmas 1540, after the conclusion of his initial campaign in south Leinster. The council meeting was preoccupied with the formulation of legislative proposals for his projected parliament. The prompt revival of the scheme in these circumstances indicates that it formed part of the preconceived liberal blueprint, a thesis borne out by subsequent events.[5] The proposal to proclaim the kingly title was designed, therefore, in pursuit of the objective of a group within crown government in Ireland, to extend the crown's sovereign jurisdiction throughout the island by conciliation, not by conquest.

The considerations that prompted the change of the king's title are stated in the preamble to the act thus: 'Lack of naming the king's majesty and his noble progenitors kings of Ireland...hath been great occasion that the Irishmen and inhabitants within this realm of Ireland have not been so obedient to the king's highness and his most noble progenitors, and to their laws, as they of right and according to their allegiance and bounden duties ought to have been.'[6] The change from 'lord' to 'king' was intended to affirm the sovereign nature of the constitutional bond between the English crown and Ireland with a view to having that sovereignty acknowledged among the Irishry. The programme for assimilating the local lordships was directed to the same end. The act was linked to the local programme in three specific ways.

A letter from the lord deputy and council in October 1541, describing the political outlook of the Irishry, focuses attention on

---

[5] *S.P. Henry VIII*, iii, p. 277 (*L.P.*, xvi, no. 367).
[6] *Statutes at large, Ireland*, i, p. 176.

the primary constitutional significance of the act in the context of the liberal programme. It explains that 'they imagined to have, as it were, another kingdom and sect of themselves, ever adversaries and enemies to your regal jurisdiction and subjects, devising to be in misery and wretchedness in avoiding subjection'.[7] The background against which this must be set is the duality of the structure of the medieval Lordship, divided constitutionally and jurisdictionally, between the community directly linked to the crown, the Englishry, and the alien community, the Irishry. The change of the royal style provided the liberal formula for abolishing that duality, with sure constitutional underpinning. On the one hand, the notion of kingly sovereignty was incompatible with the existence of local lordships exempt from internal jurisdiction. On the other hand, it powerfully facilitated the extension of constitutional status to the Irishry. Since the act affirmed the king's sovereign relationship with the island as a whole, it paved the way for the removal of local or ethnic considerations as criteria of constitutional status. By this means it also paved the way for the removal of the fundamental source of political tension within the island, the insecurity arising from the non-constitutional nature of the dynastic lordships. As Sir Thomas Cusack put it to the English privy council, 'being accepted as subjects, where before they were taken as Irish enemies,... is the chiefest mean, by good wisdom, to continue them in peace and obedience'.[8] By the substitution of the notion of kingship for that of lordship, the act for the kingly title confronted the reality of a subject Englishry and an alien Irishry with the constitutional ideal of a single community of subjects under the sovereign jurisdiction of the crown. What the act effected virtually, in respect of the national constitution, surrender and regrant was designed to actualise in respect of the dynastic lords and their lordships.

The substitution of the notion of kingship for that of lordship had implications for the external sovereignty of the island also. It was intended to strengthen the bid of the liberals for the loyalty of the lords of the Irishry against competition from foreign potentates. Here the pope enters the story, though as a competitor for temporal and not for spiritual jurisdiction. As a result of the

---

[7] *S.P. Henry VIII*, iii, p. 339 (*L.P.*, xvi, no. 1284).

[8] *S.P. Henry VIII*, iii, p. 326.

twelfth-century papal grant, the 'regal estate', the sovereign temporal jurisdiction (*imperium*) of Ireland, was commonly regarded among the Irishry as residing in the papacy. The status of the English sovereign was accordingly rendered ambiguous. Whereas in England he enjoyed full sovereignty, in Ireland his overlordship was widely regarded as subordinate and limited. No doubt the clash between papacy and crown over spiritual jurisdiction added a further complication; but the connotations of his title had anyway tended to diminish the political status of the English overlord throughout the middle ages. The immediate background to the act for the kingly title from this point of view was not only the attempts of 1534–5 and 1539–40 to exploit the religious conflict for diplomatic purposes, but also the attempts of certain of the disobedient magnates from the beginning of the century to establish ties of fealty and protection with an alternative overlord.[9] The change of royal style affirmed unambiguously the sovereignty of the English crown in Ireland, and thus declared any other external political relationship *ultra vires*. While surrender and regrant removed the ambiguity of the local dynast's personal constitutional status, the act for the king's title removed the ambiguity about the constitutional status of the crown. It left the dynastic lord in no doubt about the exclusive and sovereign nature of the jurisdictional relationship he contracted with the crown by the acceptance of title and tenure.

The third way in which the change of the royal style lent support to the liberal reform relates to the implications of sovereignty for the king himself, rather than for the island. Henry VIII was at pains to ensure that the act for the kingly title should not seem to be investing him with a status he already enjoyed in his own right. He regarded the papal grant as an irrelevance since, as he claimed, his title in Ireland, as in England, was based on an original conquest. Therefore, the assumption of the kingly title simply made explicit the sovereignty implicit in the title of 'lord'. The king soon came to realise that if the change added nothing to his authority it added significantly to his responsibilities. By making explicit his status as sovereign he was committed to making it a reality also. He was in honour bound to exercise the functions of king of Ireland.

9 Above, pp. 19–20, 31.

The implications of this for the liberal reform programme emerged in the sequel to the proclamation of the title in June 1541. Sir Thomas Cusack was dispatched to court as soon as the parliamentary session ended to present a sheaf of bills dealing with reform for the consideration of the privy council, and to break the news as gently as possible about the cost of implementing the liberal programme. He painted a rosy picture for the indefinite future, but he could offer no immediate prospect of balancing the Irish budget. As it was, only half the current expenditure on government could be found from Irish revenues. The assimilation of the disobedient territories would add to running costs, at least in the first instance, since the army would have to be maintained at the present level, and the machinery of government would have to be expanded. Meanwhile, for the initial period of adjustment, little could be expected from the assimilated lordships by way of rents and taxes. Even in those areas where payment of the subsidy might be demanded 'where as it is in the English Pale 13*s*. 4*d*. the plough land, it may not be above 2*s*., till such time they be inured withal, and that they forget all their own customs and laws'.[10] Cusack wanted money immediately to pay the army, and a sufficient indication of more to come to enable the reformers to continue with their project.

The effect of all of this was to cause Henry VIII to stall once more, just after he had reconciled himself to waiving the crown's ancient titles, as the liberal formula demanded. A dispatch conveying that decision to the lord deputy, and delegating authority to him to settle with dynasts on that basis, was followed by a second furious communication rescinding the decision. Instead, all applications for tenure were to be referred to England for consideration, and to the king himself for final decision. Guidelines were provided on the terms to be sought in the preliminary negotiations, so as to ensure maximum advantage to the crown. Meanwhile the whole question of the revenues was to be reinvestigated with a view to ensuring that the newly assimilated territories would pay their way and that the Irish budget would balance.[11]

The outcome of this episode has to be viewed against the entire

---

[10] *S.P. Henry VIII*, iii, pp. 313, 323, 326. *L.P.*, xvi, nos. 1119, 1120.
[11] *S.P. Henry VIII*, iii, pp. 313, 318, 323, 330. *L.P.*, xvi, no. 1120. Above, pp. 203–4.

background of Henrician policy in Ireland. On the two previous occasions in the course of the reign when crown government in England deliberated upon the feasibility of a general reform – in the Surrey episode in 1520, and under Cromwell in 1535–7 – the outcome was negative. On both occasions, failure to obtain a guarantee of a substantial increase in the Irish revenues to offset the cost of the venture, by means of additional taxes, was a major factor in reaching a negative decision.[12] Though it took six months of struggle, the king agreed to go ahead on this occasion, despite the failure of his efforts to get an assurance of increased revenues from Ireland.[13] In pushing Henry VIII into this historic decision, the assumption of the kingly title was clearly a major factor. That consideration figured prominently in the discussions between the king, the English privy council and Cusack that resulted from the latter's trip to court.[14] The attitude of Henry VIII is revealed in his subsequent dispatch to the council in Ireland. He was full of reproach for them for having 'devised, by an act, to invest in us the name and title of king of Ireland', since, as it now appeared, the revenues there were not 'sufficient to maintain the state of the same', most especially to extend the crown's jurisdiction unilaterally. However, the deed could not be undone, and Henry VIII concentrated on ways of extracting better terms from the submitting lords.[15] As we have seen, he was eventually brought to abandon that attempt also, and the policy of surrender and regrant was allowed to proceed on the basis of the commonwealth liberal formula.[16]

The assumption of the kingly title, therefore, increased the pressure on government in England to commit itself to reform in Ireland. It sharpened the sting of the moral censure which the movement for reform in Ireland levelled against the crown's neglect. Henceforth, kingly duty would be a much-used weapon in the armoury of persuasives deployed by Anglo-Irish political reformers.

Seen in the historical context, therefore, the change in the royal style from 'lord' to 'king' represents the attempt of the commonwealth liberals to adapt the constitutional frame of the island to the specifications of their programme of reform. By

---

[12] Above, pp. 65–7, 112–15.   [13] *S.P. Henry VIII*, iii, pp. 362, 366, 394.
[14] S.P. 60/10, nos. 35, 36. *S.P. Henry VIII*, iii, p. 326.
[15] *S.P. Henry VIII*, iii, p. 337.   [16] Above, pp. 202–3.

making explicit the sovereign status of the English crown in Ireland, they repudiated the divided structure of the medieval Lordship and replaced it with a constitution which envisaged the island as a political unity, its inhabitants a single community of subjects, governed by the unilateral jurisdiction of the crown. By making the sovereignty explicit also they increased the crown's commitment to giving it reality. The effect of the change in the short term was to secure necessary royal approbation for the commonwealth liberal programme of general reform. The constitutional and political significance of the act in the long term, after the crown abandoned the liberal programme, will appear later.

The reform of parliament

The parliament of 1541 marks a milestone in Irish constitutional history not only because of the statute for the kingly title but also because of the reform of the institution itself. Both are, of course, related. The liberal concept of a united community of subjects under the unilateral jurisdiction of the crown dictated not only the reformulation of the king's constitutional relationship with the island, but also an adaptation of the institutions of government. Here the implications of the constitutional change were most immediately reflected in the institution of parliament, and in the first place in the attendance.

Before reflecting on the significance of the appearance of the Irishry at the opening session of the parliament, it would be as well to get the record straight about the scale on which it occurred. The numbers were small, if encouraging. They had no representatives in the commons, of course, since the necessary machinery of election had not as yet been established in the disobedient territories. In the upper house only one Gaelic lord took his place *ex officio*. This was MacGillapatrick, of Carlow, who was created baron of Upper Ossory on Trinity Sunday, two days before parliament opened on 13 June.[17] By the time parliament met he was the only one of the lords in respect of whom the process of surrender and regrant had got as far as the issue of a patent of title and tenure. Others came, or sent delegates, in response to St Leger's pressing invitation. There was a gratifying response from

---

[17] *Cal. pat. rolls Ire., Henry VIII*, p. 71.

the areas where the conciliatory campaign had concentrated since the lord deputy's arrival nine months previously, most of all from Leinster. O'Reilly of Cavan came in person. There were delegations from the Cavanaghs and the O'Mores. The O'Farrells also were almost certainly represented, since two leading members of the sept received denization ('naturalised' subject status) on the Sunday following the opening of parliament, the day of public celebration of the proclamation of the kingly title.[18] Domestic upheavals seem to have kept the other four major Leinster septs away. The O'Carroll chief had just been assassinated, and O'Connor was much involved in the ensuing power struggle. The latter turned up later on in the session, with the leaders of the two rival O'Carroll factions, to seek the arbitration of parliament. In south Leinster, Turlough O'Toole had been assassinated, and this may have detained the O'Byrnes as well.[19] Apart from the Leinster lords, the two magnates contacted by St Leger at Limerick in the spring also responded to the summons. McWilliam of south Connacht – Anglo-Irish but Gaelicised and lacking feudal tenure – came in person, and O'Brien of Thomond sent a distinguished delegation. The presence of O'Meara, a minor lord from Tipperary, may be accounted for as part of O'Brien's delegation. However, a total blank was drawn with those Gaelic Irish of the southwest whom St Leger had not as yet contacted; and the solitary fruit of the lord deputy's first tentative initiative in Ulster was Feidhlim Roe O'Neill, the leader of the disaffected element of the O'Neill kin.[20] Although this attendance was modest, scarcely more could have been expected, given the brief duration of the conciliatory initiative when parliament was convened. In any case, its primary significance lies not in its scale but in the fact that it occurred at all.

Historians have made surprisingly little of the presence of Gaelic lords in the parliament of 1541. It is seen in terms of an exercise

[18] Ibid., p. 72.
[19] *A.F.M.*, v, pp. 1460–1. *Cal. Car. MSS*, i, no. 155.
[20] For the identification of Feidhlim Roe O'Neill, see *S.P. Henry VIII*, iii, p. 355. The list of those who attended is based on reports to the king of the opening of parliament from the Irish council, *S.P. Henry VIII*, iii, pp. 304, 306. The editors of the foregoing add a list which purports to be of the attendance in the Lords; but since that list provides an attendance, especially of ecclesiastics, far in excess of the figures mentioned by St Leger, and since St Leger had no reason to minimise, it is taken to represent those summoned rather than those who attended, *L.P.*, xvi, no. 974(2).

in public relations concerned with the proclamation of the kingly title. This it was: but it was more. The antiquarian Sir James Ware showed greater perception, writing almost a century after the event. He pointed out that 1541 marks the beginning of Gaelic representation in parliament. It marks, therefore, a revolutionary constitutional innovation. Parliament was no longer conceived as the representative assembly of the colony alone, but of the inhabitants of the whole island. It mirrored the constitutional change effected by the act for the kingly title, the repudiation of the divided medieval Lordship, and the inauguration of a single polity of subjects composed of Englishry and Irishry alike.

Though not of the same fundamental constitutional significance, the return of the estranged Anglo-Irish feudatories which this parliament also marks emphasises its new representativeness. The earl of Desmond appeared at parliament for the first time since the mid fifteenth century. He brought back with him his Munster underlords, Barry, Roche, Fitzmaurice, as well as Lord Bermingham of Athenry. Their return does not only signalise the arrest of political fragmentation within the colony. Taken in conjunction with the first appearance of lords of the Irishry, it also points to the changed character of parliament, from a localised institution into a nationally representative assembly.

The new representativeness of parliament in 1541 was prompted not only by the new constitutional concept of a united polity, but by the governmental demands which this imposed. Having hitherto served the needs of a dwindling colony, it was now to function as an instrument of national government.

The contrast between the nature of the reform of the parliamentary institution in Ireland in 1541–3 in response to the exigencies of commonwealth liberalism, and the reform of its English counterpart in the previous decade as an instrument of Cromwellian unitary sovereignty, emphasises the uniqueness of the constitutional revolution of the 1540s in Ireland. The exigencies of the liberal policy in Ireland dictated the revival of precisely those features of the medieval parliament which the English institution shed with its swaddling clothes. One was its peripatetic quality. A late medieval statute restricting the convening of parliament to Dublin or Drogheda, and the number of sessions to a total of two, was repealed.[21] The assembly went on circuit in 1542, convening

---

[21] *Statutes at large, Ireland*, i, p. 205.

for a three-week session in Limerick, and for a week at Trim in June. The other medieval revival was a renewed emphasis on the deliberative and judicial functions of parliament, which in England had been detached almost completely, and separately institutionalised, leaving parliament supremely a legislative body. In a letter to the king in 1541, referring to the prorogation of parliament to Limerick, St Leger indicated the purpose behind these reforms: 'The assembly thereof [in Limerick] shall not only do great good to confirm the obedience of the earl of Desmond and many others in those parts...but also be an entry to bring that quarter to much civility and quiet, both by the sight of the honourable assembly, and the determination of variances, strifes, and debates among the inhabitants in those parts, which be now great, in default of administration of justice.'[22] The promoters of liberal reform saw the revival of the judicial function of parliament as part of their strategy for securing political stability and social order by means of good government rather than by force of arms. Primarily, the king's council in parliament provided a court of sufficient status to arbitrate in the disputes of the magnates. O'Connor brought the warring factions of the O'Carrolls to seek arbitration at the first session. The assassin of Turlough O'Toole, his rival for the lordship, came to the second session at Limerick under safe conduct, to plead his case, and there, 'by the consent of all the lords, Irish and English', he received his pardon on condition of payment of a large compensation to O'Toole's kin and forfeiture of his claim to the lordship. O'Neill and his underlords came to the session at Trim to submit their disputes to arbitration.[23]

At the same time, by bringing parliament into the localities, and by associating local lords with its deliberations, its possibilities as a centripetal and unifying device were exploited. It became a means for associating local lords with one another and with the central administration in the task of government. The revival of the peripatetic capacity of parliament, and of its deliberative and judicial functions, was directed to the same end as the extension of its representation. For the first time it was envisaged both as a national assembly and as an instrument of national government administration. Again reform was directed both towards express-ing the constitutional concept of a united polity and towards

---

[22] *S.P. Henry VIII*, iii, p. 311 (*L.P.*, xvi, no. 1044).

[23] *S.P. Henry VIII*, iii, pp. 306, 311, 432, *Cal. Car. MSS*, i, nos. 155, 169. *Acts of the privy council in Ireland, 1556–71*, ed. J. T. Gilbert (London 1897), p. 274.

bringing it nearer to realisation by providing agencies of cohesion. The wielders of local power were to be brought to participate in central government, and central government was to be enabled to exercise jurisdiction in the localities.

Reform of government administration

In two respects the adaptation of the Irish council followed the pattern of parliament. A major innovation in its composition mirrored the elimination of the constitutional divide between the Irishry and the Englishry. O'Neill and O'Brien, after their creation as earls of Tyrone and Thomond, were brought on to the Irish council. The earl of Desmond's inclusion after his reconciliation, though constitutionally less significant, nevertheless emphasises the new concept of a nationally representative government.[24] Like parliament also, the council revived a medieval feature to meet the administrative needs imposed by the liberal policy. It began to function once more as a Great Council, composed of administrators and lords of the realm. In this capacity it served as an instrument of cohesion and jurisdiction, and outside the sessions of parliament it provided an instrument of arbitration in the disputes of the lords themselves that was more acceptable. by virtue of its composition, than the ordinary council which had occasionally attempted to supply that need. Such a body is described in the annals deliberating upon the affairs of Donegal early in 1543, and those of Connacht at the end of the year. A Great Council was convened by St Leger at Limerick in the autumn of 1544 to settle the question of the succession in Clanrickard. Presumably the awards in the disputes between O'Carroll and MacGillapatrick recorded in the *Acts of the privy council* under that year also were made by the same kind of augmented council. The following year O'Neill and O'Donnell were before the council in Dublin seeking settlement of their disputes.[25] Finally, before St Leger's departure to England in the spring of 1546 he convened such a body at Dublin to ensure the preservation of political stability in his absence.[26]

---

[24] *Acts of the privy council*, p. 275.
[25] *S.P. Henry VIII*, iii, p. 506. *Cal. Car. MSS*, i, no. 186.
[26] *S.P. Henry VIII*, iii, pp. 560, 562, 563. *Cal. Car. MSS*, i, no. 185(ii). *A.F.M.*, v, pp. 1482–3. *Loch Cé*, ii, pp. 338–9. *Acts of the privy council*, p. 278.

The advance into the lordships of the campaign for the dissolution of the religious orders shows central government adapting its administrative procedures to the new situation. Whereas the project was implemented throughout the colony under Cromwell in 1539–40 by means of a commission of officials from the central administration, the new areas were tackled as an exercise in cooperative administration between central government and the local magnate. The great lordships were treated individually, and commissions were established comprised partly of members of the central administration and partly of representatives of the local lord. In this way the project was advanced in Desmond, Thomond and Connacht.[27]

Thus, through the council and through such *ad hoc* commissions, the machinery of the central administration began to extend into the hitherto disobedient areas. Little attempt was made to push the financial aspect of government. In accordance with the liberal strategy, the immediate concern was to secure social and political stability. Prosperity would follow peace. When crown government had proved itself by providing both, the king's new subjects could reasonably be asked to pay for the service.

The same conception underlay the design for the adaptation of the instruments of local government as that which underlay the adaptation at the centre. Two regional councils, one for the south and another for the west, were intended to act as the hubs of local government. The councils were to be composed of administrators from the central administration, mainly judicial officials, who were to act in conjunction with the local leadership, lay and ecclesiastical. In the event, the liberal scheme was not implemented. The king was generous with blessings upon it, and upon proposals to have the central courts go on circuit in vacation time. But he made it clear that the cost would have to be borne from Irish revenues. It took St Leger until the last months of the reign to cope with that proviso, and then the death of the king prevented the scheme from taking effect.[28] Meanwhile something analogous was improvised to secure political stability in the south west and north. It took the form of boards of arbitration comprised of men of good local standing, ecclesiastics, civil dignitaries, members of

---

[27] See my *Dissolution of the religious orders*, pp. 162–76.
[28] *S.P. Henry VIII*, iii, pp. 362, 366, 385, 394, 465, 490.

the nobility, who had experience of public administration. The local dynasts bound themselves to submit their disputes to these bodies as an alternative to the more traditional method of settlement – to some, no doubt, more congenial – i.e. cattle raid and skirmish.[29]

So far as local government more generally is concerned, the factotum of local administration, the sheriff, begins to make his appearance in the Gaelic and Gaelicised lordships at this period. Such officials, chosen from the local sept, are found functioning in south Leinster, in the Limerick–Tipperary area, and in south Connacht.[30] At the same time special provision was made for the administration of justice. A legal code was devised, along the lines originally envisaged by the king in 1520, assimilating elements of brehon and march law, and adapting and moderating crown statutes. It ranged widely over the area of local government – the Church: benefices, tithes etc.; criminal justice: homicide, theft etc.; social order: retainers, vagabonds, dress; the local lordship: dues and services, judicial jurisdiction, distraint. These provisions were promulgated in the form of ordinances, throughout most of the south and west.[31] In this project, as in the other arrangements devised for local government, the liberal strategy of joining the local leadership with the central administration is noteworthy. The ordinances were promulgated on the authority of the lord deputy and the Irish council, of course, but their implementation was entrusted to the leaders in the locality, to the earls of Ormond and Desmond in their areas, acting in conjunction with the metro-politan of Cashel, and under these 'all the bishops and captains or governors of countries'.

Finally, it is worth drawing attention, in passing, to the contrast between the liberal strategy for local government and that which was implemented by the local presidential system of the Elizabe-than period. The monolithic structure of the latter, composed exclusively of agents of central government, its military character, and its autocratic and Draconian style of government, indicate the chasm that separates the liberal policy of the 1540s from the radicalism that superseded it.

[29] *S.P. Henry VIII*, iii, p. 422, *Cal. Car. MSS*, i, no. 172. Davies, *A discovery of the true causes*, pp. 244–5.
[30] *S.P. Henry VIII*, iii, p. 569. *Cal. Car. MSS*, i, no. 185(ii).
[31] Lambeth, MS 603, pp. 23 Aff., 28ff. (*Cal. Car. MSS*, i, no. 157). S.P. 60/10, no. 21 (*L.P.*, xvii, no. 848). Davies, *A discovery of the true causes*, pp. 242–3.

The reconstitution of the Irish Church

The assumption prevails that St Leger's main interest in the religious Reformation was to prevent it from disturbing political tranquility. His alleged rejoinder to Archbishop Browne about religion marring all is often cited. Despite the shaky basis for the story – it depends on the testimony of Browne, ambiguously supported by John Alen – it rings true. But the matter at issue was the implementation of the Edwardian religious programme after it had entered its radical phase with the introduction of the first Prayer Book.[32] What follows should explain why St Leger, though he had dragged his feet on the introduction of Edwardian protestantism, felt justifiably aggrieved at charges of having neglected the religious policy.

St Leger took it for granted that the royal ecclesiastical supremacy formed an essential aspect of the royal sovereignty upon which the liberal programme was based. So did his co-architect of conciliation. It was not for the want of something better to say that Sir Thomas Cusack gave such prominence to the ecclesiastical supremacy in his opening address as Speaker at the parliament of 1541. He was setting the scene for the introduction on the following day of the bill for the kingly title.[33] The political revolution was not envisaged in isolation from the ecclesiastical one. For this reason a clause repudiating papal jurisdiction formed an invariable part of the conditions of the indentures of preliminary submission subscribed by local lords preparatory to application for a patent. Although isolated gestures had been made in the course of the Cromwellian administration, it was through the conciliatory policy of the 1540s that royal ecclesiastical supremacy was systematically applied to the Irish Church beyond the obedient colony.

In the ecclesiastical as in the political settlement, the liberal formula was directed towards changing the infrastructure while preserving the superstructure. Holders of benefices by papal provision were not disturbed but were persuaded to surrender their bulls and have their appointments ratified by patent, the ecclesiastical equivalent of surrender and regrant. Although that

---

[32] S.P. 61/4, no. 36(2); S.P. 61/3, no. 45. 'Radical' is a relative term. In comparison to the second Book of Common Prayer the first one was a moderate compilation. However, it constituted a radical break with traditional liturgical practice, in its use of the vernacular if in nothing else.

[33] *S.P. Henry VIII*, iii, p. 304 (*L.P.*, xvi, no. 926).

method had been generally applied in England in the early Cromwellian period, its application in Ireland necessitated, as in the case of surrender and regrant, a major concession of disputed rights to the localities. This was partly because Archbishop Browne and his group, in so far as they had concerned themselves with the Irishry, had resorted to attempts to set up royal nominees as rivals to the locally backed papal provisors.

However, the new departure represented by the liberal strategy must be set in a fuller context. The history of conflict between crown and locality in the sphere of ecclesiastical appointments stretched further back. Since the end of the fifteenth century the crown had been exerting pressure in Rome to ensure its right of nomination to Irish bishoprics against local nominees, even to ones in the disobedient territories.[34] Under the royal supremacy it arrogated the power of provision to itself, only to concede the right of patronage, at the liberals' persuasion, to the local lords. By the terms of the patents granting title and tenure, the patentee received the right of nomination to all benefices in the gift of the crown, except bishoprics, and even the bishoprics were disposed of in accordance with the wishes of the local lord. A letter from the lord deputy and council in 1543, supporting the suit of O'Donnell for a bishopric for his chaplain, expressed the conviction that dictated the liberal approach in the matter: 'it should be well done, for a time, favourably to grant their suits, till they be brought in ure to receive the same of his highness'.[35]

The most spectacular example of the liberal policy in operation is provided by the series of royal patents granting or confirming ecclesiastical promotions issued at the behest of the lords who went to court to make formal submission in 1542–3.[36] Especially notable was the collation of George Dowdall to the primatial see of Armagh. When Dowdall became archbishop of Armagh in 1543, exactly a century had elapsed since a local-born cleric had held it. In the meantime it had gone to a succession of Englishmen, apart from one Italian, Octavian, provided by the pope in 1479.[37] Almost immediately on his arrival in Ireland St Leger indicated his favour towards breaking the pattern at Armargh. Originally

[34] W. E. Wilkie, *The cardinal protectors of England* (Cambridge 1974), pp. 63–75.
[35] *S.P. Henry VIII*, iii, p. 471. *L.P.*, xviii(i), nos. 634, 981(2).
[36] See my *Dissolution of the religious orders*, pp. 212–13.
[37] Gwynn, *The medieval province of Armagh*, pp. 260–3.

he recommended the son of the Anglo-Irish baron of Delvin. But Dowdall's part in reconciling O'Neill brought him to the lord deputy's attention, and he returned from the trip to court with O'Neill in 1542 with a promise of succeeding to the dying incumbent, Cromer.[38]

The other side of the coin is the success achieved through the liberal tactic in defeating the first onslaught of the Counter-Reformation in Ireland. As a result of the diplomacy of the Geraldine League, the papacy aggressively asserted its ecclesiastical jurisdiction in Ireland for a three-year period beginning in mid-1539. An opening salvo was fired as early as October 1538 with the provision of Art O'Friel – a canon of Derry, and O'Donnell's emissary to Rome – to the metropolitan see of Tuam in opposition to the royal nominee, Christopher Bodkin.[39] On that occasion provision was made to three vacant sees, Elphin, Clonmacnois and Dromore. In addition, in Down and Connor an absentee Englishman was deprived in favour of a local, Art Magennis, while the provisor to Clonmacnois was nominated administrator of Killaloe, replacing Bishop James O'Corrin, who had submitted to the crown.[40] The following month, in an even more aggressive gesture, the primate, Archbishop Cromer, was suspended from his see of Armagh until he should clear himself from suspicion of heresy, and a Scot, Robert Wauchop, a leading counter-reformer, was deputed to administer the diocese.[41] The momentum of the counterattack was maintained the following year. At Cork a papal candidate was opposed to the royal nominee, Dominick Tirrey, whose appointment had gone unchallenged at Rome for the previous four years. At Kilmore a rival was also offered to Edward Nugent, a pre-Reformation appointee who had submitted to the crown. And when William Miagh filled the vacancy at Kildare in 1540 by royal patent, a papal provisor was immediately put forward. A challenge was offered to Richard Farrell, the new royal

[38] Ibid.

[39] Gwynn, cit., pp. 224–6, 237–8.

[40] Gwynn, cit., pp. 239–40; *S.P. Henry VIII*, iii, p. 122. Gwynn's puzzlement at the pope's action at Killaloe can be dispelled. The royal appointee to Killaloe complained to Archbishop Browne in January 1539 that Lord Deputy Gray had given preference to the papal provisor there, 'a Grey friar, confessor to one of the Garrantynes, and a rank traitor'. This description confirms that the bishop in question was O'Corrin, and the action at Rome indicates that he received preference from Gray by submitting to the royal supremacy, *S.P. Henry VIII*, iii, p. 122 (*L.P.*, xiv(i), no. 303).

[41] Gwynn, cit., pp. 241–6.

appointee at Ardagh, in similar circumstances the following year.[42] Meanwhile, on the pastoral front, Ignatius Loyola had been occupied in mounting a missionary expedition to Ireland since 1540.[43]

From the second half of 1539 onwards, therefore, the battle for ecclesiastical supremacy in Ireland was joined on a fundamental jurisdictional issue: to whom were the bishops of the Irish Church to acknowledge allegiance? By the end of Henry's reign the answer to that question seemed beyond doubt. Through the liberal strategy, papal nominees were brought to submit to the crown on the same conditions as in England, that of having their bulls ratified by royal patent. Where the situation was complicated by the existence of rival papal and royal candidates, St Leger was usually successful in finding an acceptable compromise. At Ardagh and Kildare the papal provisor was made a suffragan of the metropolitan, and appointed to an agreeable benefice with the prospect of an episcopal appointment should a suitable vacancy arise.[44] At Clonfert a similar arrangement was made, though there the royal nominee was asked to stand down in favour of the papal one, who, as a Burke, had stronger local backing.[45] Where the papal provisor held out, which apparently happened at Cork (Lewis McNamara) and Tuam (Art O'Friel), and which certainly happened at Armagh, effective jurisdiction was exercised by the royal and not the papal candidate. It is possible to study the administration of the diocese of Armagh in some detail at this period, and it is clear that Dowdall was able to assert his jurisdiction as a royal nominee, not only in the districts *inter Anglos*, but *inter Hibernicos* also.[46] It should be added that St Ignatius's missionary expedition was a flop. Two envoys landed somewhere in the north, probably at Derry, in 1542, but retired after a month. The failure of that mission signalled the beginning of the end of the first serious attempt by the papacy to affirm its ecclesiastical supremacy in Ireland.

The basically different orientation of the crown's Irish policies

[42] Gwynn, cit., pp. 130, 246–7. *S.P. Henry VIII*, iii, p. 149 (*L.P.*, xiv(ii), no. 352).

[43] Gwynn, cit., pp. 248–9.

[44] Gwynn, cit., pp. 130, 247. *L.P.*, xx(i), no. 475.

[45] *Cal. pat. rolls Ire., Henry VIII–Elizabeth*, p. 82; *S.P. Henry VIII*, iii, p. 477. The royal nominee at Clonfert was compensated by the rectory of Ardbrahan in the diocese of Kilmacduagh, *Fiants, Henry VIII*, nos. 298, 352.

[46] Gwynn, cit., pp. 248–75.

in the 1530s and in the 1540s is reflected in the different preoccupations of their religious programmes. The liberal emphasis
on extending royal ecclesiastical supremacy into the Irishry was of
a pattern with the liberal policy in general, designed to abolish
the duality of the medieval Lordship. It was of a pattern also in
dropping the authoritarianism of the earlier campaign, and its
drive for uniformity with English religious practice. The dropping
of the chief promoter of the Cromwellian Reformation campaign,
Archbishop Browne, followed as a necessary consequence. In this
connection the significance of the contact between St Leger and
Bishop Staples of Meath again appears. In a series of reshuffles that
marked the inauguration of St Leger's second administration late
in 1546, Browne was replaced by Staples on the ecclesiastical
commissions then appointed – a deep humiliation for Browne,
who as archbishop of Dublin and as metropolitan of the Leinster
dioceses had a double claim to recognition as chief ecclesiastical
agent of the crown.[47] However, the appointments only confirmed
a situation that had existed in practice since St Leger's arrival. It
was Staples' line and not Browne's that the liberal policy followed
on the Reformation. Staples' Reformation policy has already been
noted from his letter to St Leger in the summer of 1538, criticising
Browne's Cromwellian campaign, then at its height in the Dublin
metropolitan area.[48] Instead of imposing in Ireland official injunctions devised for the Church in England, he wished to
concentrate on the fundamental tenet, the royal ecclesiastical
supremacy, and to secure genuine conversions to it. This was the
basis on which the liberal policy proceeded. Political leaders and
ecclesiastics alike were to be brought to acknowledge the royal
supremacy in the jurisdictional sphere by accepting its authority
in the dispensation of ecclesiastical office. Internal conversion was
to be obtained, as Staples recommended, by the liberal weapon
of persuasion and education.

As we have seen, the policy was a resounding success in the
sphere of ecclesiastical appointments. But the catechetical support
programme hardly got started. The period 1540–6 was a time of
plans and proposals rather than of concrete achievement. Although
evidence of this aspect of the religious policy is sparse, it is sufficient
to show the liberals' constant concern with it in the 1540s, and

[47] *L.P.*, xxi(ii), no. 476(45)(49).   [48] Above, pp. 155–9.

the nature of the projects mooted to advance it. In contrast to the attempts to provide Reformation evangelists from England in the Cromwellian campaign, and again in the reigns of Edward and Elizabeth, St Leger and his supporters looked to mobilise Irish resources, with as little disturbance as possible to the *status quo*. This had obvious difficulties. In his outline of policy before the English council in 1541, Sir Thomas Cusack proposed legislation requiring every bishop to preach at certain times yearly, either personally or by substitute, under penalty of a fine of £10.[49] No such legislation was introduced before parliament concluded in November 1543. The snag was, who was to teach the teachers? John Travers, another supporter of the liberal approach, in policy proposals submitted in 1542, suggested that the archbishop of Dublin, Bishop Staples of Meath, and 'such others as favoureth the gospel' should instruct the Irish bishops.[50] These two documents probably lie behind the king's admonition in 1542 to Arbhsbishop Browne in particular, and to the whole Irish council in general, to have 'special regard' to the provision of 'good and Catholic teaching ...to [the knowledge of] God's laws and ours together, which shall daily more and more frame and confirm them [i.e. the people] in honest living'.[51] But Travers' suggestion was not seriously taken up. St Leger had no wish for a preaching campaign in Browne's style, and Staples did not have the physical robustness to undertake such a programme.[52] O'Brien of Thomond, the first and staunchest adherent of St Leger's programme among the Gaelic lords, suggested another line of approach. When he went to court to be created earl in 1543 he urged, obviously primed by St Leger, that 'Irishmen educated in Oxford and Cambridge be sent thither to preach'.[53] This was a scheme which St Leger himself was encouraging. He patronised at least one Anglo-Irish

---

[49] *S.P. Henry VIII*, iii, p. 326.

[50] *S.P. Henry VIII*, iii, p. 431 (*L.P.*, xvii, no. 690). For Travers' connection with St Leger in the 1540s, see my *Dissolution of the religious orders*, pp. 176–7, 193–4.

[51] *S.P. Henry VIII*, iii, p. 394 (*L.P.*, xvii, no. 460).

[52] By early 1538 Staples had developed a hernia which prevented him from riding, and he had to travel in a litter. This made long-distance travel difficult and painful, and he asked to be excused from regular attendance at council meetings, *L.P.*, xiii(i), no. 1161. In general his health seems to have been frail. When he made the journey to Dublin in connection with the religious policy of 1548 he caught a fever, as a result, according to himself, of being housed in a room at St Patrick's 'bounding upon a common jakes', S.P. 61/1, no. 156.

[53] *S.P. Henry VIII*, iii, p. 463 (*L.P.*, xvi(i), no. 633).

Oxford graduate (Cantwell) and sued for wages for himself and his manservant to enable him to set up as a peripatetic schoolmaster in the border areas of the south.[54]

No substantial progress was made, however. The obstacles were too great and the time was too short. Meanwhile, the tolerant attitude in the lordships to the papally committed friars counterbalanced the advance of the royal ecclesiastical supremacy in the sphere of ecclesiastical appointments.[55] Even without such a formidable enemy within the camp it would have taken a generation for the liberal religious policy to turn its defeat of the Counter-Reformation into victory for the Reformation. The liberal policy was not granted so long. With the abandonment of the conciliatory political programme and the reappearance of militarism in the reign of Edward VI, conditions in the Gaelic and Gaelicised areas turned once more in favour of the purveyors of the Counter-Reformation ideology of faith and fatherland that had fired the Gaelic League of 1539–40. English policy rather than papal saved Gaelic Ireland for Catholicism.

It saved Anglo-Ireland also, though here it was the radicalism of the Edwardian policy in religion rather than politics that was decisive. Under that test, faith in the royal supremacy foundered, even in one so closely associated with liberalism as Archbishop Dowdall. When the pressure to implement the Edwardian religious innovations could no longer be resisted, he went into exile: he returned under Queen Mary to spearhead the Counter-Reformation. Dowdall simply presents in sharper relief the general pattern within the Anglo-Irish community. This had an important repercussion for the developing commonwealth liberal tradition. Elizabethan commonwealth liberalism departed from the Henrician pattern in distinguishing between king and supreme head, and in removing the provision for religious loyalty from its programme for reconciling the Irishry to the crown.

---

[54] *S.P. Henry VIII*, III, p. 526 (*L.P.*, xx(i), no. 1108).
[55] See my *Dissolution of the religious orders*, pp. 166–9, 171.

The practice of government

The contrast between the different constitutional concepts that
underlay the Cromwellian policy of the 1530s and the liberal
policy of the 1540s is nowhere better illustrated than in the history
of the central administration in Ireland in the two periods. As we
saw, the trend of Cromwell's policy, in accordance with his
concept of unitary sovereignty, was to reduce the central administration in Ireland to the status and the function of a regional
council of the English kingdom. The centralised structure of Irish
government was undermined, and its jurisdiction was rigorously
subordinated to the control of the English administration.

The effect of St Leger's administration was to arrest this trend.
So far as the English executive was concerned, Dublin was firmly
reestablished as the centre of crown government in Ireland. It was
no longer bypassed by direct contact between the English executive
and the Irish localities. Furthermore, the lord deputy and the Irish
council asserted their role as the policy-making agency for Ireland.
The stubbornness and the success with which they resisted
dictation from England is in startling contrast to the earlier period.

This has already been evident from the history of the liberal
policy of conciliation. The history of St Leger's parliament
provides another illustration. In contrast to the Reformation
parliament of 1536–7, Poynings' Law was not suspended, so
that the Irish executive, not the English one, remained in firm
control of the situation, and the legislative programme devised by
the Irish executive was not set aside on this occasion in favour of
a programme devised in England. Furthermore, measures from
England were blocked not by parliament itself, but by the Irish
executive. The remarkable independence of the local executive
was demonstrated in its rejection of two major English bills. One
was designed to translate the reactionary English act of 1540
upholding clerical celibacy. When the king wrote to enquire what
had become of it, he was told, with staggering audacity,
considering the personage addressed, that it was unsuitable for Irish
conditions, and that for the next session of parliament the Irish
executive would themselves devise a bill 'penned in such a sort,
as we think shall be reasonable, and possible to be performed'. The
other measure was intended to repeal an act of the parliament of
1536–7 which provided a statutory guarantee for leases granted

in the redistribution of confiscated lands. The suspension of
Poynings' Law in 1536–7 had been exploited in order to avoid
referring the bill to England for prior authority, though at the time
it had the approval of the royal commissioners, headed by St
Leger. The king now suspected malpractice and wanted the act
repealed so as to enable the leases granted at the time to be
reinvestigated. The lord deputy took a contrary view, fearing to
upset the vested interests, and also feeling that such a move would
seriously undermine the trustworthiness of the seals and statute.
Part of the interest of the episode is to note that his view eventually
prevailed. Part of it also is to note the way in which he cited
Poynings' Law to reject the authority of the English executive to
transmit bills directly for presentation in the Irish parliament, and
to uphold the function of the Irish executive as the initiator of
legislation for parliament in Ireland.[56]

Meanwhile the internal reform of government, again in contrast
to the Cromwellian period, had the effect of firmly establishing
the function of the Dublin executive, as a central administration.
A resident bureaucratic council with permanent headquarters in
Dublin was established to supervise the day-to-day working of
government.[57] The Irish executive received a further boost
through the reconstitution of chancery's equity jurisdiction. The
emphasis of the liberal programme on the creation of social
stability through the administration of justice is reflected in other
projects to revitalise the Irish judicial system. The central courts,
like the council, were provided with permanent headquarters. An
Inn of Court was established for the study of the law. The task
of preparing the Irish statutes for publication was undertaken.[58]

All of this did much to reaffirm the status of the Irish
administration as the executive of a sovereign crown government
in Ireland. Here also, the act for the kingship had exercised a major
influence in providing the programme of reform with a
constitutional concept and constitutional underpinning. As a result
the Irish executive could claim the status of the government of
a sovereign community.

---

[56] *S.P. Henry VII*, iii, pp. 394, 406, 428, 433, 442. See my 'The beginnings of modern
Ireland' in B. Farrell (ed.), *The Irish parliamentary tradition* (Dublin 1973), pp. 75–8.
[57] *S.P. Henry VIII*, iii, pp. 412, 465, 489, 580. *Cal. pat. rolls Ire., Henry VIII*, p. 132.
[58] *S.P. Henry VIII*, iii, pp. 385, 394, 398, 412, 416, 463. *Cal. pat. rolls Ire., Henry VIII*,
p. 132.

Parallel with these developments, the central administration was beginning to assume active responsibility for the government of the localities and to have its function in that respect recognised. The *Annals of the Four Masters* recognise an altogether new departure when they record under the year 1543 the resort of Manus O'Donnell to the Great Council in Dublin for the settlement of the internal disputes of the sept. No less remarkable, they record his submission to the judgement given on that occasion even though it entailed the release of rival members of the sept whom he had held in prison since an abortive coup in 1539.[59] The following year O'Neill is found writing to the king about the insubordination of his underlords and the provocation of O'Donnell's allies, all of whom, he declared, were taking advantage of the fact that he was now a subject of the crown and was debarred from using force against them.[60] The importance of such evidence is not that it proves either lord to have become a paragon of civil virtue but that it indicates the early stages of a process of adaptation to a new system of government. The central administration now seeks to regulate the conduct of local lords not only in relation to the traditionally loyal community, but in relation to their local peers and their subordinates. From Cork and Kerry in the remote southwest, where a modified judicial council was established, to Tyrone in the northeast, where an elaborate legal framework of indentures was devised to regulate relationship within the lordship, crown government had begun to assert sovereign jurisdiction.

At the same time local lords were being brought to participate in government at the centre. In a letter to Henry VIII in May 1545, St Leger refers to the presence of O'Neill in Dublin 'for the affairs of the realm'.[61] An unprecedented development lies behind the casual remark. This was only partly that the lord deputy should take counsel with a Gaelic magnate about the affairs of the realm. O'Neill's resort to Dublin for the purpose represents a notable achievement in itself. For the first time the magnates of the hitherto disobedient lordships, Desmond, O'Brien, McWilliam, O'Neill, O'Donnell, were prepared to enter the precincts of royal towns, and to do so regularly, in pursuit of their own business and

---

[59] *A.F.M.*, v, pp. 1478–9.
[60] *S.P. Henry VIII*, iii, p. 494. *L.P.*, xix(i), nos. 79, 452.
[61] *S.P. Henry VIII*, iii, p. 517.

the affairs of the realm.[62] To facilitate their visits to Dublin, the Irish council obtained approval for a scheme to provide each of the great lords with a property in the vicinity of the city on the occasion of the grant of title and tenure to him by patent.[63]

This practice of government has to be seen in association with the process examined earlier whereby the institutions of government underwent adaptation to facilitate, on the one hand, the unilateral jurisdiction of the crown throughout the island and, on the other, the participation of all the politically significant elements of the island's community in crown government. Both practice and institutional adaptation were complementary aspects of the same process, by which the commonwealth liberals set out to mould the island for the first time into a cohesive political unit. Others were to complete the task, but according to a very different model. The Elizabethan conquerors made all things new. The Henrician liberals essayed a more delicate operation, to transform what was already there by changing the infrastructure while leaving the superstructure intact.

Reform and Reaction

The historical uniqueness of the 1540s as an episode in the history of crown government in Ireland lies not only in the kind of constitutional and institutional engineering that took place but in the response which the process elicited. The implementation of surrender and regrant, and the complementary project for extending the unilateral jurisdiction of crown government throughout the island, represented an unprecedented interference in the internal affairs of the great lordships. Extraordinarily, in the light of what happened in the 1530s and what was to follow for the rest of the century, this process went hand in hand with an unprecedented softening of attitudes towards the crown and its government.

The trips of the magnates to court and their recourse to parliament and to the council at Dublin are symptomatic of the erosion of the old hostility and suspicion. However, the best proof

---

[62] On the evidence of Sir John Alen in 1546 – one of St Leger's severest critics – O'Neill was now resorting to Dublin at least once a year, S.P. 60/11, no. 53, fo. 147.

[63] The sites and demesnes of dissolved religious communities proved useful for the purpose: see my *Dissolution of the religious orders*, p. 190.

of the new attitude is provided by the reaction to the external crisis of 1543–6. The attitude of the hitherto disobedient magnates in this period provides a remarkable contrast with the diplomacy which they had practised throughout the earlier part of the century. From the time when continuous documentation begins, early in the 1520s, Desmond and O'Brien in the south and O'Neill and O'Donnell in the north are seen to be engaged in attempts to involve the emperor or the kings of Scotland and France in Irish affairs. In the 1530s the papacy became an additional focus for dissident diplomacy in consequence of the repudiation of papal supremacy. Diplomatic activity reached a new level of intensity in the period 1538–40 in connection with the Geraldine League.

In 1543–6, in contrast, no attempt was made to exploit a situation that was diplomatically more favourable than ever before. England was at war simultaneously with Scotland and France. Gerald Fitzgerald on the continent provided a way into the highest echelons of European politics, and the English army had scarcely crossed the French frontiers before Irish ports were buzzing with rumours of French schemes to send him to Ireland at the head of an invading force.[64] At the same time the Scottish king was said to be preparing to unleash his unruly islanders upon the Ulster coast.[65]

So far as the European powers were concerned, it should be said, there is no evidence that Ireland was taken more seriously than it ever had been. The real objective of their diplomacy continued to be to exploit dissident elements within the country, not to hazard a full-scale invasion. The difference on this occasion was that the magnates of the Irishry did not rise to the bait. On the contrary, O'Neill and O'Donnell in Ulster kept Dublin informed of the overtures made to them from Scotland.[66] Furthermore, a call to the great lords to provide troops for service against the king's enemies met with such a whole-hearted response as to be an embarrassment to a government that had more recruits on its hands than were required.[67]

A further indication of the development of new attitudes of good will and cooperation is provided by the Great Council

---

[64] *S.P. Henry VIII*, iii, pp. 501, 504.
[65] *S.P. Henry VIII*, iii, pp. 506, 512, 515, 517.
[66] *S.P. Henry VIII*, iii, pp. 506, 515, 517.
[67] See my *Dissolution of the religious orders*, pp. 213–14.

convened at Dublin by St Leger in the spring of 1546, on the occasion of his recall to England to face charges against his administration by the Ormond faction, aided and abetted by John Alen. The purpose of the Council was to ensure political stability during the lord deputy's absence. Cusack was able to point to the response it produced as a vindication of the liberal programme. Thither came Desmond, Thomond and Tyrone, and the leaders of the septs of Leinster, so that, as Cusack declared, 'those which would not be brought under subjection with 10 thousand men, cometh to Dublin with a letter'. From their own lips the hitherto disobedient Irishry attributed their conversion to the liberal programme, 'ascribing, that if such truth and gentleness had been showed to them by the governors and rulers that were before his [St Leger's] time they had been reformed as well then as now'.[68]

Thus, in response to the conciliatory initiative a new attitude of solidarity began to develop between the crown and the Irishry. It was a tender plant, destined to be shrivelled in the bud by the hard frost of radicalism.

[68] *S.P. Henry VII*, iii, pp. 562, 563.

9

The origins of Irish political nationalism

The abandonment of conciliation

Tragically, the days of 'truth and gentleness' were numbered. St Leger succeeded in vindicating his policy in England and returned to Ireland at the end of 1546 to revitalise the programme which had been forced into passivity by external pressures at the end of 1543.[1] However, while the battle for conciliation was being won in England, the war was being lost in Ireland. In St Leger's absence William Brabazon assumed control of the administration and, in conformity with his extreme radical proclivities, proceeded to blast the fragile shoots that had come forth in the spring of the liberal initiative. St Leger returned to find O'Connor and O'More in open war, goaded by the provocation of Brabazon.[2] The relationship of cooperation and trust between government and local leaders, so patiently built up over the previous six years, had been sabotaged.

St Leger might have saved the situation as he had done twice before, in 1540, and again in 1544 when a similar though less serious situation had developed in his absence. But the fate of the liberal initiative was sealed by the death of Henry VIII at the end of January 1547, within a month of the lord deputy's return. This study has devoted some space to demonstrating that the commonwealth liberalism of the 1540s was significantly different from the royal liberalism of the 1520s, and that Henry VIII

---

[1] *S.P. Henry VIII*, i, p. 851, 876, iii, p. 580. *L.P.*, xxi (ii), nos. 19, 35, 122, 155, 212, 365, 476(11)(43). *Cal. pat. rolls Ire.*, *Henry VIII*, p. 132.

[2] This is not the place to undertake the analysis of that tortuous episode, though such an analysis would serve to strengthen the suggestion of deliberate provocation put forward by D. G. White in 'Edward VI's Irish policy' *I.H.S.*, xiv(1964–5), pp. 198–9.

accepted the later policy with considerable reluctance. Yet when it came to the point he was amenable. Despite the tantrums and the rantings St Leger never quite lost the king's confidence or his support. It was to be altogether different during his intermittent periods as lord deputy in the reigns of Edward VI and Mary.

The immediate effect of the king's death was to change the new administration which had been devised to inaugurate the second spring of the liberal policy into a caretaker administration during the period of transition. In June, Sir Edward Bellingham was sent to take charge of military operations and to advise the lord deputy on policy generally. From then until the beginning of 1548, when Bellingham took over completely, St Leger was hamstrung. The new lord deputy, a stiff, unbending protestant, approaching Irish politics as a soldier, completed from the best of intentions the work which Brabazon began from the worst. Under him the crown set out on a course that was to lead to a thoroughly radical policy by launching the project for garrisoning and colonising Offaly.[3] In the sphere of religion also, the administration of Bellingham set crown policy on the path of radicalism. St Leger had actively promoted the royal ecclesiastical supremacy, confident – rightly so, as the response showed – that general acquiescence to the jurisdictional principle could be secured. However, he was not disposed to interfere directly with traditional religious forms. The liberal strategy for reform in this sphere, as we saw, was one of gentle attrition, aimed at enabling the Church in Ireland to outgrow what reformers regarded as its legacy of medieval formalism and superstition by providing better religious instruction and by fostering education generally. For this humanist milk Bellingham substituted the strong meat of protestant preaching and liturgical innovation, a diet that was to become coarser still with the change of regime in England at the end of 1549 and Warwick's headlong rush towards protestantism.[4]

The instability of the Dublin administration in the mid-Tudor period, and the vacillation and uncertainty that characterised the conduct of Irish government during that time, reflected the instability of government in England at the same time. St Leger

---

[3] White, cit. Canny, *The Elizabethan conquest of Ireland*, pp. 34–5. Cf. Davies, *A discovery of the true causes*, pp. 69–70.

[4] See my 'The Edwardian Reformation in Ireland', *Archivium Hibernicum*, xxiv (1976–7), pp. 83–99.

was sent back briefly to replace Bellingham in 1550. It turned out to be another caretaker administration to bridge the transition between the protectorate of Somerset and the all-but-kingship of Warwick. The latter sent a supporter of his own, Sir James Croft, to replace St Leger in 1551. On the death of Edward VI, St Leger had a final fling in the early years of Mary's reign, until he gave way finally to Lord Fitzwalter, soon to become earl of Sussex. In the course of his two later administrations St Leger tried to revitalise his conciliatory initiative. But the time was too short, too much of it had to be spent in undoing the damage of his immediate predecessors, and he had powerful enemies working against him in England. All of this vitiated the effectiveness of his efforts. His recall in 1556 marks the end of the crown's flirtation with liberalism as an Irish policy. Sir Thomas Cusack struggled manfully into the 1560s, but liberalism was never again sponsored by the head of an Irish administration. The modified radicalism of the earl of Sussex in 1556 paved the way for the emergence of the classic strategy of conquest and colonisation under Henry Sidney a decade later.[5]

The entry on Sir Anthony St Leger in the *Dictionary of National Biography* concludes by remarking that he was 'the only deputy out of a long succession who appreciated fully the good and bad points of Irish character'. The author was Robert Dunlop, one of the ablest historians to concern himself with the history of crown government in Ireland in the sixteenth and seventeenth centuries. Dunlop's observation was intended as a reflection on St Leger's approach to Irish politics, not on his social attitudes, and Dunlop spoke as an authority on Anglo-Irish relations throughout the entire early modern period. His observation implies, therefore, a devastating judgement upon the long line of St Leger's successors, upon the policies they pursued, and upon the governments in England that appointed them. Dunlop sought to avoid such an inference by placing the blame for the failure of the conciliatory initiative upon the lords of the Irishry and upon the Gaelic political system. The irresponsibility of the former and the tenacity of the latter frustrated the attempt at peaceful assimilation and forced the crown to apply another solution.[6]

---

[5] Canny, *The Elizabethan conquest*, pp. 45–65. White, cit, pp. 197–211.

[6] Dunlop, 'Some aspects of Henry VIII's Irish policy', pp. 301–5. Cf. Idem, 'Ireland to the settlement of Ulster' in *Cambridge Modern History*, iii (Cambridge 1905), pp. 584–5, 587.

In the light of the examination undertaken here of the response to the liberal initiative among the Irishry in the early 1540s, Dunlop's remarks about their lack of political adaptability and maturity seem rather glib.[7] Again, had he paid more attention to the circumstances in which the initiative ground to a halt after 1543, and in which crown policy took a new direction under Edward VI and Mary, he could not have failed to be impressed by the strength of the pressures working against conciliation within crown government itself. Sadly, as the foregoing review indicates, one major factor here was constituted by greed and a developing colonial ideology, especially among the new English element in Ireland. Sir William Brabazon provides the prototype of a species of minor demon whose influence on the course of Irish history was to be altogether more baneful than the major demons whom the historiography presents for our execration.[8] More excusable, perhaps, was the ineptitude and muddle-headedness of the English administrations under Edward VI and Mary. The fumbling attempts to secure the western borders of the Pale which led eventually to the colonisation of Laois and Offaly was the fatal blunder of the mid-Tudor period. Not only did it alienate permanently the expropriated border septs, the powerful O'Connors and O'Mores, but it also confirmed the worst suspicions about the crown's designs among the Irishry as a whole.[9] Thus the move designed to secure the breach resulted in releasing the flood. The radicalisation of the religious policy under Edward VI was another factor that worked powerfully against the conciliatory initiative. St Leger clearly understood the potential of a radical religious programme for heightening tension between the crown and the Gaelic and Anglo-Irish communities alike. His importunate protests to the English council were unavailing, and the tragi-comedy of John Bale's career as protestant evangelist and bishop of Ossory in 1552–3 nicely illustrates the consequences.[10] Lastly, there was the pressure of the crown's financial exigencies. So straitened were the circumstances of the crown from the 1540s onwards that even the comparatively light cost of the liberal programme tended to be regarded in London as an insupportable

---

[7] Above, pp. 222–30, 255–7.

[8] For examples of such people in the Elizabethan period, see Canny, *The Elizabethan conquest*, pp. 118–22.

[9] White, 'Edward VI's Irish policy', passim.

[10] My 'The Edwardian Reformation in Ireland'.

burden. Under Henry VIII funds were withheld in respect of
crucial aspects of the programme, such as the regional
presidencies.[11] Under Edward VI attempts were made to revive
a Pale system as a cheaper alternative.[12] Understandable though
this may be, it proved to be a case of penny wise and pound foolish,
since the recall of St Leger was invariably the signal for a
deterioration of the political situation in Ireland and the consequent
escalation of military expenditure.[13]

The result of all of this – of the vacillation between conciliation
and peremptory government, of the tampering with religion, and
especially of the programme of expropriation and colonisation in
Laois and Offfaly – was to erode the credibility of crown government among the Irishry to the extent that, as the second half
of the century ran its course, the prospects for a successful revival
of the liberal initiative became increasingly remote. The logic of
this situation impressed itself with varying degrees of clarity on
a succession of lord deputies and influential observers in Ireland
and in England in the reign of Elizabeth, increasing the receptiveness of government to a radical approach in dealing with the
Irish problem. Probably, as Canny argues, the die was already cast
by the mid-1570s, the Desmond rebellion of the early 1580s being
the symptom rather than the cause of the crown's commitment

---

[11] Above, p. 243.

[12] White, cit. Canny, *The Elizabethan conquest*, pp. 34–5.

[13] A table of government expenditure in Ireland for the period 1541–56 shows that the
cost of the military establishment in St Leger's initial administration hovered around
£8,000 annually, apart from 1545 when troops for the Scottish campaign added some
£5,000. In 1547, when Bellingham was sent as lord marshal, military expenditure rose
to £12,877 1s. 10d. When he took over as lord deputy the following year, the cost
escalated to £18,450 3s 11d., to which some £6,000 was added in 1549 for the building
of fortifications. The bill came down to £18,080 14s. 10d. when St Leger returned
in 1550–1 but again shot up, this time to the region of £40,000, when he was displaced
by Sir James Croft. In St Leger's final term of office under Queen Mary, military
expenditure stood around £35,000, until a drastic overhaul of the system by an English
commission reduced the bill to £16,061 5s. 9d. in 1555–6. However, it proved
impossible to keep costs at this level. In 1560–1 the military establishment cost £21,741
19s. 9½d., and Lord Deputy Sussex was estimating his needs at the same time as £2,875
per month. (For the table of government expenditure, 1541–56, see B.L., Add. MS
4767, fo. 125. For military expenditure in 2 Eliz. see cit., fos. 116–17. For Sussex's own
estimate of his military needs see S.P. 63/1, no. 5.) The same point is made in a different
form by the contemporary who complained that the government of Ireland required
no more than a garrison of 500 under Henry VIII and 800 or 900 under Edward VI
and Mary, but that by the opening year of Elizabeth's reign it stood at 2,160, B.L.,
Add. MS 4767.

to the radical formula in accordance with which the Elizabethan 'settlement' in Ireland was finally achieved.[14]

It cannot be said with certainty that the conciliatory formula would have solved the Irish problem had the momentum of the liberal initiative been sustained beyond the early 1540s. On the other hand, history continues to demonstrate, lamentably, that the radical alternative was no solution at all.

The liberal legacy

The liberal enterprise proved to be a transient episode in the history of crown policy in Ireland. In its conception, in its strategy, and in its programme, it could not have been more remote from the final crown settlement, the colonial state of the eighteenth century, spawned by Sir Henry Sidney's radical solution in the 1570s. Nevertheless, the events of the 1540s had lasting consequences for the course of Irish history. That it took the radical solution to the end of the seventeenth century to reach finalisation draws attention to the long-term significance of the liberal legacy.

The constitutional legacy – the kingdom

The act for the assumption of the kingly title in 1541 has already been set in its immediate context. It was directed towards the reconstitution of the island as a political entity in accordance with the requirements of the liberal programme. The intention was to provide a national frame for the assimilation of the dynastic lordships by making explicit the sovereign status of the crown in Ireland. However, in that process a fundamental constitutional change was effected which had political consequences long after crown government ceased to have any use for the formula of surrender and regrant.

The nature of the change thus effected draws attention once more to the different implications which the act contained for its two subjects, the English king and the Irish Lordship. The king insisted that the act added nothing to his sovereignty. However, as we have seen, it altered the nature of political relationships within the island, as well as augmenting the claim which the island could make upon the king. Similarly, at the most fundamental

---

[14] See Canny, *The Elizbethan conquest*, passim.

constitutional level, if the act did not alter the constitutional status of the king, it did alter the constitutional status of the island.

In this respect it is instructive to note the reaction in England to the enactment. Everything goes to show that it was regarded, more or less, as a non-event. The only evidence of reaction on Henry VIII's part was one of dissatisfaction. The phraseology of the act seemed to imply that parliament had conferred the kingly title upon him, instead of proclaiming what was his by rightful inheritance. At his insistence the statute was reframed to take the form of a petition from parliament requesting him to add to his style his just title of king of Ireland. In this form the statute was reenacted in the second session of parliament at Limerick in the spring of 1542. To emphasise the point, the change of style was announced by royal proclamation in England before the redrafted act was passed in Ireland.[15]

Apart from this the only evidence of the effect produced by the event within government circles in England relates to necessary administrative formalities. The impression is that it was treated as a matter of routine administration, the revision of a statutory formula with consequent adjustment of legal instruments. This impression is strengthened by references to the event in diplomatic dispatches. Not a cheer was raised at court, it seems. Had any special celebrations marked the occasion, they must have been noted by Chapuys when he mentioned the event in a dispatch to the emperor in mid-July 1541. However, Chapuys treated the episode in a very casual fashion: to him it was remarkable only for the fact that it caused an interruption in public business when the official seals were withdrawn for alteration. Indeed, he prefaced his allusion to the matter with a remark that he had no news of importance to report. Marillac, the French ambassador, used the same tones the following spring in reporting the second episode caused by the king's insistence on repeating the whole process.[16]

---

[15] The published statutes contain the first version of the act, passed in Dublin in June 1541, *Statutes at large, Ireland,* i, pp. 176–7. Although the original is now lost, it was collated with the published act in the nineteenth century and no discrepancies were noted. The original in question must have been that of the first version, since it contained the subscription of O'Brien's proctors, who attended the first session of parliament, Quinn (ed.), 'Bills and statutes of Henry VII and Henry VIII', p. 164. The revised version does not survive either, but its form is suggested by the royal proclamation issued from Westminster in January 1542. P. M. Hughes and J. F. Larkin (eds.), *Tudor royal proclamations* (New Haven 1964), i, pp. 307–8.

[16] *Calendar of state papers, Spanish,* vi, no. 173. *L.P.,* xvi, no. 1005, xvii, nos. 71(22), 84.

The manner in which the event was marked in Dublin is in striking contrast. A public holiday was proclaimed, and a general pardon for prisoners. The act was promulgated in St Patrick's Cathedral after a solemn procession thither of the members of government and those assembled for parliament. A congregation of two thousand crowded in for the high mass and the intoning of the *Te Deum*. Many more, one may be sure, participated in the secular festivities. There were cannonades and bonfires, free wine dispensed in the streets and feasting in houses.[17]

The contrast in reactions to the act underlines its different implications for its joint subjects. Henry VIII and his courtiers saw no reason for celebration since the act served little for the king's enhancement. What he was he remained: king. And the act itself insisted that the replacement of the archaic form of 'lord of Ireland' in his style by that of 'king' did not make him any more of a king than he already was. Where the act effected a real change was in the status of the island. Ireland became a kingdom. In the act for the kingly title the designation 'this realm of Ireland' was used for the first time to replace the designation used hitherto of 'land of Ireland'. Henceforth, in statute and in official correspondence, Ireland was referred to as a realm.[18] This was not, as in the alteration of the king's style, a mere playing with words. Whatever had been its constitutional status as a Lordship, Ireland was now a sovereign kingdom. The change had permanent consequences for the constitutional structure of the island, internally and externally, which ensured that the liberal programme of the 1540s exercised a continuing political influence, despite the abandonment of the policy officially.

The internal constitutional change was pointed out, and its political consequences hinted at, by the antiquarian Sir James Ware early in the seventeenth century. He noted that as a result of the act for the kingly title in 1541 the appellation 'Irish enemy', the generic term regularly applied to the Irishry in the medieval

[17] *S.P. Henry VIII*, iii, p. 304. *L.P.*, xvi, nos. 912, 926. *Cal. Car. MSS*, i, no. 158.

[18] The change of designation was not rigorously observed in the legislation of the parliament of 1541. Most of the bills had been drafted before parliament opened. In any case, the form of the new royal style was not determined until the royal proclamation in January 1542, and was not enjoined for use for official purposes until the following July. In some of the acts passed by the parliament at the later sessions, the designation in the original bill was altered from 'land' to 'realm', Quinn (ed.), 'Bills and statutes of Henry VII and Henry VIII', p. 162. By the next parliament, that of Philip and Mary in 1557, the custom of referring to Ireland as a 'kingdom' was invariable.

statutes, was deprived of constitutional validity, and was dropped from statutory terminology thenceforward.[19] The same constitutional change resulting from the act of 1541 was reflected in the statutes in another way also. Their exclusive formulation – the device which had ensured, ever since the fourteenth century, that statutes applied to the Englishry only – was abandoned. From 1541 onwards, parliament was to legislate for the Irishry as well as for the Englishry.[20] The significance of all of this is that the constitutional arrangement codified in the statutes of Kilkenny in 1366 was now superseded. The legal distinction between loyal subjects and Irish enemies, and the partition of the island (in effect) into two jurisdictional entities which the distinction assumed, were incompatible with the new status of Ireland as a kingdom. The implication of that transformation was that the Gaelic Irish came within the law.

The long-term political significance of the internal constitutional change was that it provided a legal means of thwarting the purveyors of conquest and colonisation. Irish rebels there might still be, if by their own acts they made themselves so, but the whole population of the Irishry could no longer be consigned, *ipso facto*, to a state of enmity with the crown. On the contrary, as members of the kingdom they could claim the protection and privileges of subjects under the law. At the same time some of the most powerful members of the Gaelic nobility had been provided with sound legal tenure through surrender and regrant. Thus, the radical policy had been substantially preempted, though not permanently frustrated; and Edmund Spenser, at the end of the century, turning his mind from poesy to politics, bemoaned the work of the 1540s as the great impediment to the advance of the radical programme.[21]

In the external sphere, the definition of Ireland's status as a kingdom provided a constitutional bulwark against the onslaughts of unionism. The assertion of the superior jurisdiction of English institutions of government over their Irish counterparts could be

[19] W. Harris (ed.), *Ware's works* (Dublin 1764), ii, p. 88. As in the change of designation from 'land' to 'realm', the statutes of the parliament of 1541 did not observe the change consistently.

[20] In this respect also the change was not consistently observed until the Marian parliament of 1557.

[21] Edmund Spenser, *View of the present state of Ireland*, ed. W. L. Renwick (London 1934), pp. 9–10, 23.

and was repudiated on the basis of Ireland's sovereign status. More generally, also, it provided the Anglo-Irish separatist tradition with constitutional underpinning. A succession of able Anglo-Irish lawyers were able to exploit its possibilities in the agitation against the continuing presence of the English garrison, as well as against the Anglicisation of Irish government, pursued steadily from 1557 onwards. Constitutional arguments, of course, were ultimately no match for the political and military power of a determined government. Nevertheless, the jurisdictional union envisaged by Thomas Cromwell took over two and a half centuries to be fully accomplished, when the colonial parliament of 1801 surrendered the sovereign constitution of the island that had been proclaimed by the Anglo-Irish parliament of 1541.

The long-term effect of the definition of Ireland's status as a kingdom remains to be considered in its most important aspect. This was in providing a constitutional principle on which to base an ideology of Irish nationalism. Before examining the emergence of that phenomenon, however, it is first necessary to consider another part of the liberal legacy that contributed to the nationalist ideology – the liberal concept of the commonwealth.

The political legacy – commonwealth liberalism
The legacy of the 1540s consisted not only in the changed constitutional status of the island, but in the concept of political reform which it bequeathed to the Anglo-Irish reform movement. This gave the movement a new aspiration and a new programme.

As we have seen, the humanist aspiration towards the betterment of society, centring on the notion of the commonwealth, gave rise within the Anglo-Irish reform milieu to the concept of a general reformation, a scheme of political and social reform that would embrace not only the colonial community but the community of the Irishry also. It was in pursuit of this objective that the idea of a new conquest, whereby crown government might exercise unilateral jurisdiction throughout the island, came to be mooted within the Anglo-Irish movement of political reform as early as the second decade of the sixteenth century.[22] What distinguished the programme of general reform of the 1540s from earlier proposals was that it employed a liberal rather than a radical

---

[22] Above, pp. 49–57.

formula. Where the programmes urged unsuccessfully upon
Cromwell in the 1530s proposed conquest as the means of
achieving the crown's unilateral jurisdiction, and colonisation (or
at least military rule) as the method of implementing reform, the
programme of the 1540s set out to achieve unilateral jurisdiction
by conciliation, and reform by persuasion and cooperation. Thus
the humanist concept of the commonwealth with its strong social
orientations, gave rise in Ireland to a new political aspiration and
a new political programme. The aspiration was towards the
unification of the island's distinct politico-cultural groups into a
cohesive national community under the unilateral jurisdiction of
the crown. The programme was designed to achieve this effect by
changing the political infrastructure of the island while leaving its
political superstructure intact.

   Although the crown turned aside from the path of conciliation
irrevocably in the Elizabethan period, the political aspiration
thrown up by the work of the 1540s continued to exercise a
dominant influence on Irish politics to the end of the seventeenth
century, and indeed in a transmuted form continues to do so.
The aspirations of commonwealth liberalism came to dominate
the mainstream Anglo-Irish movement of political reform. The
commonwealth liberal lobby of the 1540s generated the commonwealth group which emerged as the main source of opposition to Lord Deputy Sidney in the parliament of 1569–71 and
continued thereafter as the focus of constitutional resistance to the
crown's radicalism. To trace the influence of commonwealth
liberalism on the politics of the Elizabethan period is beyond the
scope of the present study. Here it is proposed to focus attention
on its role at the period of the watershed, when radicalism became
finally entrenched in government under Lord Deputy Sussex, and
when the ideology of nationalism first made its appearance within
the Anglo-Irish movement of political reform. This will be done,
in the first instance, by examining the responses to Sussex's policy
of two major figures of Anglo-Irish politics who had been closely
associated with the liberal enterprise: George Dowdall, archbishop
of Armagh and primate of Ireland, and James Fitzjohn, earl of
Desmond.

   Although the critical episode in Dowdall's case comes later than
that of Desmond, it is best treated first, because it provides a
convenient means of sketching in the background to the period

as a whole. It is necessary to consider the episode at some length because it has led to a very serious misunderstanding of the political significance of the advent of Sussex as head of the Irish administration, and of Dowdall's views on Irish policy, as a representative figure of the Pale political establishment. The primate has been presented as the advocate of 'a "Spanish" policy' of conquest and colonisation, and Sussex as an opponent of 'a harsh unyielding policy towards the Irish'.[23] In fact, their roles were exactly reversed.

The clash between the lord deputy and the primate centres on a number of submissions on the subject of Irish policy which the latter presented to the privy council in England in the summer of 1558.[24] In order to interpret these documents correctly it is necessary to appreciate the circumstances which threw them up. They were written at a time of great personal crisis and demoralisation for the archbishop, within weeks of his death, which may very well have been hastened by events. Dowdall had gone into exile under Edward VI in protest against the liturgical innovations. He was restored under Mary and returned to Ireland in triumph to inaugurate the Counter-Reformation. However, he went back to a bleak political situation. The O'Connors and the O'Mores were in revolt, and there was an alarming influx of Scottish colonists to the north. Dowdall's return coincided with the termination of yet another brief caretaker administration led by St Leger, and his replacement by Sussex bent on radical reform.[25]

Sussex's policy was one of moderate radicalism. He envisaged a plantation of Laois and Offaly, the territories of O'Connor and O'More, on the western borders of the Pale, and of areas of Ulster also. The rest of the country was to be held down by a network of English garrisons and brought to conform to English government. To this task he applied himself and his army with determination. His activities provoked a storm of resentment from Anglo-Irish and Gaelic Irish alike.[26]

In the period between 1556 and 1558, Dowdall became a focus of opposition to the new lord deputy's policy. In his view the

---

[23] Quinn, 'Ireland and sixteenth century European expansion', p. 26.
[24] Two have survived in contemporary copies, both of which were based on an earlier submission which is lost. S.P. 62/2, no. 44; T.C.D., MS 842, fos. 75–82. Another copy of the latter is in B.L., Harleian MS 35, fos. 195ff.
[25] S.P. 62/1, no. 10. B.L., Add. MS 4763, fo. 109.
[26] S.P. 62/1, nos. 22, 22(11)(24)(31).

situation was quickly deteriorating to the chaos of 1539–40, with
the English army on the rampage inside the Pale, and the Irishry
organising themselves to descend upon it from without. Meanwhile, attempts to check the lord deputy in the council succeeded
only in inflaming Sussex's fury and confirming his suspicion that
the archbishop was a collaborator with the enemy. Acting on
information about Dowdall's conciliatory contacts with the northern leaders made through the Gaelic dean of his cathedral at
Armagh, Sussex sent his troops to ransack the cathedral and the
churches in the town in search of incriminating evidence.
Dowdall's letters of protest to Cardinal Pole and the English
chancellor produced a summons to present his case before the
privy council.[27]

When Dowdall presented himself before the council in 1558,
circumstances could hardly have been less favourable to him.
Sussex had preceded him to London, where he succeeded in
vindicating his policy in Ireland against the criticisms of St Leger.
His backers were in the ascendant on the council, and when
Dowdall submitted his own lengthy statement against Sussex's
administration it was passed on to the lord deputy informally for
his comments. He got his brother-in-law and close collaborator
in Dublin, Sir Henry Sidney, to provide a detailed refutation, and
to bully a large representative group of councillors into putting
their signatures to it. Sussex returned this to the privy council with
a demand to be relieved of his Irish appointment if Dowdall was
not made an example of to opponents of his regime.[28] The
archbishop was further compromised by the fact that England was
once more at war with France and Scotland and, in contrast to
the 1540s, Gaelic dynasts were once more showing a keen interest
in attracting the support of European allies against the crown.[29]

This background is crucial in interpreting the line taken by
Dowdall before the privy council in the summer of 1558. His
tactics were dictated by the realisation that his adversary enjoyed
great personal support in the privy council, while his own loyalty
was in doubt, and the policy of conciliation for which he stood
was discredited and out of favour. The problem was how to get
a hearing for a denunciation of Sussex's hard-line policy against

27 S.P. 62/1, no. 61.   28 S.P. 62/2, nos. 32, 32(i).
29 S.P. 62/2, no. 10.

a background of Gaelic rebellion and foreign intrigue, as well as of suspicion of himself as a Gaelic fellow-traveller.

Bearing these circumstances in mind, the point of his opening gambit – the source of much confusion about his attitude – can be appreciated. The papers he presented to the privy council began by abhorring Gaelic disloyalty and by conceding that the ideal crown policy for Ireland would be one of conquest and colonisation. By this he hoped to establish his credentials, and to demonstrate the distinction between his political stance as an Anglo-Irishman and that of the Gaelic Irish. It was of obvious importance to Dowdall to play up the distinction, and to emphasise the historic loyalty of the Anglo-Irish community. It is significant, incidentally, that it was necessary for him to do so. The political climate was now such that the distinction between the loyal Anglo-Irish community and the Gaelic 'disobedients' was becoming blurred in England with good reason, as we shall see.

This cleared the way for the second stage of the tactic. Here he adopted an argument already used by St Leger and Cusack, which was now becoming a common ploy of the moderates. Having given theoretical assent to the doctrine of conquest and colonisation in order to establish his political orthodoxy, he went on to rule it out as impractical. In this context he took a stance diametrically opposed to what Sussex stood for, and propounded conciliation as an absolute criterion for government in Ireland. 'Considering that clemency and good discretion is more meet in a governor than rigour or cruelness to rule the lawless and barbarous people of that country, the deputy must behave himself accordingly to win the love and favour of all the country and specially of mere Irish.'[30] Accordingly, the colonisation of Laois and Offaly must be called off and the O'Mores and the O'Connors must be restored to grace, 'for whosoever takes the rule of Ireland in hand he must according the gospel *remittere usque ad septuagies septies*'.[31]

Finally, Dowdall's alternative to Sussex's moderate radicalism has to be considered. It would nicely round off the thesis if he had proposed the restoration of commonwealth liberalism. In fact, he ruled it out also, and proposed instead a return to the conservative policy of Skeffington. The Irishry were to be bound to the crown by the traditional indentures, though by a strategy of conciliation,

---

[30] T.C.D., MS 842, fo. 78.   [31] Ibid., fo. 77.

not one of compulsion. With their cooperation the Scottish intruders could be expelled, the country made secure against foreign intrigues, and the hated English army wound down.

There are two possible explanations for Dowdall's reversion to conservatism. It may have been simply tactical. Dowdall was arguing his case in the aftermath of an unsuccessful bid by St Leger himself to vindicate his policy against Sussex. In those circumstances the archbishop would have been well advised to plump for the classic medieval compromise. On the other hand he may have become genuinely convinced, as a result of the chequered history of the liberal programme, that the Irishry were irreformable because, as he said, 'the pride and ravenous behaviour of their forefathers is so printed in their hearts'. If this was so, it does not seem that his disillusionment was as complete as might appear. His submission to the council ended with an appeal for the foundation of a university and free schools as 'expedient for that whole realm', an indication that he was keeping the needs of general reform in mind. Finally, he continued to back the architect of the liberal policy, for he urged the council to consult St Leger for further advice on the political situation.[32]

The main significance of the episode is that it illustrates the response of a highly influential figure within the Pale to the adoption of a radical policy by the crown. Whatever hesitation he may have had about the feasibility of continuing the commonwealth liberal programme of general reform, he was unambiguously in favour of a policy based on conciliation, and flatly opposed to a forceful solution. Furthermore, the thread of continuity is clear between the response and the policy launched in the 1540s. Finally, the reception accorded Dowdall's attempt to voice widespread local resentment was ominous. Autocratic action by the lord deputy, connived at in England, was to force the majority element in the Anglo-Irish movement for political reform to regard itself increasingly as an opposition, and as an increasingly frustrated one.

The earl of Desmond provides a second case study through which the changing scenario of Irish politics in Mary's reign is exemplified. Desmond's reaction to Surrey's radicalism need not detain us long, since the Dowdall episode has served to fill in the

---

[32] Ibid., fo. 82.

background. However, it has its own special significance. In the first place, it demonstrates more clearly the continuity between the sponsorship of commonwealth liberalism in the 1540s and the emergence of the movement of Anglo-Irish opposition in the 1550s. If Dowdall had second thoughts about the feasibility of the liberal programme, Desmond had none. His long submission to the privy council in 1556 made the ritual protestation of political orthodoxy, by subscribing to the doctrine of conquest and colonisation, and then went on to advocate the greater practicality of the liberal formula. To 'train in' all the Irishry by 'fair means' was the better way, since not only was a conquest a hazardous operation, but the gains would hardly offset the charges of the enterprise.[33]

As well as illustrating the continuity between the officially sponsored liberal movement of the 1540s and the movement of opposition to official policy in the 1550s, Desmond's resistance to Sussex also illustrates a new unity in the emerging movement of Anglo-Irish opposition. It is clear from the common line taken by Dowdall and Desmond that the two were in contact. Not only did they both make the same gesture towards conquest and colonisation, but, more tellingly, each made the same appeal for the dispatch of a royal commission from England to investigate the conduct of Sussex's administration.[34] The forging of such a link between the leading Anglo-Irish nobleman of the day and a major figure of the political milieu of the Pale must be underlined. The reforming element in the Pale which Dowdall represented had traditionally displayed an attitude of hostility towards the great Anglo-Irish dynasts as impeders of the movement of political reform. They had played an important part in the downfall of Kildare in the 1530s. The joint opposition of Dowdall and Desmond in the 1550s reflects the transition taking place in the attitude of the Pale group which was to culminate in their espousal of the demand for the restoration of an Anglo-Irish nobleman as head of the Irish administration. The circumstances in which the transition began need to be underlined also: it was precipitated by common resistance to the radical policy of the English lord deputy towards the Irishry.

---

[33] S.P. 62/2, no. 11. For Desmond's participation in the resistance to Sussex and his defence of the liberal programme, see also S.P. 62/1, nos. 25, 26, 27, S.P. 62/2, nos. 8, 12, 30.   [34] Ibid.

That the resistance of Desmond and Dowdall was representative rather than individual is indicated by the evidence of opposition related to the Marian parliament of 1557–8. Unfortunately, what transpired in the course of the parliament itself is shrouded in a veil of mystery; but the existence of mystery itself gives ground for suspicion. The almost total lack of evidence about the proceedings of Sussex's two parliaments in 1557–8 and 1560 is in pointed contrast to the two preceding Henrician parliaments and to the two subsequent Elizabethan ones. The lacunae can hardly be put down to chance, especially since his administration is generally quite well documented.

In the case of the 1560 parliament, scraps of evidence provide ominous indications of intimidation and of gross abuse of parliamentary management to overcome local resistance.[35] The silence enshrouding the parliament of 1557–8 cannot be penetrated even to that limited extent; but there is plenty of evidence of a movement of resistance before parliament convened at all. Significantly, the class of Pale professional gentry were closely associated with this. The two pieces of legislation against which opposition was directed are also highly significant. One was the act prohibiting marriage and fosterage with the Gaelic Irish. Sussex discovered that the original had been extracted from the records and therefore could not be implemented. The second was the bill for planting Laois and Offaly. The transmiss twice disappeared on reaching Dublin from England, and the circuit had to be made for a third time before it could be presented to parliament.[36] There is one other matter of significance relating to the movement of opposition and the preparatory phase of the Marian parliament. That is the contrast between the kind of parliament projected in an unofficial scheme for reform presented to the English privy council in 1556 and the actuality which transpired. The scheme was formulated from the standpoint of commonwealth liberalism. It envisaged a parliament that would adopt the methods of the St Leger parliament of 1541–3 in order to make it an instrument of national government and of community cohesion. It was to go on circuit, once more, to regional centres – to Limerick for the south, Athlone for the west, and Armagh or Dundalk for the

---

[35] See my 'The beginnings of modern Ireland', pp. 80–1 and note 11.
[36] S.P. 62/1, nos. 29, 38, 46. B.L., Cotton MS Titus B. XI, fos. 413ff.

north. At these various centres, local leaders were to participate in devising a system of government for the region that would be tailored to local conditions and at the same time assimilated to the central administration. In order to create a good atmosphere beforehand, Philip and Mary were to address letters to all the lords of the Irishry, assuring them that they were as highly regarded by their majesties as any other of their subjects.[37] The actuality was a parliament that met briefly in Dublin to enact a programme of legislation legitimising Mary's claim as queen, repealing the Reformation legislation, and confiscating the lands of the Gaelic Irish of Laois and Offaly.

The history of the parliament of 1556–7, therefore, corroborates the evidence discussed earlier. It illustrates the continuity between the movement of commonwealth liberalism 'in government' in the 1540s and the movement of opposition to radicalism in the 1550s. The opposition of the 1550s, in turn, must obviously be seen as the origins of the movement of constitutional protest of the 1560s and the 1570s, and of the commonwealth group which looked for support to the Gaelic Irish, who by 1569 were trickling into parliament as a result of the extension of the shire system.

What remains to be considered is the motivation that inspired the movement of resistance in its initial phase. The vested interests are obvious enough. Sussex's radical policy entailed the continued presence of the English army, and the imposition, therefore, of a social and economic burden that seemed unendurable to the gentry class of the Pale. For Desmond's part, his letters to the queen and the privy council betray his anxiety to assume a role of political preeminence. The presence of a substantial English military force, under the direct control of the lord deputy, cramped his style. All of this is so obvious as hardly to require saying. What the sceptical mind of the academic historian finds more difficult to grasp is that there was an ideological dimension also. If the movement of conciliation towards the Gaelic Irish began in the 1540s from considerations of practical self-interest, by the 1550s it had been subsumed under a new ideology of nationalism.

[37] S.P. 62/1, no. 13.

The ideological sequel – nationalism

The submissions of Archbishop Dowdall and the earl of Desmond to the privy council in 1557–8 exhibit a feature which, while commonplace by then, was exceedingly rare in similar documents twenty years earlier. They were both characterised by an expression of patriotic sentiment. Their concern for political reform, they declared, was promoted by 'natural affection' for their 'native country'. Such a patriotic protestation can be traced in a treatise on Irish reform submitted to Cromwell in the first half of the 1530s, but it is conspicuous for its novelty in this respect in comparison with the vast bulk of similar material emanating from Anglo-Irish sources at the time.[38] It seems significant that the author of the 1530 treatise, though Irish-born and professing devotion to Ireland, was the son of an Englishman and wrote his treatise while resident in England. Just as the concept of the commonwealth gained common currency in Anglo-Irish politics under English influence in the early decades of the century, so in the middle decades England gave the Anglo-Irish the concept of the *patria*, the native country, and in doing so prompted the upsurge of a new kind of political patriotism.[39]

The nature of the new patriotism must be stressed, since it had highly important implications in the Irish context. Hitherto the focus of national sentiment within the Anglo-Irish community was the ethnic group, an orientation which accorded with the

[38] *S.P. Henry VIII*, ii, p. 166 (*L.P.*, vi, no. 1587).

[39] Especially after Hexter's famous broadside against Pollard it was for long scarcely decent to mention the upsurge of national sentiment as a feature of Tudor history. Hexter did not deny its occurrence, nor could he in face of the evidence; but he suggested that Pollard may well have exaggerated its importance, even in England. J. H. Hexter, *Reappraisals in history* (London 1961), pp. 26–44. A. F. Pollard, *Factors in modern history* (3rd edn, London 1932), pp. 13–31. However, recently scholars have come once more to emphasise its importance, e.g. D. M. Loades, *Two Tudor conspiracies* (London 1970); idem, *Politics and the nation*. J. Pocock, 'England' in O. Ranum (ed.), *National consciousness, history and political culture in early modern Europe* (Baltimore and London, 1975), pp. 98–117. A timely reminder of the importance of the theme in the European context was issued by J. H. Elliott, 'Revolution and continuity in early modern Europe', *Past and Present*, no. 42 (1969), pp. 36–56.

It seems significant that the patriotic protestation that occurs at the outset of the treatise mentioned in the preceding note closely resembles in form the patriotic protestation of Edmund Dudley at the beginning of *The tree of commonwealth*, p. 21. For an early English example of the humanist treatment of the patriotic theme, see Sir Thomas Elyot, *The boke named the Governour*, ed. H. H. S. Croft (London, 1880), Bk II, c. 8.

medieval sense of the word 'nation'. It was concerned with the original Anglo-Norman invaders, with the history of the colony and of its community. This kind of community consciousness, as we have seen, found expression in the ideology of Anglo-Irish separatism, in the movement to preserve the political autonomy of the Lordship against encroachments from England. Its influence on Anglo-Irish attitudes towards Gaelic Ireland was complex. The colonists proudly identified with the heritage of the ancient Gaelic civilisation – its golden age of saints and scholars – which provided them with a valuable counter to English cultural arrogance. On the other hand, pride in the historical colonial community produced a strong element of *parti pris* in relations with the existing Gaelic community, although, as we have seen, it did not produce a fixed, ideologically conditioned state of war between the two races. In contrast to this medieval type of ethnic consciousness the treatise submitted to Cromwell in 1533 expresses quite a different form of national sentiment. The author excuses his meddling with the subject of Irish reform by presenting himself as 'coveting the weal of my native country...as I was born there'. The focus of devotion has shifted from ethnic to local origin, from the race to the land, regarded now not merely for its attributes, natural or cultural, but for its innate value as the *patria*, the native land. Furthermore, attaching to the idealisation of the native land was a moral imperative, an obligation of duty and service. Thus Dowdall professed his 'natural affection' to 'poor Ireland'. Devotion to Ireland was decreed by the law of nature to those of Irish birth. It was the assimilation of this newly emerging patriotism by commonwealth liberalism that first produced an ideology of Irish nationalism.

The new patriotic sentiment was not, of course, the special monopoly of advocates of commonwealth liberalism. The treatise just mentioned, dating from the 1530s, urged a programme of reform along moderate radical lines. Even the hard-core radical element within the Anglo-Irish community, represented by Robert Cowley in the 1530s, found no difficulty in making patriotic genuflections in the 1550s in treatises such as that of Edward Walshe, which urged strict racial segregation between Gaelic and Anglo-Irish and extensive colonisation.[40] That this was

[40] Quinn (ed.), 'Edward Walshe's "Conjectures concerning the state of Ireland", pp. 315–22.

the case serves to emphasise the distinction between patriotic sentiment and nationalist ideology – a distinction immediately apparent to anyone acquainted with a cross-section of Scots or Welshmen, or even Ulster protestants. A nationalist ideology emerged within the Anglo-Irish community in the mid sixteenth century when patriotism was adopted as the fundamental justification for a constitutional principle of national sovereignty and a political programme of national unification.

Of all the political programmes thrown up by the drive for political reform in Ireland in the first half of the sixteenth century, commonwealth liberalism was the one which could most fully assimilate the new patriotism. In the first place, there was an obvious correspondence between the affirmation of the island's constitutional sovereignty as a kingdom, which that programme emphasised, and protestation of devotion to it as the native land. More significantly, however, this new concept of the nation could be used to provide an emotionally satisfying justification for the integrative aspirations of commonwealth liberalism, and an antidote to Anglo-Irish group consciousness which acted against them. It responded to the concept of the island's fragmented communities as a unified, coherent national community. At the same time, by shifting the focus of national piety from the race to the *patria* it directed national sentiment towards what the two historic ethnic communities of the island had in common rather than what was unique to each. These, then, were the elements which came together in the formation of the Anglo-Irish nationalist ideology. There was a constitutional concept of national sovereignty which emphasised the island's internal unity and its external autonomy from England, though under the English crown. This was associated with a programme of political and social reform which comprehended the ideal of a national community, and of national solidarity, despite racial diversity. Thirdly, there was a patriotic sentiment to which both constitutional principle and reform programme aptly responded. This was compounded of a positive element, a new attitude of devotion to the native land, and a negative element, an old attitude of resentment towards English overbearance.

It cannot be doubted that Desmond was self-consciously avowing such an ideology when he prefaced his most solemn protest to Queen Mary against Sussex's radical policy with a profession of zeal for the common weal of the Queen's poor realm, his native country. Here the three concepts of commonwealth, kingdom and native land are found in conjunction with a forthright advocacy of the liberal programme.[41] It may, however, be objected that Desmond cannot be taken as a representative figure. The location of the earldom, remote from the heartland of the colony; the political and cultural ambience of the family, for long alienated from the crown and closely identified with the Gaelic tradition: all of this makes it possible to argue that Desmond's political mentality was far removed from the outlook of the Anglo-Irish of the Pale and of the towns. On the other hand, we have just noted the close correspondence between Desmond's reaction to the aggressive government of Lord Deputy Sussex and that of Archbishop Dowdall, a leading political figure in the Pale. Furthermore, Dowdall also gave expression to the new patriotic sentiment in making his protest against Sussex. In fact, the evidence suggests that in the development of this new ideology the Pale continued to be, as it obviously had been since the beginning of the century, the source of creative political thought within the Anglo-Irish community. At least two years before Desmond's letter to Queen Mary, the cross-fertilisation of the three concepts of commonwealth, kingdom and native country is already evident in a lengthy reform treatise emanating from the political milieu of the Pale. Indeed, that particular document can be analysed as a manifesto of the new nationalist ideology.

The author of the treatise is unknown. But internal evidence identifies him as a member of the Pale community resident in London – almost certainly a student at the Inns of Court. He describes a visit made by a group of friends and himself to a certain Mr Aylmer from the Pale, who had come to London on a political mission. His task was to oppose before the privy council the advice urged by Sir John Alen to abandon the programme of general reform and to return to the conservative policy of Skeffington.[42] The result of the meeting was that our author produced his own treatise, opposing Alen's suggestion and presenting a programme

---

[41] S.P. 62/2, no. 11.

[42] These circumstances place the treatise in 1554 or 1555, when the Marian council was engaged in formulating an Irish policy. The treatise survives in an Elizabethan copy in Hatfield, Salisbury MS C.P. 201/116 (*Calendar of the manuscripts of the marquess of Salisbury*, i (London 1883), no. 498).

of political reform of his own. Our interest is not in the programme of political reform as such, but in the ideological frame in which it is set. Two features have a special significance. The work is permeated by the new national patriotism which, according to the author, was fully shared by his companions. It opens with the avowal, familiar from Archbishop Dowdall and Desmond, of love of the native country, and the patriotic theme is constantly repeated throughout the essay. Secondly, and as a corollary, the treatise shows how thoroughly commonwealth liberalism had assimilated the new national patriotism.

The author sets the conciliatory policy of the 1540s against the historical background of the Anglo-Norman invasion of the twelfth century, and presents it as the most significant historical development since that date. This was because the 'politic handling of Sir Anthony Sentleger' had restored the island to a monarchy.[43] However, that achievement had been vitiated. Here another note familiar from Dowdall and Desmond is sounded, the implications of which we have already noted. The breakthrough achieved in the reign of Henry VIII had not been consolidated. Instead, 'a multitude of rash needy soldiers' had been sent to reform a people that for the more parts coveted nothing so much as 'the knowledge of a law'.[44] The greater part of the treatise is taken up with the author's discussion of ways in which the historic breakthrough needed to be consolidated by a further programme of reform. In doing so he reveals how the ideological seeds buried in the liberal programme of the 1540s had come to full flower.

He singled out the two pivotal features of the liberal policy and appealed for the acceptance of their logical implications. The act for the kingly title had given Ireland the status of a sovereign kingdom, yet a whole body of legislation which conflicted with that concept still had statutory force. He was referring to the legal impediments to social intercourse between the Irishry and the Englishry imposed under the statutes of Kilkenny, and reiterated in attempts at political reform ever since. Such prohibitions, he declared, were totally incompatible with the notion of a national community. He listed a whole series of legal impediments that were repugnant to the island's sovereign constitution: the inability

---

[43] Hatfield, Salisbury MS C.P. 201/116, fo. 117v.
[44] Ibid., fo. 118r.

of the Irishry to live in the English area without denization, the strictures against marriage and fosterage, and 'such other number of statutes dividing us asunder as we inhabiting one realm should take ourselves to be, as it were, strangers of several nations'.[45] This 'pestiferous order of creating English and Irish pales' must be swept away, he declares, so that the Gaelic Irish could be reassured that they enjoyed the same security under the law as the Anglo-Irish, and could be guaranteed the same impartial justice.

Similarly, the effectiveness of the other pivot of the liberal programme, surrender and regrant, was vitiated by failure to follow it through. The 'rough hewing' of surrender and regrant had not been followed by the 'plane of severe justice'. The task of reforming the dynastic lordships must be taken in hand with renewed vigour. The author proposed a programme of local reform following the lines of the 1540s. The special interest of his proposals is the way they demonstrate once more how the constitutional principle of sovereignty, and the political programme of commonwealth liberalism, had assimilated the new patriotism. One reflection of this is the author's repudiation of the suggestion of an unbridgeable chasm between the two communities. The Gaelic Irish were reformable and could be integrated within a single polity under the crown by means of the liberal programme. He could vouch success for the enterprise because his first-hand experience of the Gaelic Irish gave him a realisation of their 'sharp wits in politic causes'. In any case two other elements forged a bond between them. One was 'Catholic reverence to the Church of God'. This is the only hint which the treatise provides of the potential of a common repugnance for protestantism as an ideological cement between the two communities. The recusant state of both would push this element more to the fore in the reign of Elizabeth. However, the main source of ideological solidarity between the two races which the author envisaged was not religion but patriotism – and so it remained later, because of the place of the English crown in the Anglo-Irish constitutional scheme.[46] Both communities owed love and loyalty to the same native land, their 'own mother'. And so the author, addressing the Gaelic dynastic lords as his 'dear countrymen', launched into

---

[45] Ibid., fo. 119.
[46] Ibid., fo. 119v. On the ambiguity of religious dissent as a factor that served to give the two communities a sense of unity of purpose, see above, pp. 181–2.

an exhortation in which he urged them to undertake the proposed reform programme for the sake of patriotic pride, to silence the slander against their native country, to falsify the old proverb that 'Ireland is a goodly country inhabited with evil people'.

In this treatise, therefore, we find as early as 1555 an ideology which embraced a developed concept of an Irish national community, a community in which the island's two ethnic groups were fully integrated, in which political status and property titles were safeguarded without discrimination under the constitution, and in which there was absolute equality before the law. This ideology embodied notions of the community's internal integrity and its external autonomy deriving from the island's constitutional status as a sovereign kingdom united to the English crown. It enjoined upon the members of the national community an attitude of moral and psychological solidarity based on common devotion to the native land.[47]

It is not suggested that the fusion of these ideas took place everywhere at once. Obviously they took time to work through the community, and they coalesced more quickly and more successfully in some cases than in others. Neither did the nationalist ideology at any stage totally pervade the Anglo-Irish community: ideologies never do. Nevertheless by the mid-1550s it was already an identifiable element in Anglo-Irish politics.

Awareness of the emergence of this new ideology in the 1550s adds a new dimension to the study of the politics of the Anglo-Irish community in the Elizabethan period. The nature of the impact of the former on the latter cannot be elaborated here.[48] What may be done is to demonstrate the continuity of the ideological tradition from the 1550s onwards. Possibly it is best to start by grasping the nettle. The attitude reflected in Richard Stanyhurst's discourse on Ireland, which appeared in the sixth volume of Holinshed's *Chronicles* in the 1580s, is usually regarded as paradigmatic of Anglo-Irish political attitudes at this time. Stanyhurst's hostility to the phenomenon of Gaelicisation is well known.[49] This is taken as establishing the continuity into the

[47] Elsewhere I have discerned the development of a different kind of nationalism, strongly ethnic in character, within the Gaelic community at this time; see my 'Native reaction to the westward enterprise' in K. R. Andrews et al (eds.), *The westward enterprise* (Liverpool 1978).

[48] It is sketched to some extent in my 'The beginnings of modern Ireland', pp. 81–7.

[49] Stanyhurst, 'The description of Ireland' in *Holinshed's Chronicles*, vi, p. 5.

Elizabethan period of a tradition of racial antagonism between the two communities stretching back to the Anglo-Norman invasion. We have already discussed the nature of the relationship between the two communities in the medieval period and need not go into the matter again. Our concern here is with the testimony that Stanyhurst provides of Anglo-Irish political attitudes in his own time.

Three points are worth making. Stanyhurst's discourse reflects the same ethos as the nationalist manifesto of the 1550s in one feature at least, in the ardour of the patriotic sentiment to which it gives utterance. In itself, that provides little indication of his precise ideological commitment. However, had writers paid more attention to it they might not have missed the subtlety of Stanyhurst's attitude to the Gaelic community. Standish O'Grady, both scholar and populariser of Gaelic Ireland at the turn of this century, showed more perception than recent scholars when he pointed out the Gaelic dimension to Stanyhurst's patriotism. Far from denigrating the Gaelic Irish, he made them the subject of a spirited if patronising defence. They were uncivilised, of course, but not so degenerate as many so-called civil societies such as the Germans, who were given over to gluttony, drunkenness and debauchery. Furthermore, they were amenable to reform by the application of the humanistic panacea of good government and social engineering. This suggests an attitude closer to the patriotic solidarity of the 1550 treatise than to the supposed historic struggle of the two nations.[50]

Finally, Stanyhurst's attitude to Gaelic culture deserves some examination. His lamentation that 'the Irish tongue should be so universally gaggled in the English Pale' has been too easily taken as evidence of colonial cultural prejudice. In fact Stanyhurst's attitude in this respect was highly ambiguous. He had no hesitation in identifying with the ancient cultural heritage of the Gael. He recounts with obvious pride the glories of the Gaelic saints and scholars. On the other hand, he could only envisage a

---

[50] I first put forward this view of Stanyhurst in 1973 in 'The beginnings of modern Ireland', p. 83. An able, full-scale study of Stanyhurst by Colm Lennon ('Richard Stanyhurst', unpublished M.A. thesis, University College, Dublin, 1976) endorsed my aproach in general but argued that I minimised the ideological gap between Stanyhurst's Old English patriotism and a full-blown nationalism which would have led him to identify with the Gaelic Irish more completely. I hope the fuller exposition of my view presented here may be more persuasive.

politically reformed Ireland that was also a culturally Anglicised
one. The exigencies of reform, therefore, not racial antagonism,
was the source of his opposition to Gaelicisation.

More important than Stanyhurst's own view in this case is the
light he throws on attitudes generally in the Pale in the matter.
The fact that this chestnut of reform treatises at the beginning of
the century could be repeated with such vehemence by Stanyhurst
as the century drew to a close is a sufficient commentary on the
ineffectualness of reform in this respect in the meantime, even
within the Pale.[51] One reason for the lack of success in repelling
Gaelic culture is indicated by Stanyhurst himself. He anticipates
the objections of practical-minded reformers to his intransigent
stance: 'You see all things run to ruin in the English Pale by reason
of great enormities in the country either openly practised or
covertly winked at; you glance your eye on that which standeth
next you, and by beating Jack for Gill, you impute the fault to
that which perhaps would little further the weal public it if were
exiled.'[52] The practical politicians' main concern was for the
eradication of 'enormities', those political and social disorders in
concern for which the reform movement first began. Their
attitude towards Gaelic culture was tolerant. Thus, Gaelic cultural
forms continued to prevail within the Pale itself, and there was
no great will, even among reformers themselves, to eradicate
them.

Something more must be said. Stanyhurst's remarks reveal not
only an attitude of tolerance towards Gaelic culture within
politically influential circles of the Pale, but one of positive
enthusiasm. He anticipates objection to his point of view partly
from pragmatic reformers but also from some 'snappish carpers'
outraged, as he says, by his 'debasing the Irish language'. There
is no difficulty in identifying a number of Stanyhurst's
contemporaries who might well have been among such 'snappish
carpers'. One was John Ussher, head of a great patrician family
of Dublin, who financed the first book printed in the Irish
language, a catechism published in 1571, together with a devotional
poem by the great Tadhg Bocht Ó Huiginn.[53] Another was

---

[51] Another testimony to the same effect from this period is provided in Lord Chancellor
Gerrarde's 'Note on the government of Ireland', S.P. 63/60, no. 29.

[52] Stanyhurst, 'The description of Ireland' in *Holinshed's Chronicles*, vi, p. 5.

[53] Bruce Dickins, 'The Irish broadside and Queen Elizabeth's types' in *Transactions of
the Cambridge Bibliographical Society*, i (1949), pp. 48–60.

Richard Creagh, member of a great merchant family of Limerick, who found time, while acting as an agent of the Counter-Reformation, to compose an Irish grammar.[54] Another worth mentioning is Christopher Nugent, the heir to the baron of Delvin. He composed a primer of Irish grammar which he presented to Queen Elizabeth in the course of his stay at court. He also provides an example of the continuing patronage of bardic poetry by Anglo-Irish lords of the Pale – some of the products of his patronage still survive in testimony.[55]

Each of these figures in his own way illustrates what little progress had been made in de-Gaelicisation at the cultural level despite the pervasive influence which the movement of political reformation had gained within the Anglo-Irish political community since Darcy penned his reform articles in 1515. Moreover, they testify to the way in which the predilections, the enthusiasms and the technology of the renaissance were being introduced to the world of Gaelic culture through the mediation of the Anglo-Irish nobility and gentry.

However, of even greater interest than any of these from our point of view is Christopher Nugent's brother, William. No doubt he was personally known to Stanyhurst, who described him in his account of Irish writers as 'a proper gentleman, and of singular good wit, who wrote in the English tongue divers sonnets'.[56] William Nugent certainly had the marks of a proper Elizabethan gentleman – noble blood, an Oxford education, a spell at court, and a taste for composing sonnets. Because of this, all the greater significance attaches to the fact that recent scholarship has identified him as the author of two accomplished poems in the Irish language.[57] In view of the attitudes of racial and cultural prejudice which historians have regarded as characterising the Anglo-Irish at this time, Nugent is important in the first instance for the evidence he provides of the continuity, at this particular juncture and in this particular milieu, of the tradition of poetic

---

[54] On Creagh, see the *D.N.B.;* also R. D. Edwards, *Church and state in Tudor Ireland* (Dublin 1935), pp. 229–33.

[55] On Christopher Nugent, see F. X. Martin, *Friar Nugent* (London 1962), pp. 5–6. Cf. E. Ó Tuathail (ed.), 'Nugentiana', *Éigse*, ii, (1940), pp. 4–14. A facsimile of the dedication of Nugent's grammar is in J. T. Gilbert (ed.), *Facsimiles of the national manuscripts of Ireland*, iv(i) (London 1882), no. 22.

[56] Stanyhurst, 'The description of Ireland' in *Holinshed's Chronicles*, vi, p. 62.

[57] Gerard Murphy (ed.), 'Poems of exile by Uilliam MacBarúin Dealbhna', *Éigse*, vi (1948), pp. 8–15. Cf. Ó Tuathail (ed.), 'Nugentiana'.

composition in Irish among the Anglo-Irish, a tradition which can be traced back to the beginning of the fourteenth century. However, Nugent's importance lies not merely in the fact that he wrote but more in the content of what he wrote. The two poems which survive are among the earliest examples of a new *genre* of Gaelic poetry which was to receive its finest expression by Anglo-Irish writers, notably Geoffrey Keating and Pádraigín Haicéad, in the opening decades of the seventeenth century. The form which Keating and Haicéad so radiantly enhanced is known as the poetry of exile.[58] Although the fact has gone totally unnoticed, the poetry of exile marks as great an ideological milestone in Gaelic literature as it does a literary one.

Set in the context of late medieval bardic poetry, the novelty of the themes of Keating and Haicéad – and of Nugent before them – is immediately apparent. It is true that poems of exile occur in the earlier verse; but there the object of the poet's yearning is a particular locality and its ruling dynasty. Although references to Ireland usually occur in such poems, they are made incidentally from a perspective that is intensely local. In the new *genre*, in contrast, particular localities are subsumed under the theme of Ireland as a whole, and the native land rather than a particular dynastic sept is idealised as the object of the poet's devotion. The point is emphasised by the contrast in race-consciousness reflected in the two kinds of poetry. As we noted in the opening chapter, the literature of the medieval period takes for granted the separateness of the two ethnic groups who inhabit the island, depicting each with its own individual identity and ethos, although coexisting and interrelating rather than locked in mortal combat, as used to be thought.[59] Nugent and the later Anglo-Irish exile

---

[58] The best known of Keating's poems of this type is ' Mo bheannacht leat a scríbhinn ', Eoin C. Mac Giolla Eáin (ed.), *Dánta, amhráin is caointe Sheathrúin Céitinn* (Dublin 1900), no. 2. A fine example of Haicéad's work in the style is ' Chum na hÉireann tamall roimh thriall dá hionnsai ', Máire Ní Cheallacháin (ed.), *Filíocht Phádraigín Haicéad* (Dublin 1962), no. 11. Strictly, the genre is not entirely without precedent in Irish literature. The theme of patriotic yearning and the idealisation of the national *patria* is found in the early medieval period, notably in the poetry associated with St Columkille. But these themes vanish almost without trace from the twelfth century onwards, to reemerge in the second half of the sixteenth century. The disappearance makes good sense in terms of the difference in political culture that exists between early and late medieval Ireland. For examples of such exile poetry, see A. O'Kelleher and G. Schoeperle (eds.), *Betha Colaim Chille* (Illinois 1918), passim.

[59] Above, pp. 21–6.

poets, in contrast, reflect a milieu that has lost its colonial consciousness and has exultantly discovered a common identity, politically, socially and culturally, with the older indigenous community of the island, the Gaelic Irish. One aspect of that common identity is religion. Even in Nugent's poems, written in the late 1560s or early 1570s, the typically ecclesial character of Counter-Reformation devotion is evident in reverential allusions to the mass, the clergy and the religious orders. However, the common identity which these writers esteemed so highly was forged not by their Catholicism but by those factors of geography and history which decreed that the two ethnic groups should claim Ireland as their common native land. For them the two ethnic heritages of the island constituted the warp and weft from which the historical process had woven a single fabric. Thus Nugent could call Ireland 'the land of Gall [Anglo-Irish] and Gael [Gaelic Irish]'.[60] As such it was the object of their common devotion.

In view of what was said earlier about the emergence of the patriotic theme in the political literature of the Anglo-Irish in mid-century, the ideological implications of a parallel development in poetry written by Anglo-Irishmen in the Irish language need not be stressed. Suffice it to say that in face of all the evidence, the dimension of nationalism must be regarded as a central feature of the politics of the Anglo-Irish from the mid-Tudor period onwards. To analyse the political history of that community in the Elizabethan period in a way that cursorily dismisses or ignores national sentiment – as recent historians have done – is like analysing the plot of *Hamlet* without taking account of the brooding spirit of Hamlet's father.[61] At the same time – to revert to a point that was emphasised already – it has to be remembered that the relationship between ideology and politics is usually a complex one. It is not suggested that all Anglo-Irish politicians were motivated by national sentiment or that all of those who were subscribed to the same political programme. In practice, the programmes of those who subscribed to a nationalist

---

[60] Murphy (ed.), 'Poems of exile', no. 2, line 9.

[61] For the cursory dismissal of nationalism in this period, see V. W. Treadwell, 'The Irish parliament of 1569–71', *Proceedings of the Royal Irish Academy*, lxv, sect. C. (1966–7), p. 86. For a writer who attempts to analyse the mental outlook of the Anglo–Irish in the sixteenth century without adverting to the phenomenon of patriotism at all, see N. Canny, *The formation of the Old English elite in Ireland*, O'Donnell Lecture (Dublin 1975).

vision of Irish politics covered a wide spectrum. Richard Stanyhurst may be taken to represent one extreme, with his patronising attitude towards the Gaelic community and his arrogant assumption of the superiority of English civility. At the other extreme William Nugent, Gaelic poet, and by 1580 rebel and recusant, can be taken to represent the militant nationalist tradition.[62] Between these two, the young lawyer whose treatise we discussed earlier represents the mainstream tradition which sought to adapt English political and constitutional institutions for the purpose of constructing an authentically national Irish polity. In the main this was the outlook of those who in the name of the commonwealth sought to resist the aggressive colonialism of the new English by constitutional means throughout the Elizabethan period. Tough political fighters though these showed themselves to be, they were essentially visionaries. To them it seemed feasible to conceive of a politically united, though culturally diverse, Irish community in which all were guaranteed equal justice and liberty before the law. The history of Ireland continues to mock the realisation of their dream, while at the same time overwhelmingly demonstrating that it constitutes the only hope for securing the island's peace.

[62] On William Nugent's participation in the widespread series of rebellions by Anglo–Irish and Gaelic dissidents alike early in the 1580s, see the examination of James FitzChristopher Nugent in the Tower of London in December 1581, S.P. 63/87, nos. 68, 69.

Bibliography

Bibliographies and guides

Asplin, P. W. A., *Medieval Ireland, c. 1170–1495*, Dublin 1971
Elton, G. R., *Modern historians on British history*, London 1970
Hayes, R. (ed.), *Manuscript sources for the history of Irish civilisation*, 11 vols., Boston 1965
Johnston, E. M., *Irish history: a select bibliography*, London 1969
Levine, M. (ed.), *Tudor England, 1485–1603* (Conference on British Studies Bibliographical Handbooks), Cambridge 1968
Moody, T. W. (ed.), *Irish historiography, 1934–70*, Dublin 1971
Read, C., *Bibliography of British history, 1485–1603*, 2nd edn, Oxford 1959

Manuscript sources

British Library, London:
    Additional MSS 4763, 4767
    Cotton MSS Titus B.I, B.XI
    Harleian MS 35
    Lansdowne MS 159
Hatfield House, Hertfordshire:
    Salisbury MS C.P. 201/116
Lambeth Palace, London:
    Carew MSS 598, 600, 602, 603, 621, 623
Public Record Office, London:
    State Papers, Henry VIII, S.P. 1
    State Papers, Ireland, Henry VIII–Elizabeth, S.P. 60–S.P. 63
    Theological Tracts, S.P. 6
Trinity College, Dublin:
    W. Shaw Mason, 'Collation of the Irish statutes', Add. MS W.8 (MS V, 2.7)
    MS 842

Published sources and calendars

Public records

Acts of the privy council in Ireland, 1556–71, ed. J. T. Gilbert, Historical MSS Commission, 15th report, London 1897

Calendar of Carew Manuscripts, ed. J. S. Brewer and W. Bullen, i–vi, London 1867–73.

Calendar of fiants (Ireland), Henry VIII–Mary, appendices to 7th–9th reports of Public Records in Ireland, Dublin 1875–7

Calendar of letters and papers, foreign and domestic, Henry VIII, ed. J. S. Brewer et al., i–xxi, London 1862–1932 ('*L.P.*')

Calendar of state papers, Spanish, vi–xiii, London 1890–1954

Hughes, P. M. and J. F. Larkin (eds.), *Tudor royal proclamations,* New Haven and London 1964

Quinn, D. B. (ed.), 'Bills and statutes of the Irish parliaments of Henry VII and Henry VIII', *Analecta Hibernica,* x (1941)

State papers of Henry VIII, i–iii, London 1830 ('*S.P. Henry VIII*')

Statutes at large, Ireland, i, Dublin 1786

Statutes of the realm (England), iii, London 1817

Miscellaneous records

Calendar of the manuscripts of the marquess of Salisbury, Historical MSS Commission, i, London 1883

Carney, M. (ed.), 'Agreement between Ó Domhnaill and Tadhg Ó Conchubhair concerning Sligo Castle', *Irish Historical Studies,* iii (1942–3)

Chambers, D. S. (ed.), *Faculty office registers of Canterbury,* Oxford 1966

Curtis, E. (ed.), *Calendar of Ormond deeds,* iv, Dublin 1937

Ellis, H., *Original letters,* 2nd ser., ii, London 1827

Gilbert, J. T. (ed.), *Facsimiles of the national manuscripts of Ireland,* iv (i–ii), London 1882

Gwynn, A. (ed.), 'Archbishop Cromer's Register', *County Louth Archaeological Journal,* x (1942–3)

McNeill, C. (ed.), *Calendar of Archbishop Alen's Register,* Dublin 1950

Annals, chronicles, contemporary literature etc.

A.F.M.: see O'Donovan (ed.) below

Annals of Ulster: see MacCarthy (ed.) below

Bale, John, 'The vocacyon of Johan Bale', in *Harleian Miscellany,* vi, ed. T. Park, London 1813

Bergin, O., *Irish bardic poetry,* ed. D. Greene and F. Kelly, Dublin 1970

Davis, Sir John, *A discovery of the true causes why Ireland was never entirely subdued,* London 1612.

Dimock, J. F. (ed.), 'Topographia Hibernica', 'Expugnatio Hibernica' in *Opera omnia Giraldi Cambrensis*, v, London 1867

Dudley, Edmund, *The tree of commonwealth*, ed. D. M. Brodie, Cambridge 1948

Elyot, Sir Thomas, *The boke named the Governour*, ed. H. H. S. Croft, London 1880

Finglas, Patrick, Baron, 'Breviat of the getting of Ireland, and of the decaie of the same' in W. Harris (ed.), *Hibernica*, i, Dublin 1747

Harris, W. (ed.), *Ware's works*, Dublin 1764

Hennessy, W. M. (ed.), *Annals of Loch Cé*, ii, London 1871

Knott, E. (ed.), *The bardic poems of Tadhg Dall Ó Huiginn*, London 1922

Loch Cé: see Hennessy (ed.) above

MacCarthy, B. (ed.), *Annals of Ulster (Annála Uladh)*, iii, Dublin 1895

Mac Giolla Eáin, E. C. (ed.), *Dánta, amhráin is caointe Sheathrúin Céitinn*, Dublin 1900

McKenna, L. (ed.), *Dioghluim Dána*, Dublin 1938

Aithdioghluim Dána, Dublin 1939

Mac Niocaill, G. (ed.), 'Duanaire Ghearóid Iarla', *Studia Hibernica*, iii (1963)

Murphy, G. (ed.), 'Poems of exile by William MacBarúin Dealbhna', *Éigse*, vi (1948)

Ní Cheallacháin, Máire (ed.), *Filíocht Phádraigín Haicéad*, Dublin 1962

O'Donovan, J. (ed.), *Annals of the kingdom of Ireland by the Four Masters*, v, 2nd edn, Dublin 1856 ('*A.F.M.*')

O'Kelleher, A. and G. Schoeperle (eds.), *Betha Colaim Chille*, Illinois 1918

O'Rahilly, T. F. (ed.), *Dánta Gradha*, Dublin 1916

Ó Tuathail, E. (ed.), 'Nugentiana', *Éigse*, ii (1940)

Roper, William, *The life of Sir Thomas More, knight*, ed. E. E. Reynolds, London 1963

Stanyhurst, Richard, 'The description of Ireland', 'The chronicles of Ireland' in *Holinshed's Chronicles*, vi, London 1808

Starkey, Thomas, *A dialogue between Cardinal Pole and Thomas Lupset*, ed. K. M. Burton, London 1968

Secondary works

Binchy, D. A., 'Secular institutions' in M. Dillon (ed.), *Early Irish society*, Cork 1954

Bradshaw, B., 'The opposition to the ecclesiastical legislation in the Irish Reformation parliament', *Irish Historical Studies*, xvi (1969)

– 'George Browne, first Reformation archbishop of Dublin', *Journal of Ecclesiastical History*, xxi (1970)

– 'The beginnings of modern Ireland', in B. Farrell (ed.), *The Irish parliamentary tradition*, Dublin 1973

– *The dissolution of the religious orders in Ireland*, Cambridge 1974

- 'The Edwardian Reformation in Ireland', *Archivium Hibernicum*, xxiv (1976/7)
- 'Cromwellian reform and the origins of the Kildare rebellion, 1553–4', *Transactions of the Royal Historical Society*, 5th ser., xxvii (1977)
- 'The Elizabethans and the Irish', *Studies*, lxvi (1977)
- 'Native reaction to the westward enterprise', in K. R. Andrews, N. Canny and P. E. H. Hair (eds.), *The westward enterprise*, Liverpool 1978

Brooks, F. W., 'The council of the north' in J. Hurstfield (ed.), *The Historical Association book of the Tudors*, London 1973

Butler, W. F. T., 'The policy of surrender and regrant', *Journal of the Royal Society of Antiquaries of Ireland*, ser. VI, iii (1913)

Canny, N. P., *The formation of the Old English elite in Ireland*, O'Donnell Lecture, Dublin 1975
- *The Elizabethan conquest of Ireland, 1565–1576*, Hassocks, Sussex 1976

Carney, J., *The Irish bardic poet*, Dublin 1967

Corish, P. J., *The origins of Catholic nationalism*, Dublin and Sydney 1968

Curtis, E., *A history of medieval Ireland*, London 1938
- *A history of Ireland*, rev. edn, London 1950

Dawson, H. C., *The making of Europe*, London 1932

Dickens, B., 'The Irish broadside, and Queen Elizabeth's types', *Transactions of the Cambridge Bibliographical Society*, i (1949)

Dolley, M., *Anglo-Norman Ireland*, Dublin 1972

Dunlop, R., 'Some aspects of Henry VIII's Irish policy' in T. F. Tout and J. Tait (eds.), *Historical essays*, London 1902
- 'Ireland to the settlement of Ulster' in *Cambridge Modern History*, iii, Cambridge 1905

Edwards, R. D., 'The Irish bishops and the Anglican schism', *Irish Ecclesiastical Record*, xlv (1935)
- *Church and state in Tudor Ireland*, Dublin 1935
- 'Ireland, Elizabeth I and the Counter-Reformation' in S. T. Bindoff, J. Hurstfield and C. H. Williams (eds.), *Elizabethan government and society*, London 1961
- 'The Irish Reformation parliament', *Historical Studies*, vi (1968)

Edwards, R. D. and T. W. Moody, 'The history of Poynings' Law: Part I, 1494–1615', *Irish Historical Studies*, ii (1940–1)

Elliott, J. H., 'Revolution and continuity in early modern Europe', *Past and Present*, no. 42 (1969)

Ellis, S. G., 'Tudor policy and the Kildare ascendancy, 1496–1534', *Irish Historical Studies*, xx (1977)

Elton, G. R., 'Thomas Cromwell's decline and fall', *Historical Journal*, x (1951)
- *The Tudor revolution in government*, Cambridge 1953
- 'King or Minister? The man behind the Henrician Reformation', *History*, xxxix (1954)

– *Reform and renewal*, Cambridge 1973
– *England under the Tudors*, London 1974 edn.
– *Reform and Reformation*, London 1977
Ferguson, A. B., *The articulate citizen and the English renaissance*, Durham, N.C. 1965
Frame, R., 'English officials and Irish chiefs in the fourteenth century', *English Historical Review*, xc (1975)
– 'Power and society in the Lordship of Ireland, 1272–1377', *Past and Present*, no. 76 (1977)
Greene, D., 'The professional poets' in B. Ó Cuív (ed.), *Seven centuries of Irish learning*, Dublin 1971
Gwynn, A., *The medieval province of Armagh*, Dundalk 1946
Hancock, W. K., *Politics in Pitcairn*, London 1947
Hand, G. J., 'The forgotten statutes of Kilkenny', *Irish Jurist*, n.s., i (1966)
– 'The status of the native Irish in the Lordship of Ireland, 1272–1331', *Irish Jurist*, n.s., i (1966)
Hayes-McCoy, G. A., *Scots mercenary forces in Ireland, 1565–1603*, Dublin and London 1937
– 'Gaelic society in Ireland in the late sixteenth century', *Historical Studies*, iv (1963)
– 'The royal supremacy and ecclesiastical revolution, 1534–47' in T. W. Moody et al. (eds.), *A new history of Ireland*, iii, Oxford 1976
Hexter, J. H., *Reappraisals in history*, London 1961
Jones, W. R. D., *The Tudor commonwealth, 1529–59*, London 1970
Knott, E., *Irish classical poetry*, rev. edn, Dublin 1960
Loades, D. M., *Two Tudor conspiracies*, London 1970
– *Politics and the nation, 1450–1660*, Brighton 1974
Lydon, J. F., *The Lordship of Ireland in the middle ages*, Dublin 1972
– *Ireland in the later middle ages*, Dublin 1973
MacAirt, S., 'The development of early modern Irish prose' in B. Ó Cuív (ed.), *Seven centuries of Irish learning*, Dublin 1971
McConica, J. K., *English humanists and Reformation politics*, Oxford 1965
McFarlane, K. B., *The nobility of later medieval England*, Oxford 1973
MacNeill, E., *Phases of Irish history*, Dublin 1919
– *Early Irish laws and institutions*, Dublin 1935
Martin, F. X., *Friar Nugent*, Rome and London 1962
– 'The coming of parliament' in B. Farrell (ed.), *The Irish parliamentary tradition*, Dublin 1973
Mathew, D., *The Celtic peoples and renaissance Europe*, London 1933
Moody, T. W., F. X. Martin and F. J. Byrne (eds.), *A new history of Ireland*, iii, Oxford 1976
Morley, H., *Ireland under Elizabeth*, London 1890

Nicholls, K., *Gaelic and Gaelicised Ireland*, Dublin 1972
Ó Corráin, D., *Ireland before the Normans*, Dublin 1972
Ó Cuív, B., 'Literary creation and the Irish classical tradition', *Proceedings of the British Academy*, xliv (1963)
Ó Tuama, S., 'The new love poetry' in B. Ó Cuív (ed.), *Seven centuries of Irish learning*, Dublin 1971
Otway-Ruthven, A. J., *A history of medieval Ireland*, London 1968
Pocock, J., 'England' in O. Ranum (ed.), *National consciousness, history and political culture in early modern Europe*, Baltimore and London 1975
Pollard, A. F., *Factors in modern history*, 3rd edn, London 1932
Quinn, D. B., 'The Irish parliamentary subsidy in the fifteenth and sixteenth centuries', *Proceedings of the Royal Irish Academy*, xlii, sect. C (1934–5)
– 'Anglo-Irish local government, 1485–1534', *Irish Historical Studies*, i (1938–9)
– 'The early interpretation of Poynings' Law, 1494–1534', *Irish Historical Studies*, ii (1941–2)
– (ed.), 'Parliaments and Great Councils in Ireland, 1461–1534', *Irish Historical Studies*, iii (1942–3)
– (ed.), 'Edward Walshe's "Conjectures concerning the state of Ireland"', *Irish Historical Studies*, v (1946–7)
– 'Ireland and sixteenth century European expansion', *Historical Studies*, i (1958)
– 'Henry VIII and Ireland, 1509–34', *Irish Historical Studies*, xii (1960–1)
Quinn, D. B. and K. W. Nicholls, 'Ireland in 1534' in T. W. Moody et al (eds.), *A new history of Ireland*, iii, Oxford 1976
Scarisbrick, J. J., *Henry VIII*, Harmondsworth 1971
Stokes, W., 'The Irish abridgement of the Expugnatio Hibernica', *English Historical Review*, xx (1905)
Treadwell, V. W., 'The Irish parliament of 1569–71', *Proceedings of the Royal Irish Academy*, lxv, sect. C (1966–7)
Walsh, P., *Irish men of learning*, London 1912
White, D. G., 'Edward VI's Irish policy', *Irish Historical Studies*, xiv (1964–5)
Wilkie, W. E., *The cardinal protectors of England*, Cambridge 1974
Wilkinson, B., *The constitutional history of England in the fifteenth century*, London 1966
Williams, E. C., *The court poet in medieval Ireland*, London 1971
Williams, P., *The council in the marches of Wales*, Cardiff 1958
Wilson, P., *The beginning of modern Ireland*, London 1912
Youings, J. A., 'The council of the west', *Transactions of the Royal Historical Society*, 5th ser., x (1960)

Unpublished theses

Bradshaw, B., 'George Browne, first Reformation archbishop of Dublin', M.A., University College, Dublin 1966
Corristine, L., 'The Kildare rebellion, 1534', M.A., University College, Dublin, 1975

Ellis, S. G., 'The Kildare rebellion', M.A., Manchester, 1974
Lennon, Colm, 'Richard Stanyhurst', M.A., University College, Dublin, 1976
Morgan, P. T. J., 'The government of Calais', D.Phil., Oxford, 1966
Quinn, D. B., 'Tudor rule in Ireland, 1485–1547', Ph.D., London, 1933
Simms, K., 'Gaelic Ulster in the late middle ages', Ph.D., Trinity College, Dublin, 1976

Index